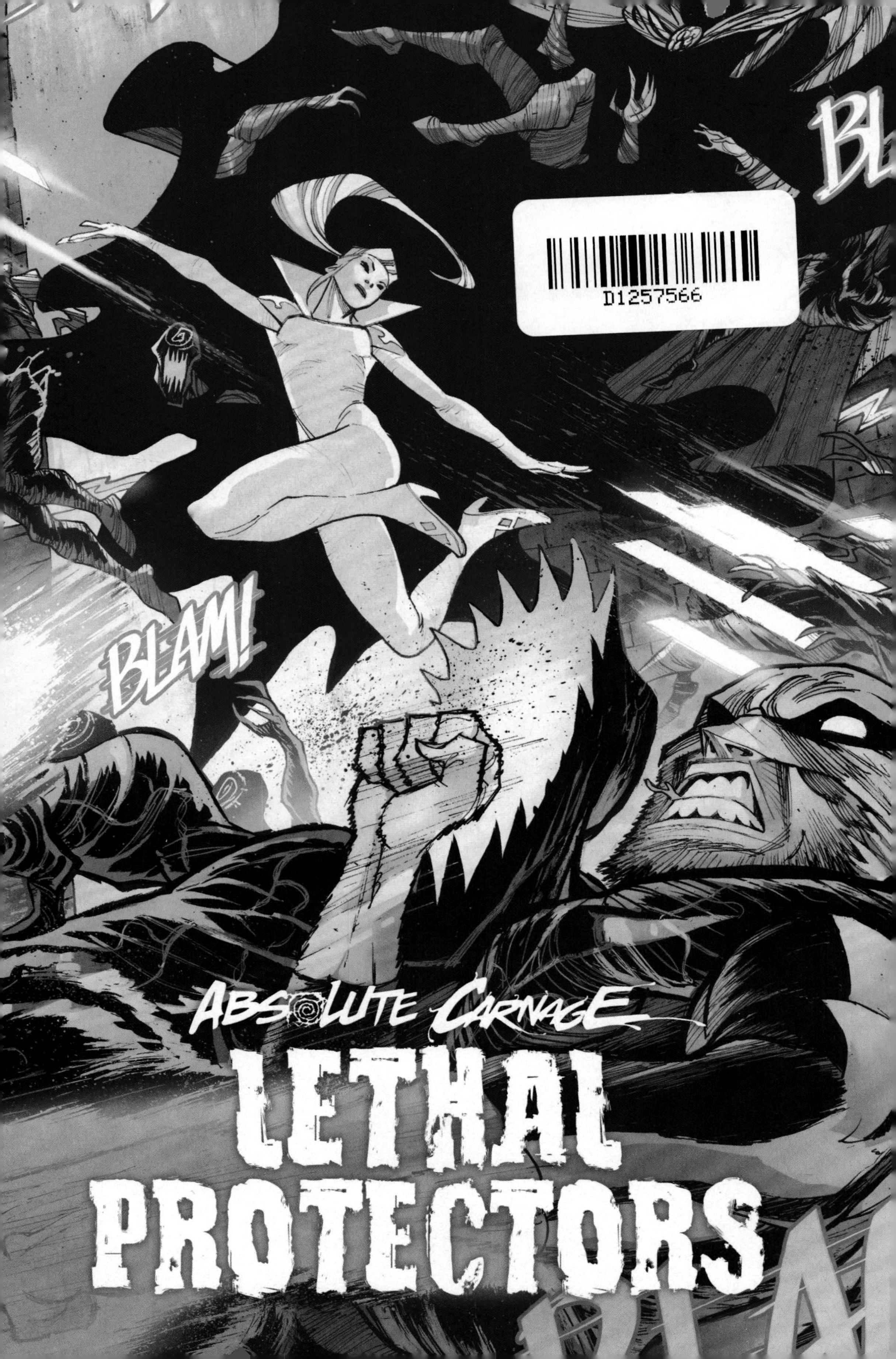
BLAM!
ABSOLUTE CARNAGE
LETHAL PROTECTORS

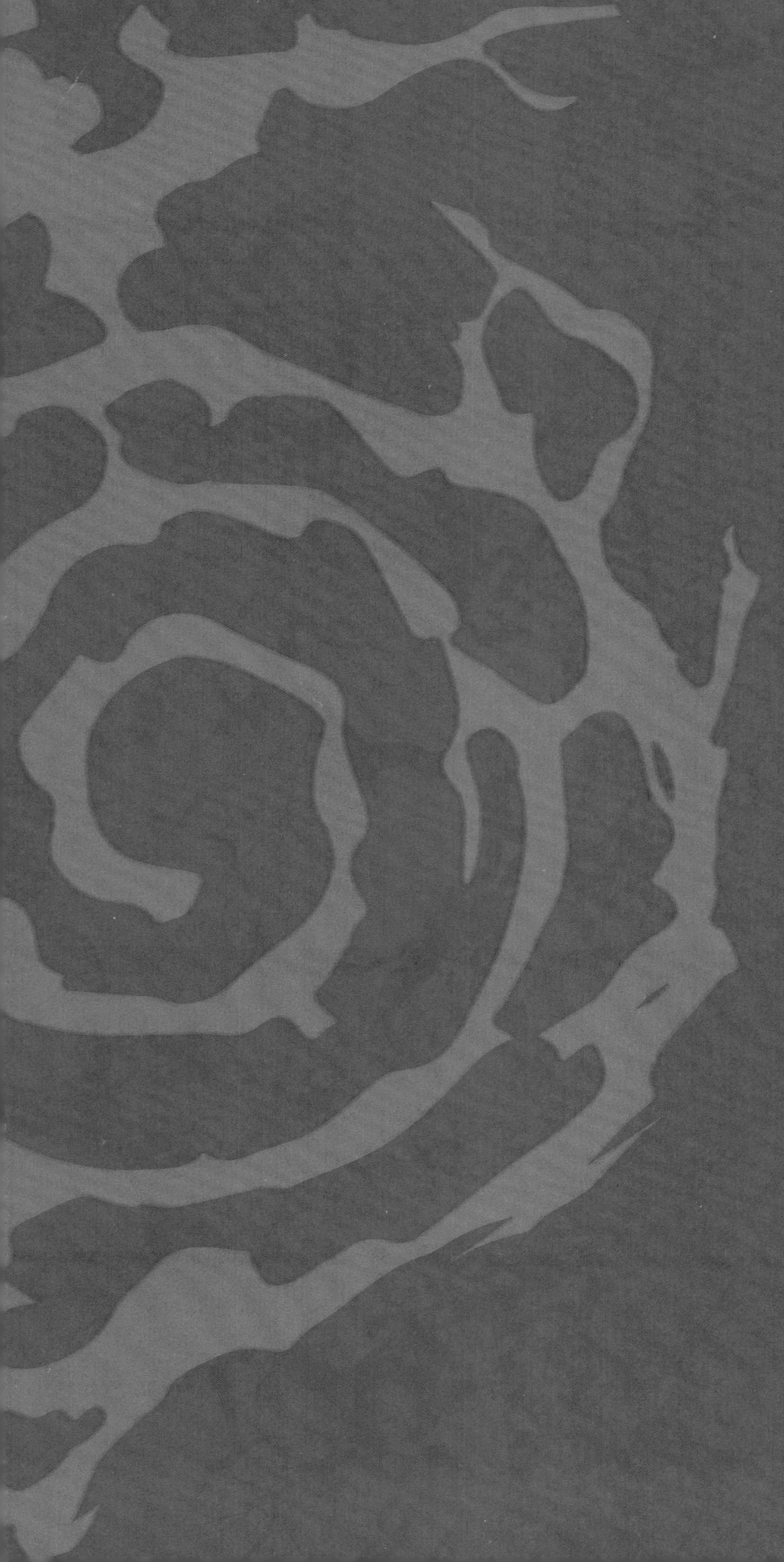

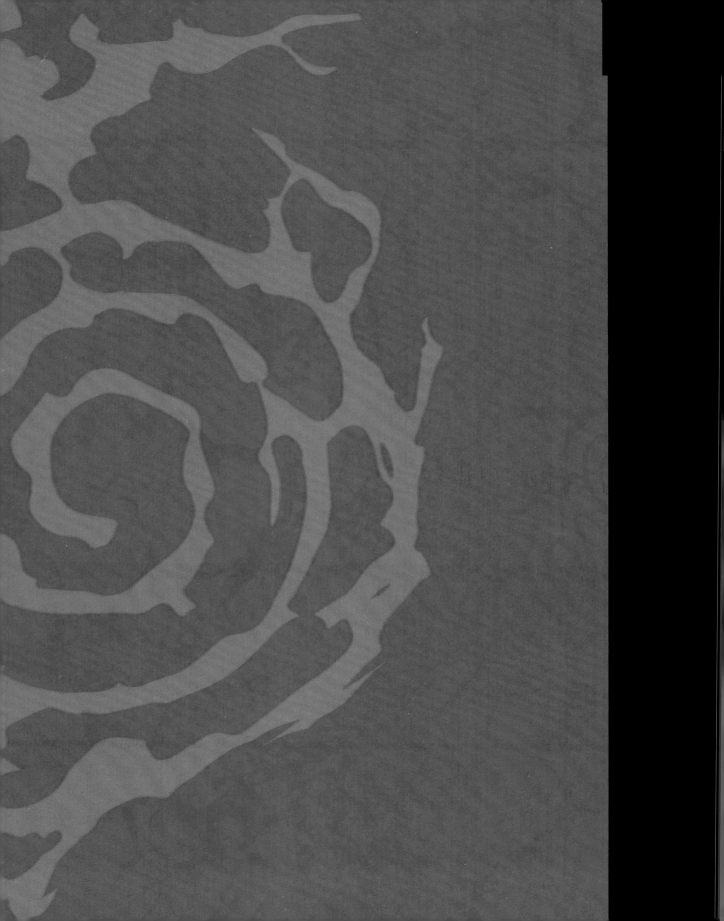

The town of Doverton, Colorado, was once taken over by the symbiotic, psychotic killer Cletus Kasady, A.K.A. Carnage.

While researching the disinterred graves in Doverton, **John Jameson uncovered a massive cult** worshipping the symbiote god, Knull.

Misty Knight was dispatched to locate Jameson after he went missing during his investigation, and she discovered him naked with gaps in his memory. They left on a road trip back to New York…but **all is not as it seems** with John Jameson…

Warning: The events of this story take place after *ABSOLUTE CARNAGE #2*.
If you haven't read it yet, proceed at your own risk!

ABSOLUTE CARNAGE
LETHAL PROTECTORS

Frank Tieri
WRITER

Flaviano
ARTIST

Federico Blee
COLORIST

VC's Joe Caramagna
LETTERER

Bengal (#1) and
Iban Coello & **Jason Keith** (#2-3)
COVER ART

Absolute Carnage: Avengers

Leah Williams & **Zac Thompson**
PLOT

Zac Thompson
SCRIPT

Alberto Alburquerque & **Guiu Vilanova**
ARTISTS

Rachelle Rosenberg
COLOR ARTIST

VC's Cory Petit
LETTERER

Clayton Crain
COVER ART

Danny Khazem
ASSISTANT EDITOR

Devin Lewis
EDITOR

Nick Lowe
EXECUTIVE EDITOR

Collection Editor **Jennifer Grünwald**
Assistant Editor **Caitlin O'Connell**
Associate Managing Editor **Kateri Woody**
Editor, Special Projects **Mark D. Beazley**

VP Production & Special Projects **Jeff Youngquist**
Book Designers Stacie Zucker with Adam Del Re
SVP Print, Sales & Marketing **David Gabriel**
Director, Licensed Publishing **Sven Larsen**

Editor in Chief **C.B. Cebulski**
Chief Creative Officer **Joe Quesada**
President **Dan Buckley**
Executive Producer **Alan Fine**

ABSOLUTE CARNAGE: LETHAL PROTECTORS. Contains material originally published in magazine form as ABSOLUTE CARNAGE: LETHAL PROTECTORS (2019) #1-3, ABSOLUTE CARNAGE: AVENGERS (2019) #1, INVADERS (2019) #7, AVENGERS (2018) #22, FANTASTIC FOUR (2018) #11 and VENOM (2018) #15. First printing 2019. ISBN 978-1-302-92013-5. Published by MARVEL WORLDWIDE, INC., a subsidiary of MARVEL ENTERTAINMENT, LLC. OFFICE OF PUBLICATION: 135 West 50th Street, New York, NY 10020. © 2019 MARVEL No similarity between any of the names, characters, persons, and/or institutions in this magazine with those of any living or dead person or institution is intended, and any such similarity which may exist is purely coincidental. **Printed in Canada.** DAN BUCKLEY, President, Marvel Entertainment; JOHN NEE, Publisher; JOE QUESADA, Chief Creative Officer; TOM BREVOORT, SVP of Publishing; DAVID BOGART, Associate Publisher & SVP of Talent Affairs; DAVID GABRIEL, VP of Print & Digital Publishing; JEFF YOUNGQUIST, VP of Production & Special Projects; DAN CARR, Executive Director of Publishing Technology; ALEX MORALES, Director of Publishing Operations; DAN EDINGTON, Managing Editor; SUSAN CRESPI, Production Manager; STAN LEE, Chairman Emeritus. For information regarding advertising in Marvel Comics or on Marvel.com, please contact Vit DeBellis, Custom Solutions & Integrated Advertising Manager, at vdebellis@marvel.com. For Marvel subscription inquiries, please call 888-511-5480. **Manufactured between 11/22/2019 and 12/24/2019 by SOLISCO PRINTERS, SCOTT, QC, CANADA.**

10 9 8 7 6 5 4 3 2 1

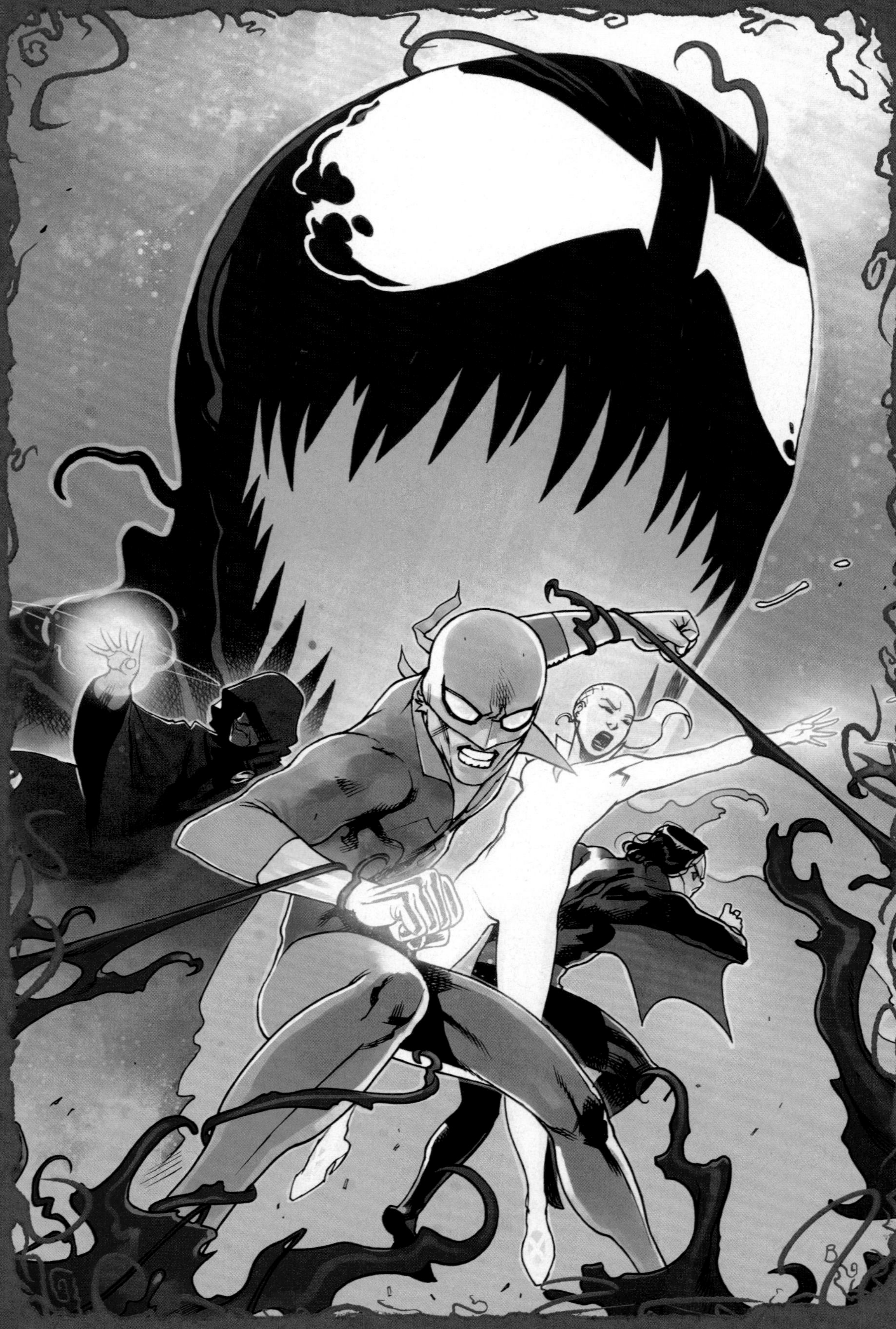

LETHAL PROTECTORS 1

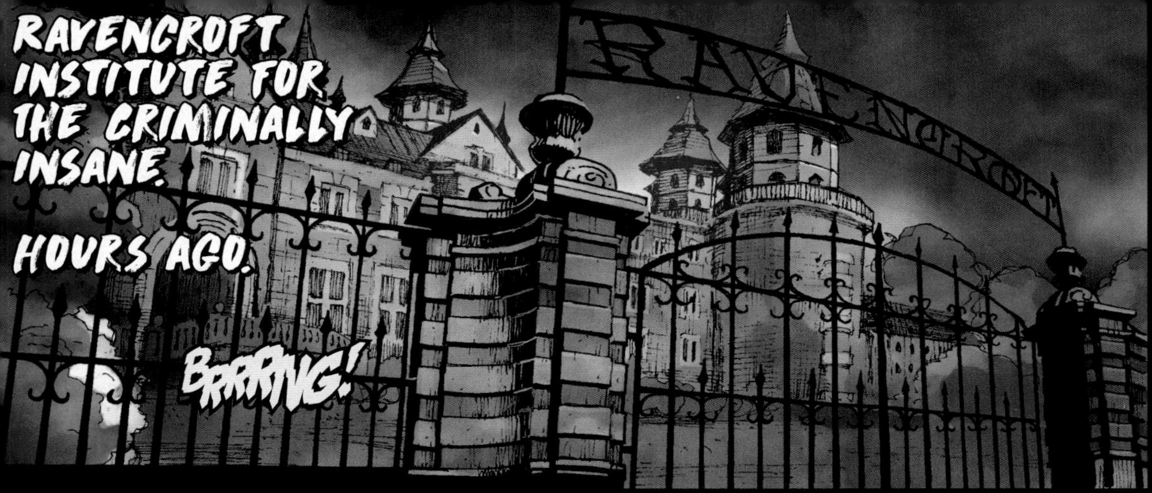
RAVENCROFT INSTITUTE FOR THE CRIMINALLY INSANE.
HOURS AGO.
BRRRING!

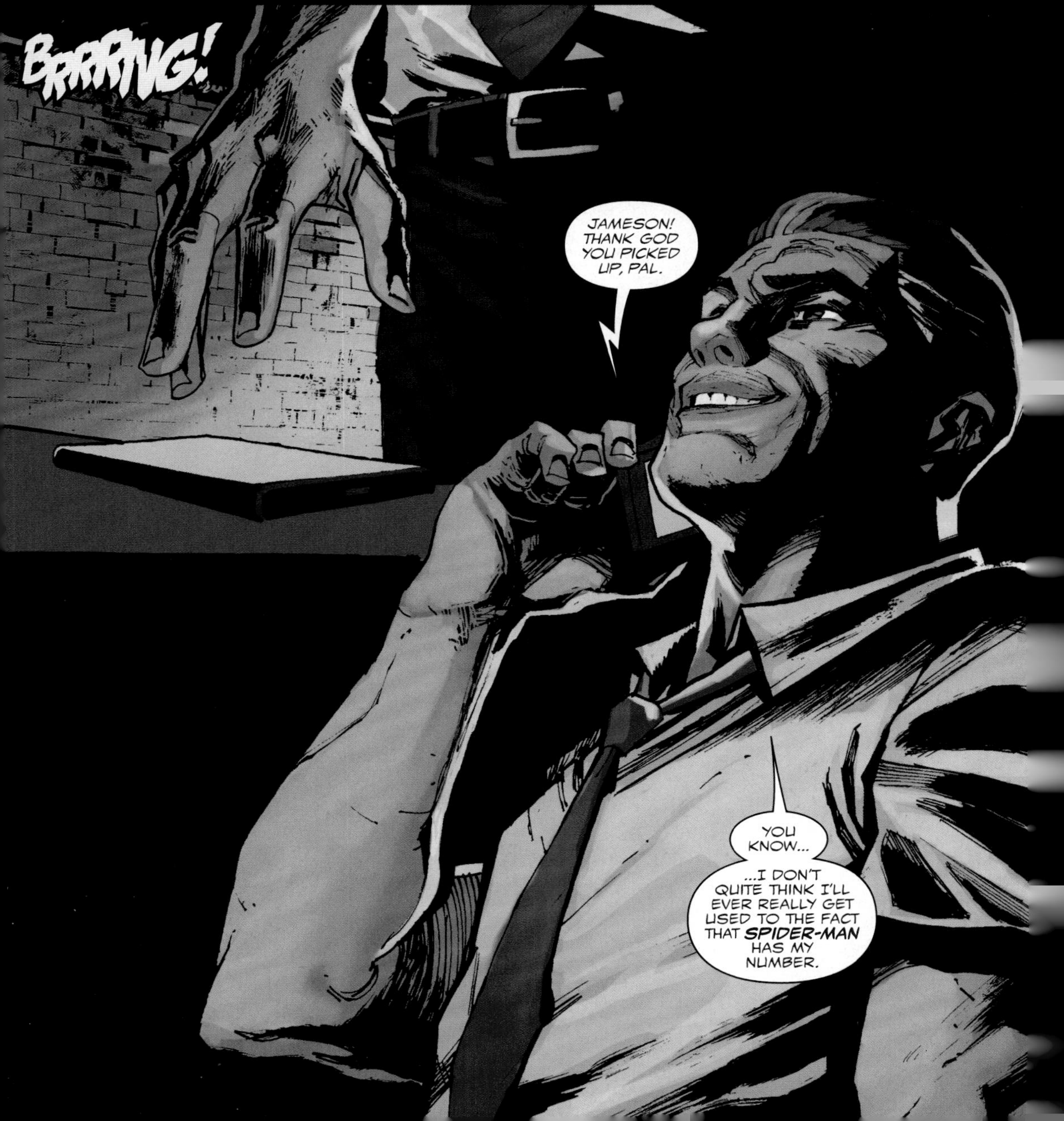
BRRRING!
JAMESON! THANK GOD YOU PICKED UP, PAL.
YOU KNOW...
...I DON'T QUITE THINK I'LL EVER REALLY GET USED TO THE FACT THAT SPIDER-MAN HAS MY NUMBER.

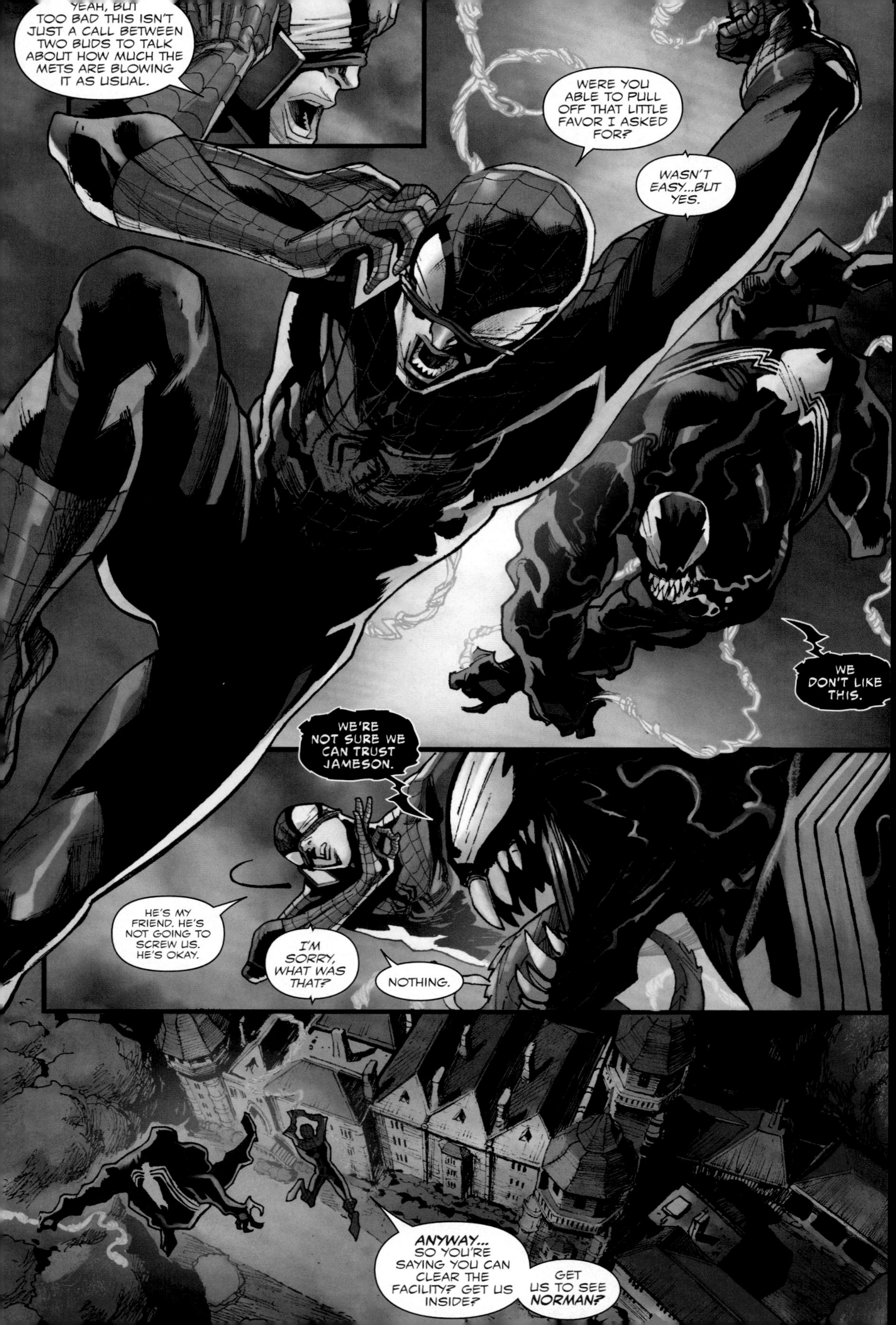

YEAH, BUT TOO BAD THIS ISN'T JUST A CALL BETWEEN TWO BUDS TO TALK ABOUT HOW MUCH THE METS ARE BLOWING IT AS USUAL.
WERE YOU ABLE TO PULL OFF THAT LITTLE FAVOR I ASKED FOR?
WASN'T EASY...BUT YES.
WE DON'T LIKE THIS.
WE'RE NOT SURE WE CAN TRUST JAMESON.
HE'S MY FRIEND. HE'S NOT GOING TO SCREW US. HE'S OKAY.
I'M SORRY, WHAT WAS THAT?
NOTHING.
ANYWAY... SO YOU'RE SAYING YOU CAN CLEAR THE FACILITY? GET US INSIDE?
GET US TO SEE NORMAN?

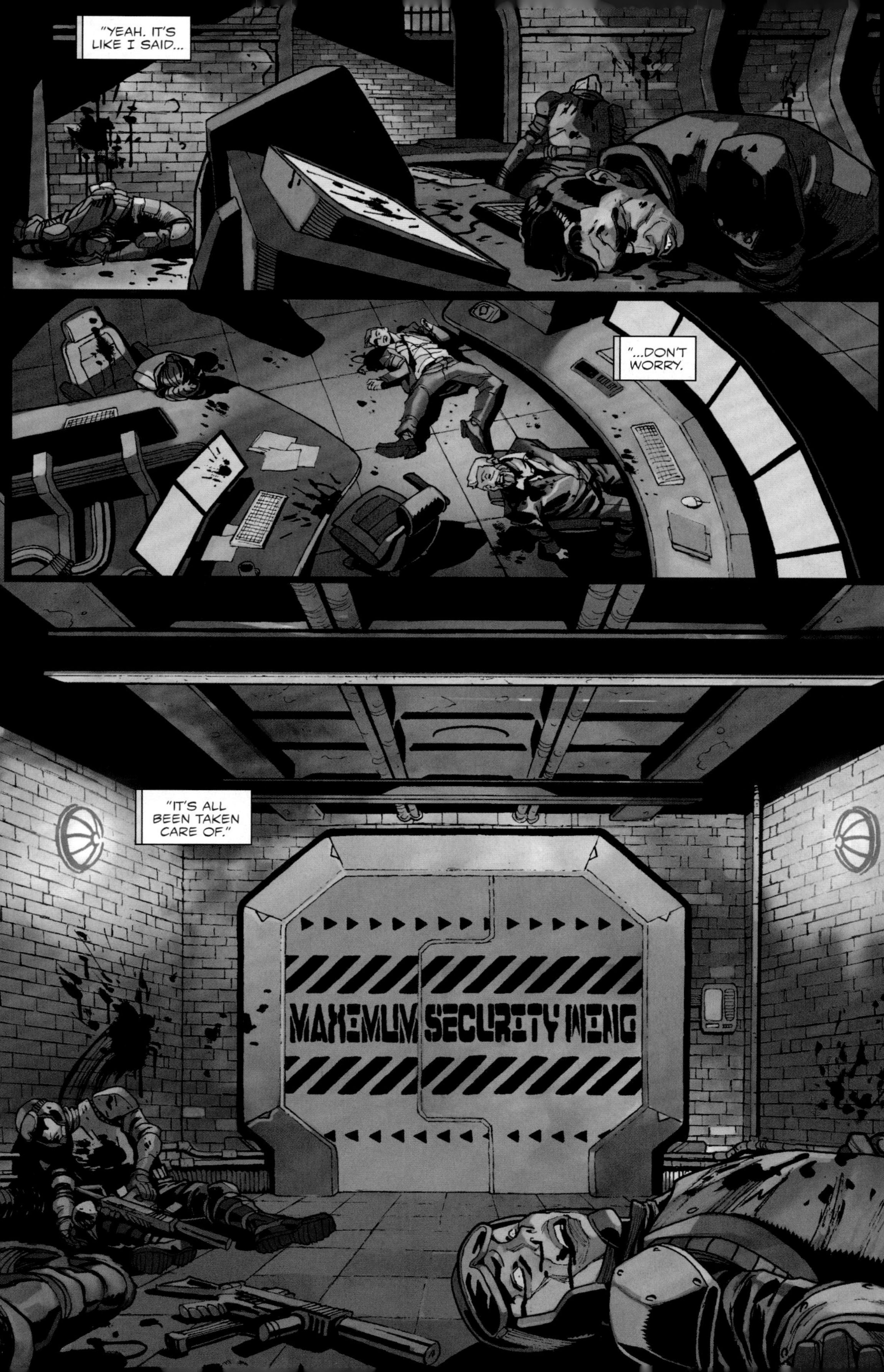
"YEAH. IT'S LIKE I SAID...
"...DON'T WORRY.
"IT'S ALL BEEN TAKEN CARE OF."
MAXIMUM SECURITY WING

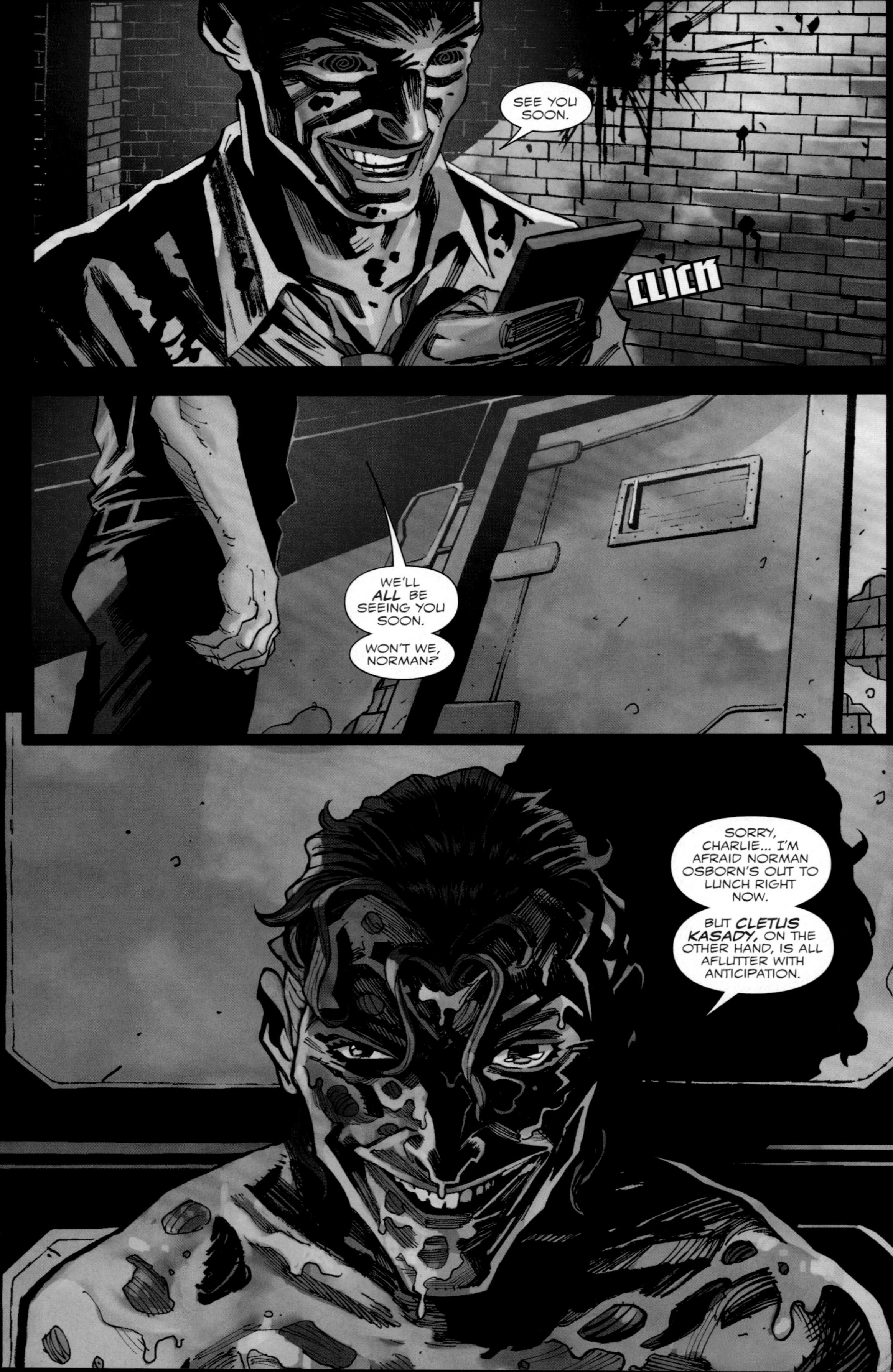
SEE YOU SOON.
CLICK
WE'LL ALL BE SEEING YOU SOON.
WON'T WE, NORMAN?
SORRY, CHARLIE... I'M AFRAID NORMAN OSBORN'S OUT TO LUNCH RIGHT NOW.
BUT CLETUS KASADY, ON THE OTHER HAND, IS ALL AFLUTTER WITH ANTICIPATION.

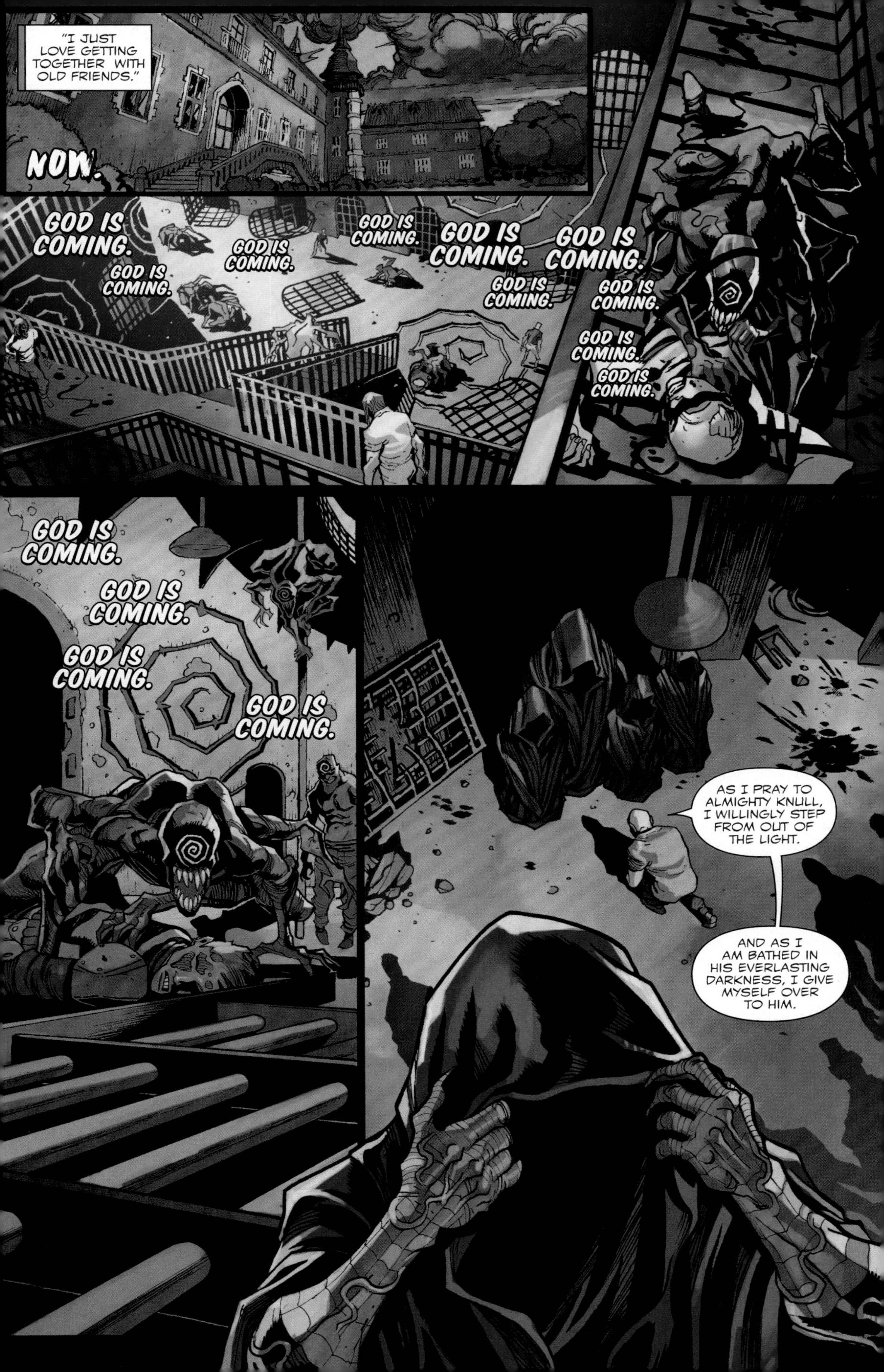
"I JUST LOVE GETTING TOGETHER WITH OLD FRIENDS."
NOW.
GOD IS COMING.
GOD IS COMING.
GOD IS COMING.
GOD IS COMING.
GOD IS COMING.
GOD IS COMING.
GOD IS COMING.
GOD IS COMING.
GOD IS COMING.
GOD IS COMING.
GOD IS COMING.
GOD IS COMING.
GOD IS COMING.
GOD IS COMING.
AS I PRAY TO ALMIGHTY KNULL, I WILLINGLY STEP FROM OUT OF THE LIGHT.
AND AS I AM BATHED IN HIS EVERLASTING DARKNESS, I GIVE MYSELF OVER TO HIM.

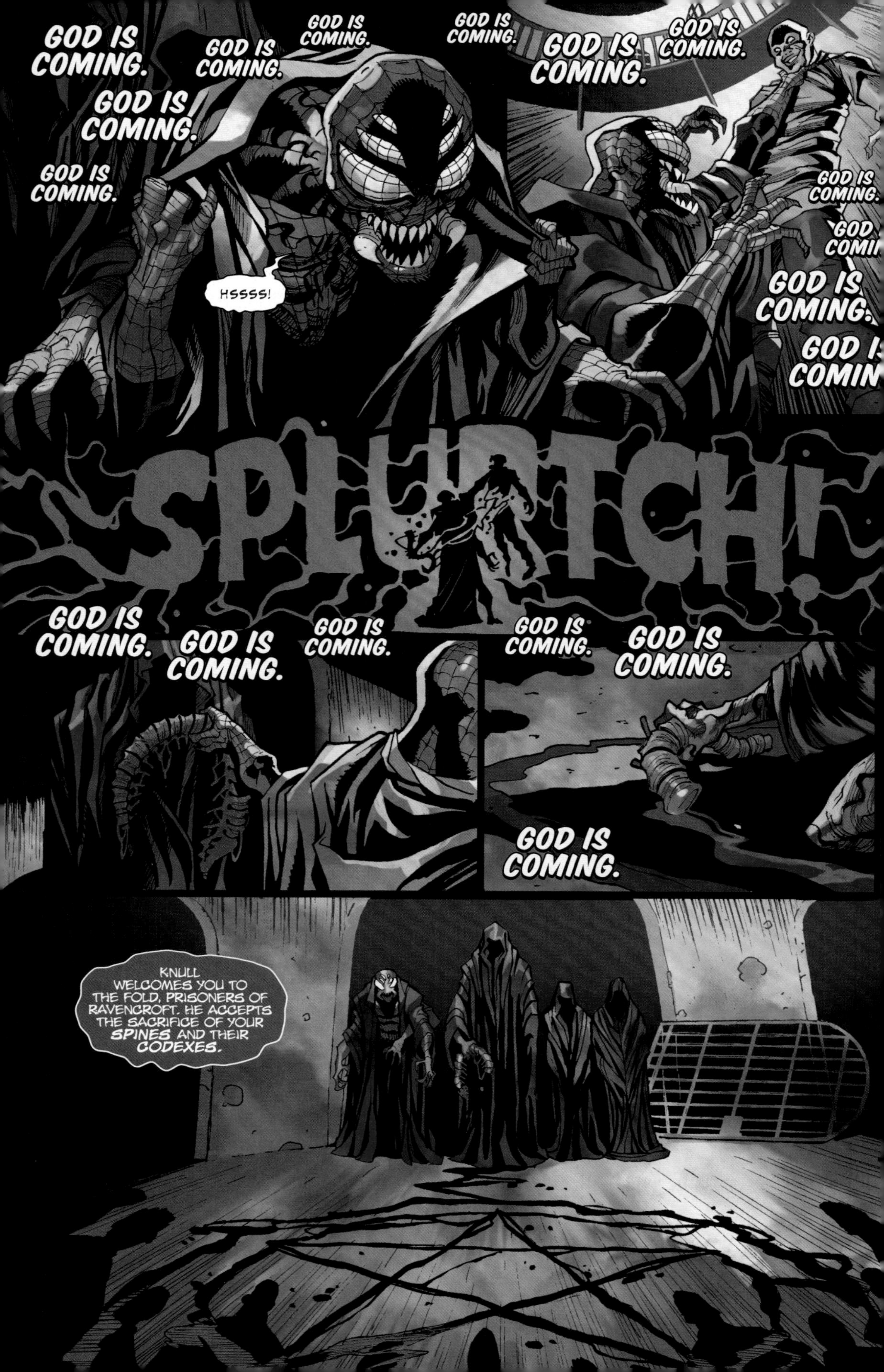
GOD IS COMING.
GOD IS COMING.
GOD IS COMING.
GOD IS COMING.
GOD IS COMING.
GOD IS COMING.
GOD IS COMING.
GOD IS COMING.
HSSSS!
GOD IS COMING.
GOD IS COMING.
SPLURTCH!
GOD IS COMING.
GOD IS COMING.
GOD IS COMING.
GOD IS COMING.
GOD IS COMING.
GOD IS COMING.
KNULL WELCOMES YOU TO THE FOLD, PRISONERS OF RAVENCROFT. HE ACCEPTS THE SACRIFICE OF YOUR SPINES AND THEIR CODEXES.

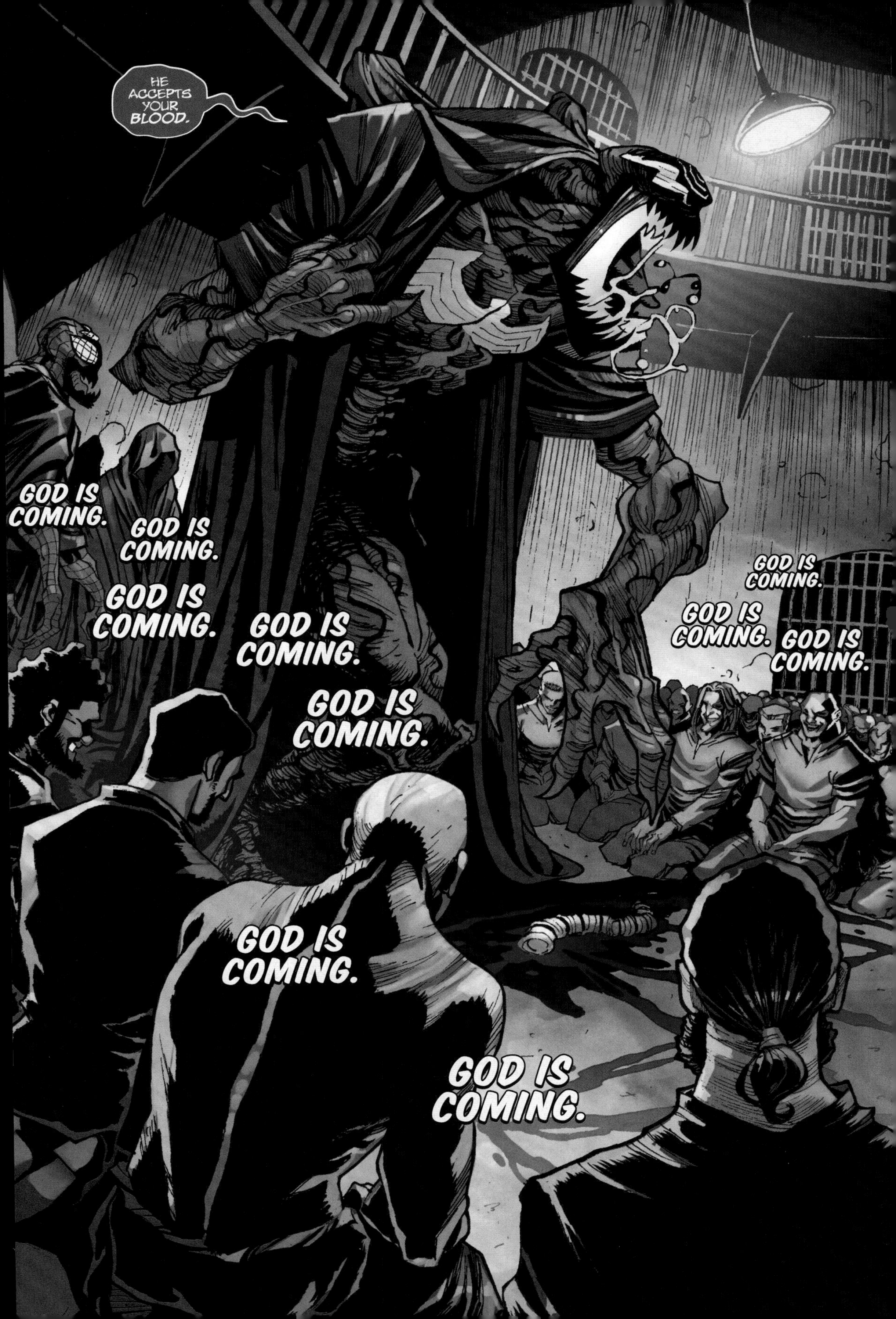
HE ACCEPTS YOUR BLOOD.
GOD IS COMING.
GOD IS COMING.
GOD IS COMING.
GOD IS COMING.
GOD IS COMING.
GOD IS COMING.
GOD IS COMING.
GOD IS COMING.
GOD IS COMING.
GOD IS COMING.

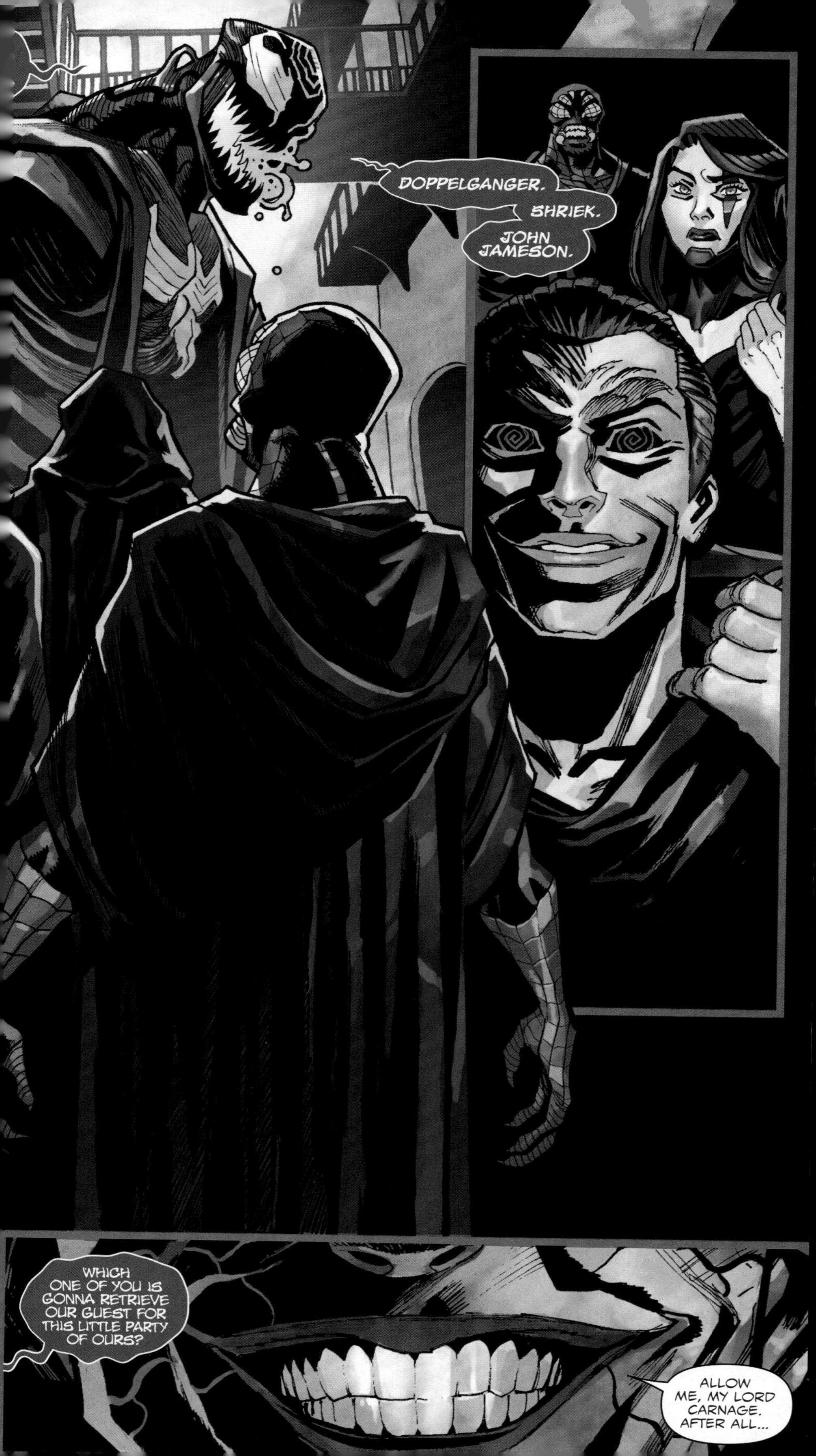
DOPPELGANGER.
SHRIEK.
JOHN JAMESON.
WHICH ONE OF YOU IS GONNA RETRIEVE OUR GUEST FOR THIS LITTLE PARTY OF OURS?
ALLOW ME, MY LORD CARNAGE. AFTER ALL...

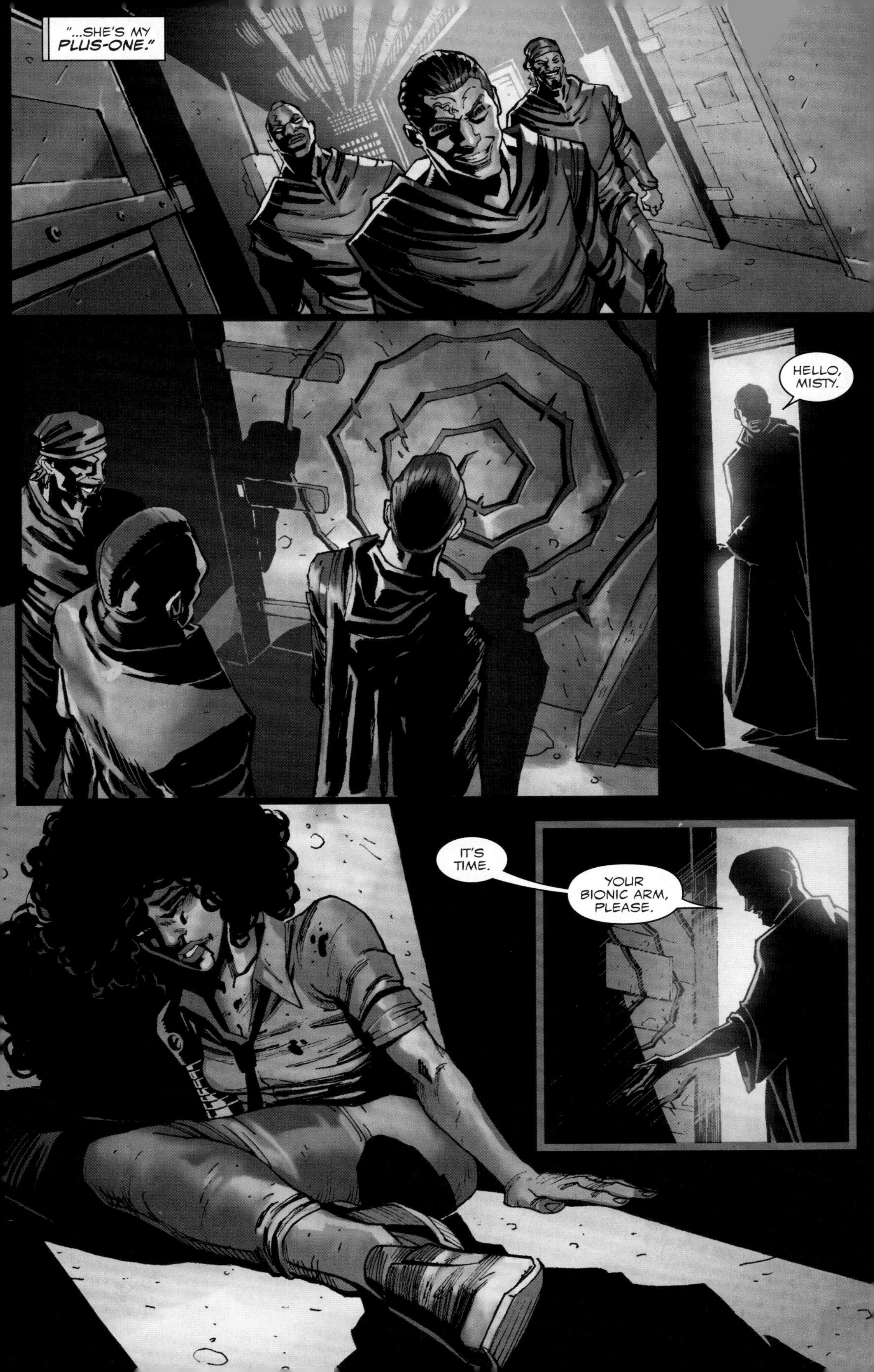
"...SHE'S MY PLUS-ONE."
HELLO, MISTY.
IT'S TIME.
YOUR BIONIC ARM, PLEASE.

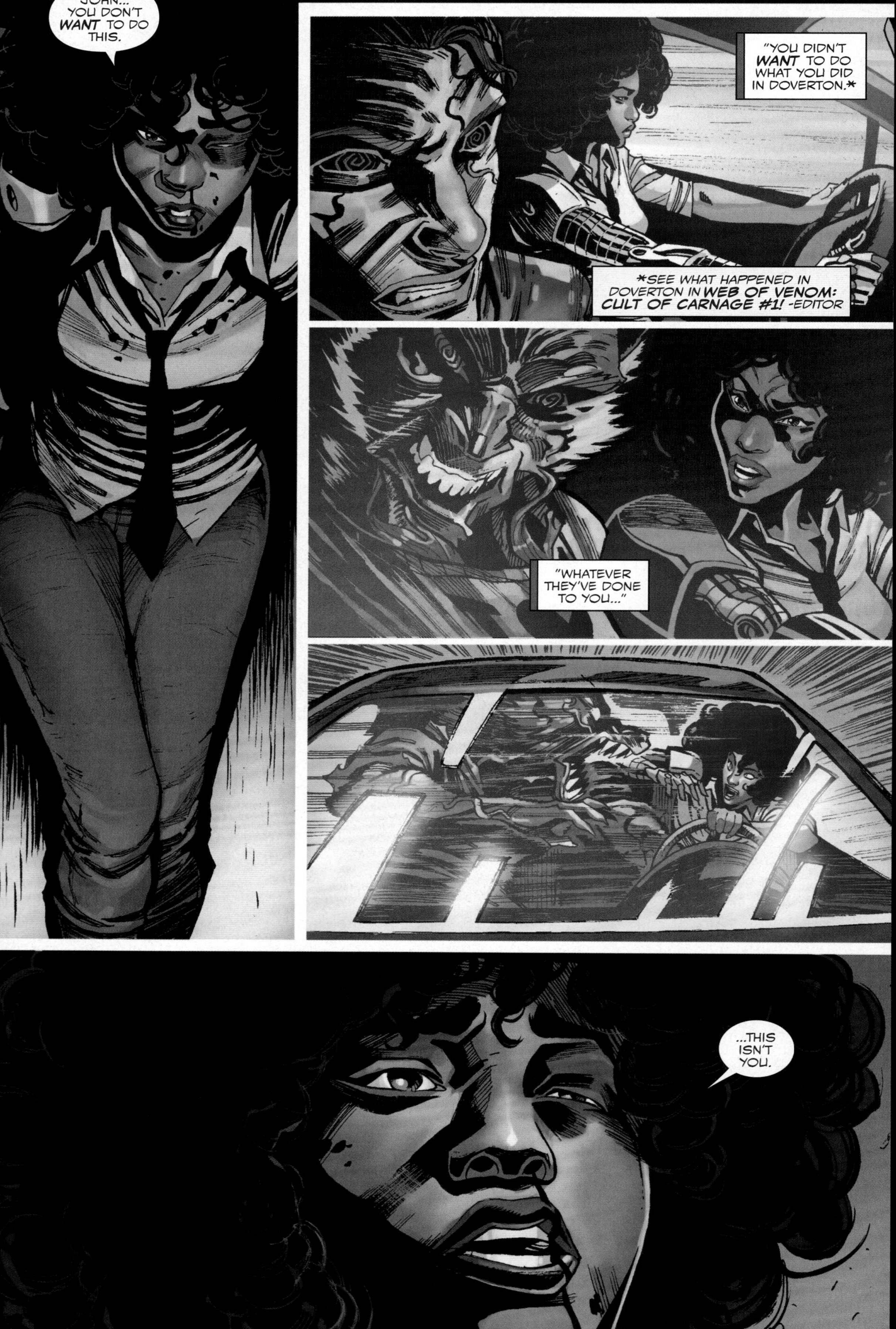
JOHN... YOU DON'T WANT TO DO THIS.
"YOU DIDN'T WANT TO DO WHAT YOU DID IN DOVERTON.*
*SEE WHAT HAPPENED IN DOVERTON IN WEB OF VENOM: CULT OF CARNAGE #1! -EDITOR
"WHATEVER THEY'VE DONE TO YOU..."
...THIS ISN'T YOU.

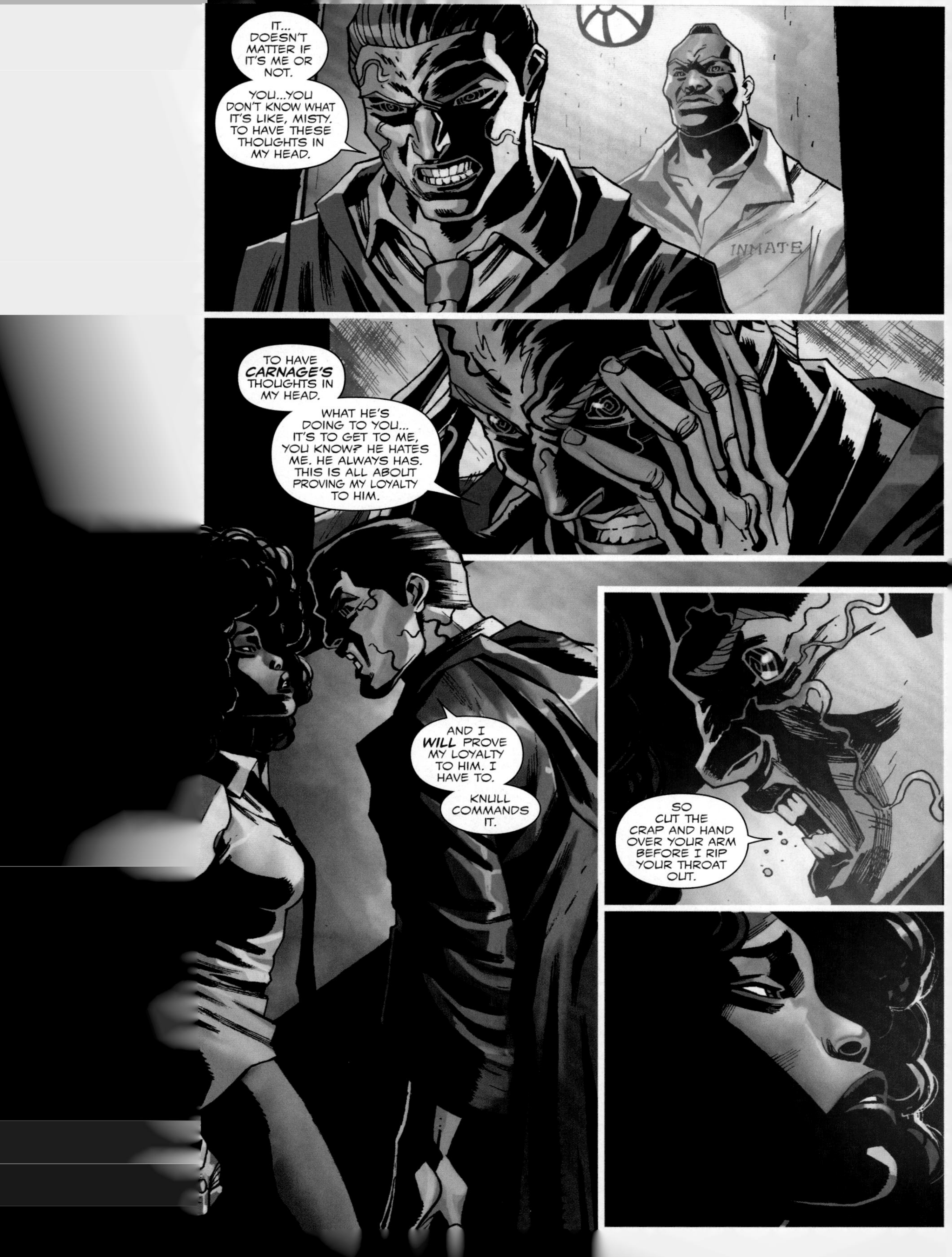
IT... DOESN'T MATTER IF IT'S ME OR NOT.
YOU...YOU DON'T KNOW WHAT IT'S LIKE, MISTY. TO HAVE THESE THOUGHTS IN MY HEAD.
INMATE
TO HAVE CARNAGE'S THOUGHTS IN MY HEAD.
WHAT HE'S DOING TO YOU... IT'S TO GET TO ME, YOU KNOW? HE HATES ME. HE ALWAYS HAS. THIS IS ALL ABOUT PROVING MY LOYALTY TO HIM.
AND I WILL PROVE MY LOYALTY TO HIM. I HAVE TO.
KNULL COMMANDS IT.
SO CUT THE CRAP AND HAND OVER YOUR ARM BEFORE I RIP YOUR THROAT OUT.

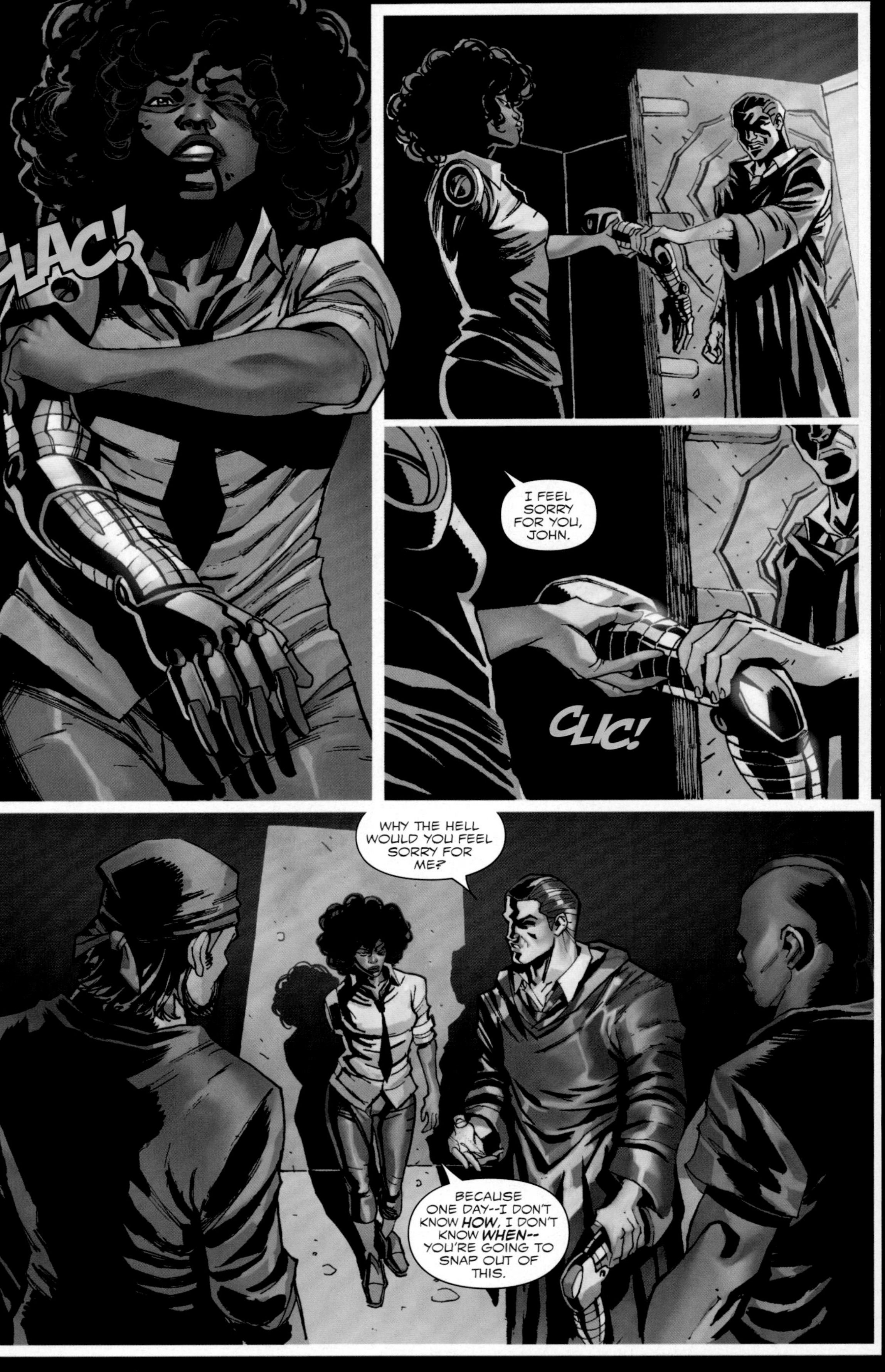

CLAC!
I FEEL SORRY FOR YOU, JOHN.
CLIC!
WHY THE HELL WOULD YOU FEEL SORRY FOR ME?
BECAUSE ONE DAY--I DON'T KNOW **HOW**, I DON'T KNOW **WHEN**-- YOU'RE GOING TO SNAP OUT OF THIS.

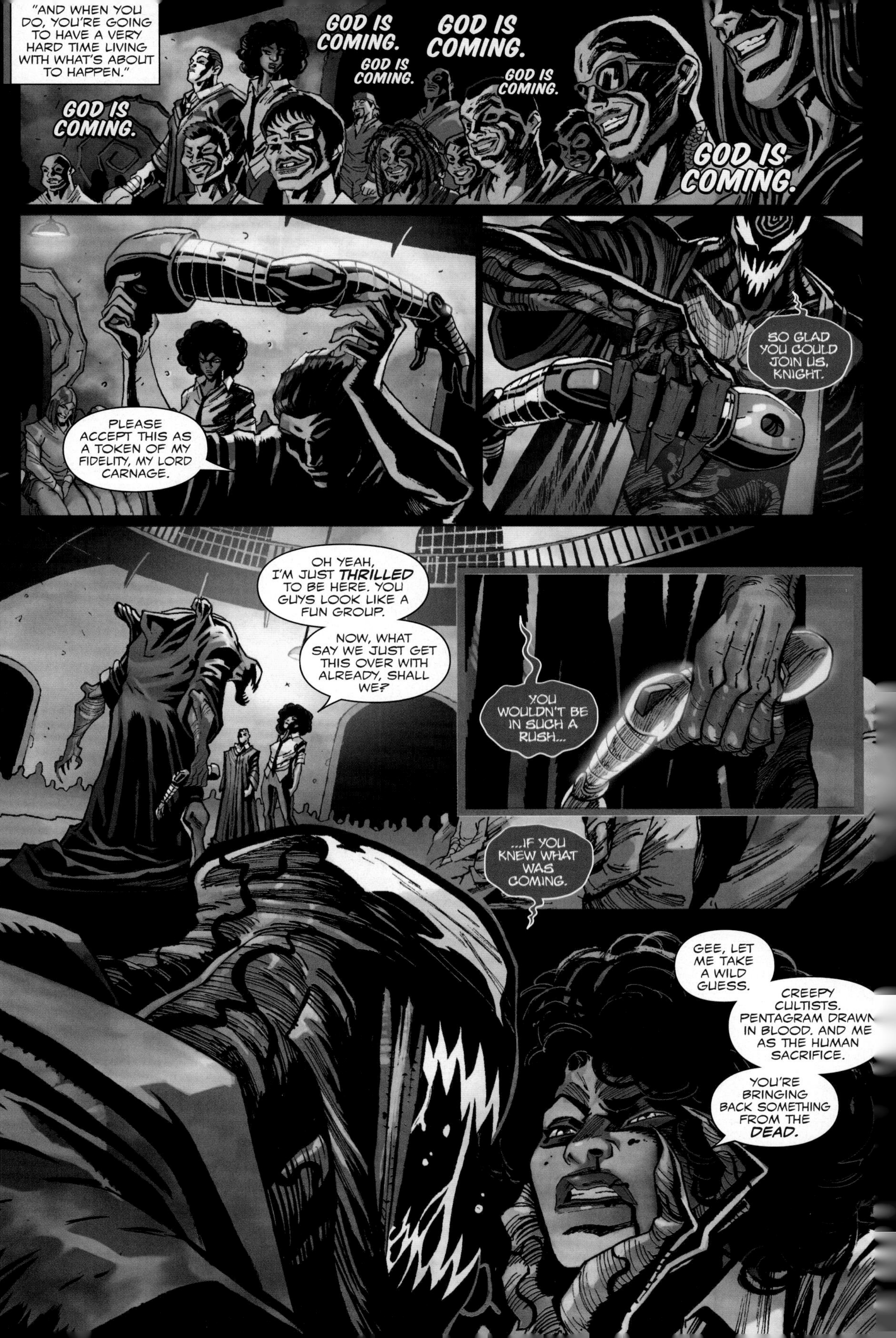
"AND WHEN YOU DO, YOU'RE GOING TO HAVE A VERY HARD TIME LIVING WITH WHAT'S ABOUT TO HAPPEN."
GOD IS COMING.
GOD IS COMING.
GOD IS COMING.
GOD IS COMING.
GOD IS COMING.
GOD IS COMING.
GOD IS COMING.
PLEASE ACCEPT THIS AS A TOKEN OF MY FIDELITY, MY LORD CARNAGE.
SO GLAD YOU COULD JOIN US, KNIGHT.
OH YEAH, I'M JUST THRILLED TO BE HERE. YOU GUYS LOOK LIKE A FUN GROUP.
NOW, WHAT SAY WE JUST GET THIS OVER WITH ALREADY, SHALL WE?
YOU WOULDN'T BE IN SUCH A RUSH...
...IF YOU KNEW WHAT WAS COMING.
GEE, LET ME TAKE A WILD GUESS.
CREEPY CULTISTS. PENTAGRAM DRAWN IN BLOOD. AND ME AS THE HUMAN SACRIFICE.
YOU'RE BRINGING BACK SOMETHING FROM THE DEAD.

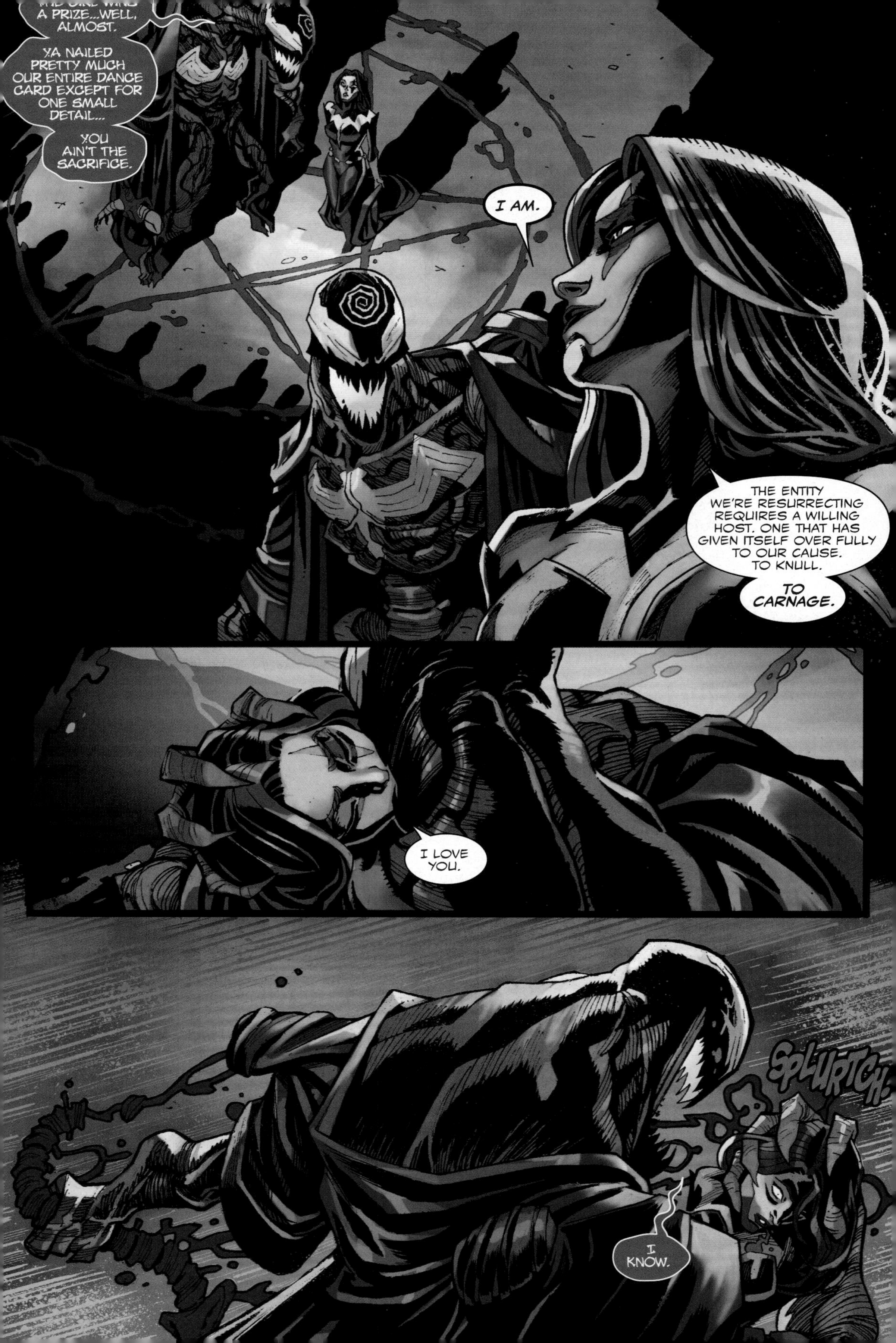
A PRIZE...WELL, ALMOST.
YA NAILED PRETTY MUCH OUR ENTIRE DANCE CARD EXCEPT FOR ONE SMALL DETAIL...
YOU AIN'T THE SACRIFICE.
I AM.
THE ENTITY WE'RE RESURRECTING REQUIRES A WILLING HOST. ONE THAT HAS GIVEN ITSELF OVER FULLY TO OUR CAUSE. TO KNULL.
TO CARNAGE.
I LOVE YOU.
SPLURTCH.
I KNOW.

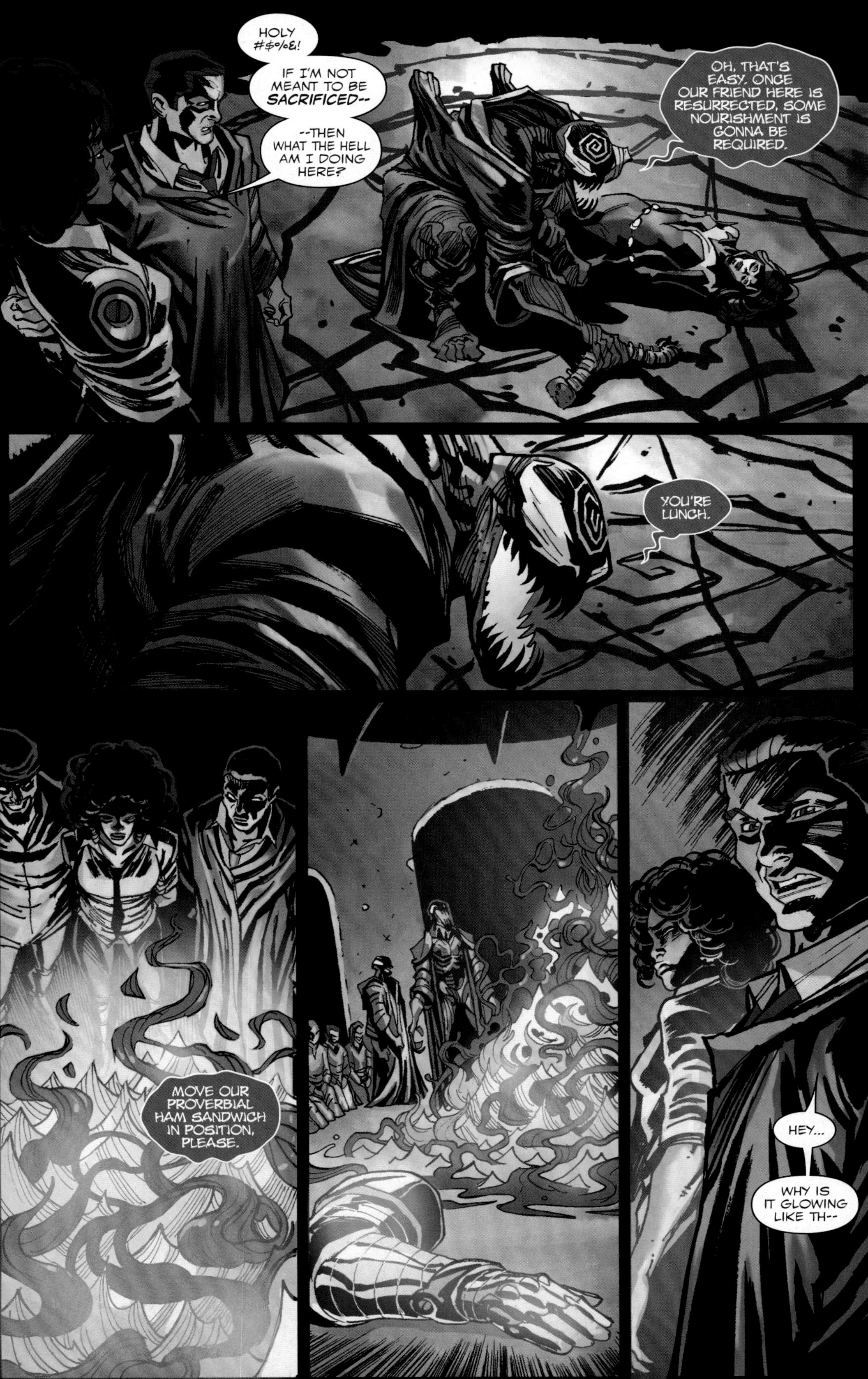
HOLY #$%&!
IF I'M NOT MEANT TO BE SACRIFICED--
--THEN WHAT THE HELL AM I DOING HERE?
OH, THAT'S EASY. ONCE OUR FRIEND HERE IS RESURRECTED, SOME NOURISHMENT IS GONNA BE REQUIRED.
YOU'RE LUNCH.
MOVE OUR PROVERBIAL HAM SANDWICH IN POSITION, PLEASE.
HEY...
WHY IS IT GLOWING LIKE TH--

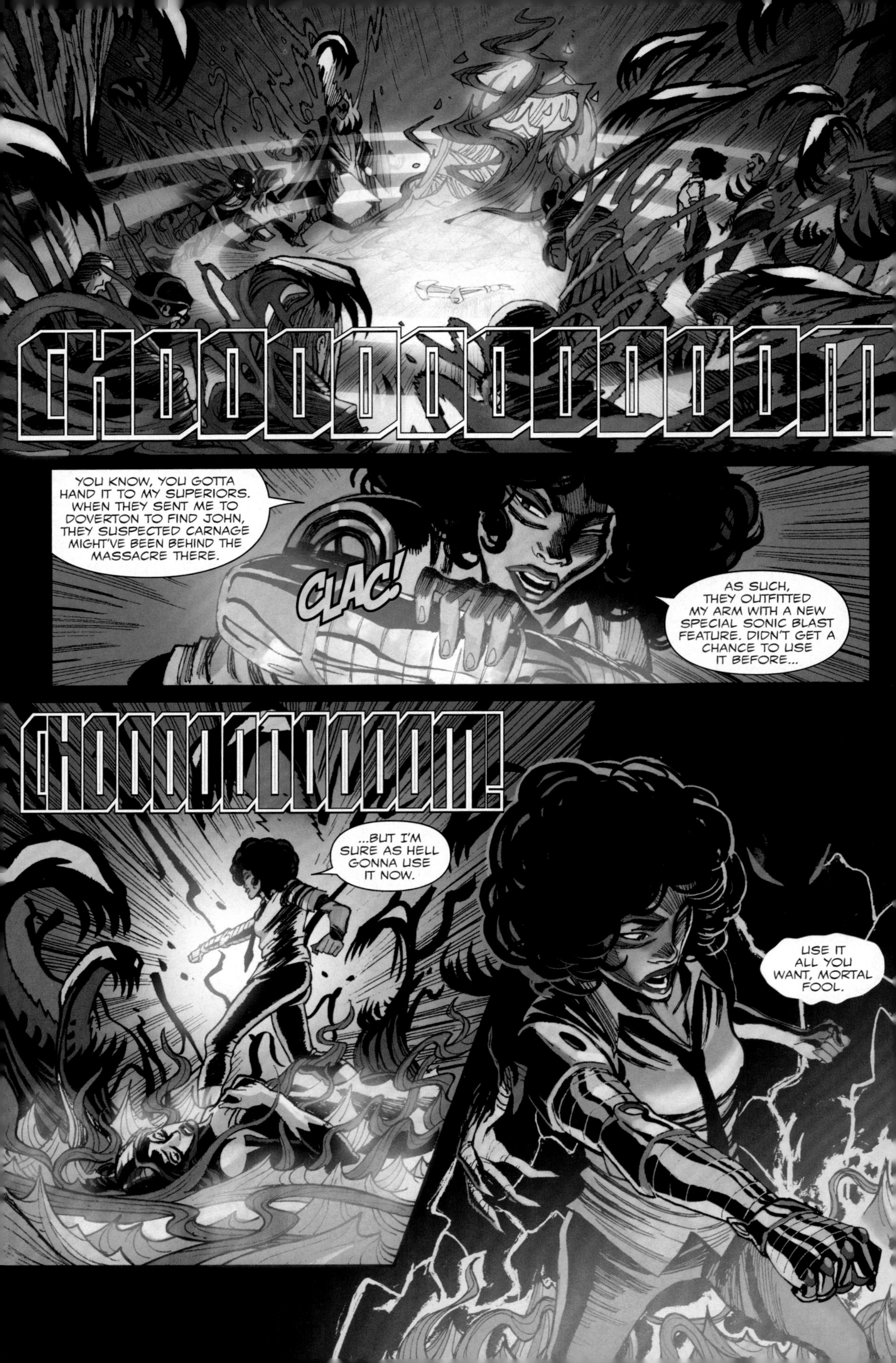
CHOOOOOOOOOOM
YOU KNOW, YOU GOTTA HAND IT TO MY SUPERIORS. WHEN THEY SENT ME TO DOVERTON TO FIND JOHN, THEY SUSPECTED CARNAGE MIGHT'VE BEEN BEHIND THE MASSACRE THERE.
CLAC!
AS SUCH, THEY OUTFITTED MY ARM WITH A NEW SPECIAL SONIC BLAST FEATURE. DIDN'T GET A CHANCE TO USE IT BEFORE...
CHOOOOOOOOOOM!
...BUT I'M SURE AS HELL GONNA USE IT NOW.
USE IT ALL YOU WANT, MORTAL FOOL.

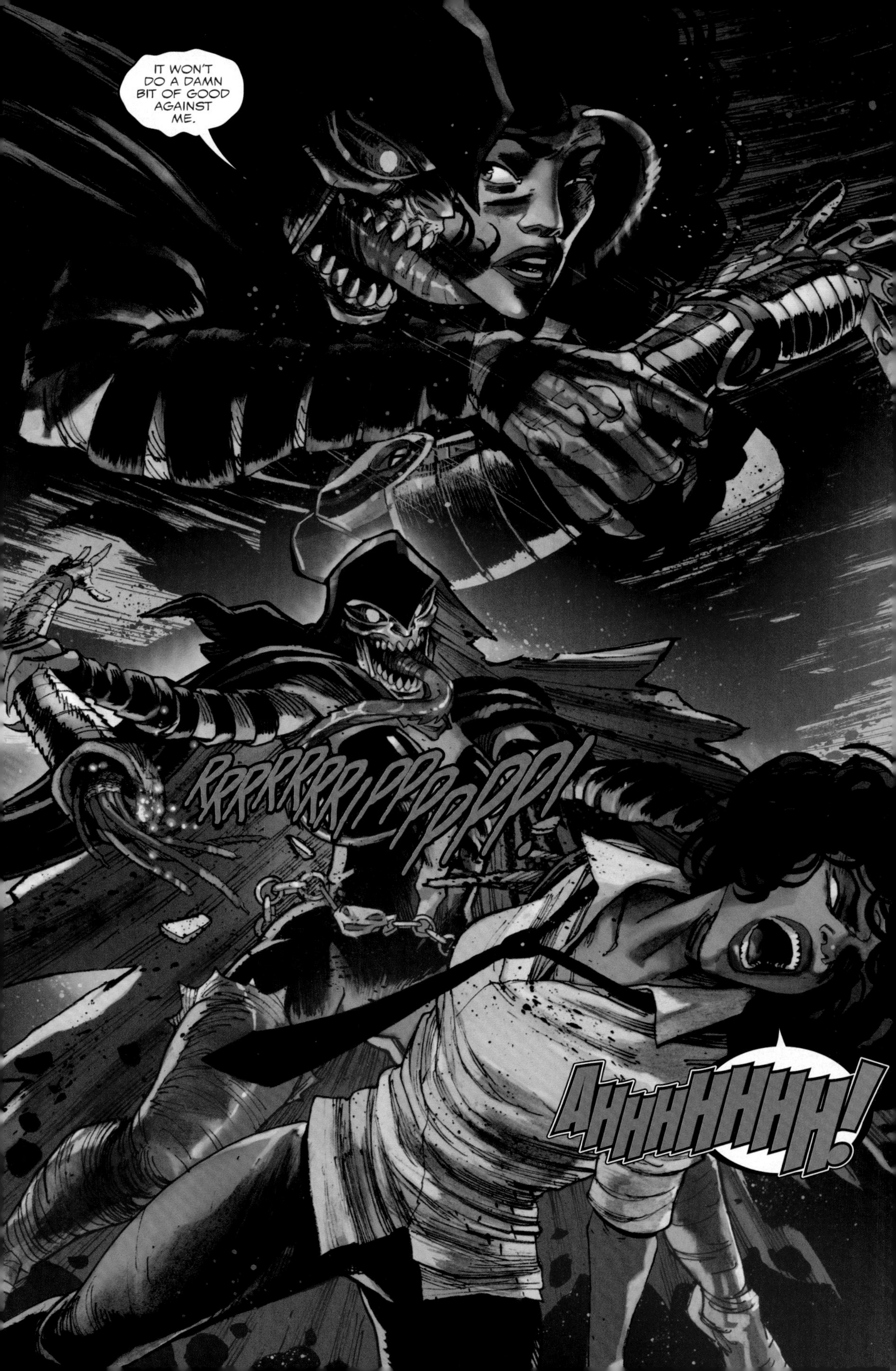
IT WON'T DO A DAMN BIT OF GOOD AGAINST ME.
RRRRRRRRIPPPPPPP!
AHHHHHHH!

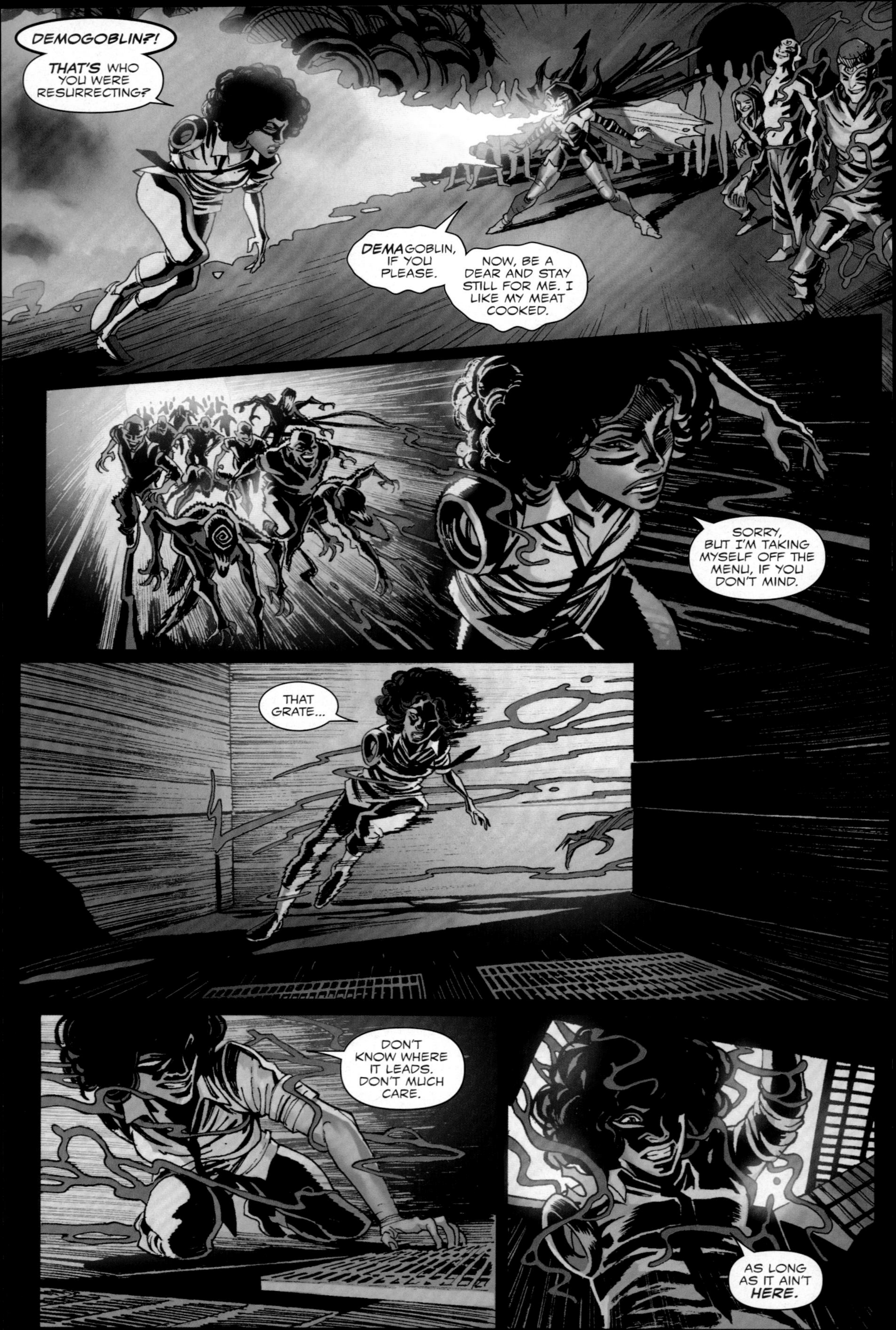
DEMOGOBLIN?!
THAT'S WHO YOU WERE RESURRECTING?
DEMAGOBLIN, IF YOU PLEASE.
NOW, BE A DEAR AND STAY STILL FOR ME. I LIKE MY MEAT COOKED.
SORRY, BUT I'M TAKING MYSELF OFF THE MENU, IF YOU DON'T MIND.
THAT GRATE...
DON'T KNOW WHERE IT LEADS. DON'T MUCH CARE.
AS LONG AS IT AIN'T HERE.

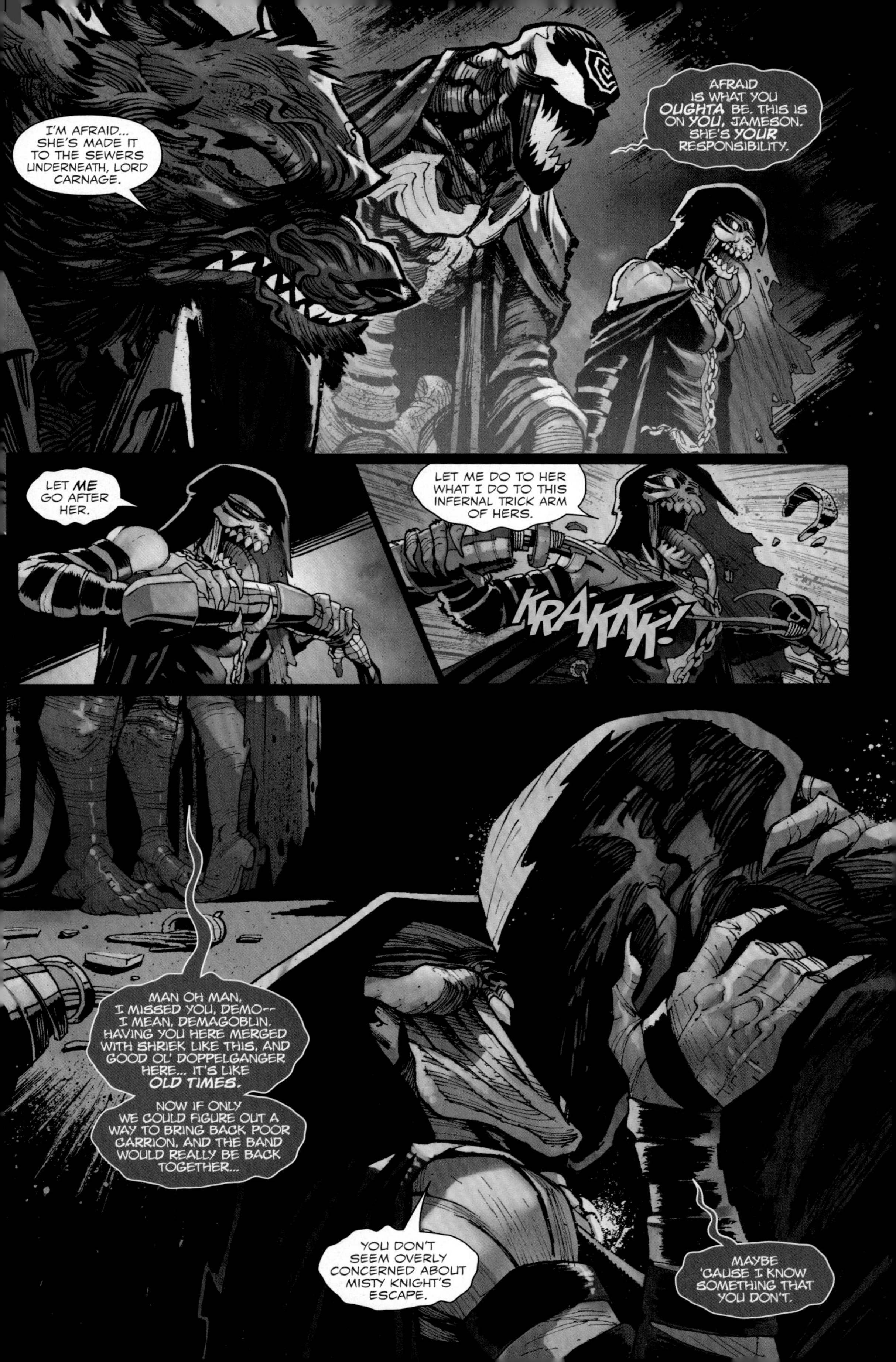
I'M AFRAID... SHE'S MADE IT TO THE SEWERS UNDERNEATH, LORD CARNAGE.
AFRAID IS WHAT YOU OUGHTA BE. THIS IS ON YOU, JAMESON. SHE'S YOUR RESPONSIBILITY.
LET ME GO AFTER HER.
LET ME DO TO HER WHAT I DO TO THIS INFERNAL TRICK ARM OF HERS.
KRAKKKK!
MAN OH MAN, I MISSED YOU, DEMO-- I MEAN, DEMAGOBLIN. HAVING YOU HERE MERGED WITH SHRIEK LIKE THIS, AND GOOD OL' DOPPELGANGER HERE... IT'S LIKE OLD TIMES.
NOW IF ONLY WE COULD FIGURE OUT A WAY TO BRING BACK POOR CARRION, AND THE BAND WOULD REALLY BE BACK TOGETHER...
YOU DON'T SEEM OVERLY CONCERNED ABOUT MISTY KNIGHT'S ESCAPE.
MAYBE 'CAUSE I KNOW SOMETHING THAT YOU DON'T.

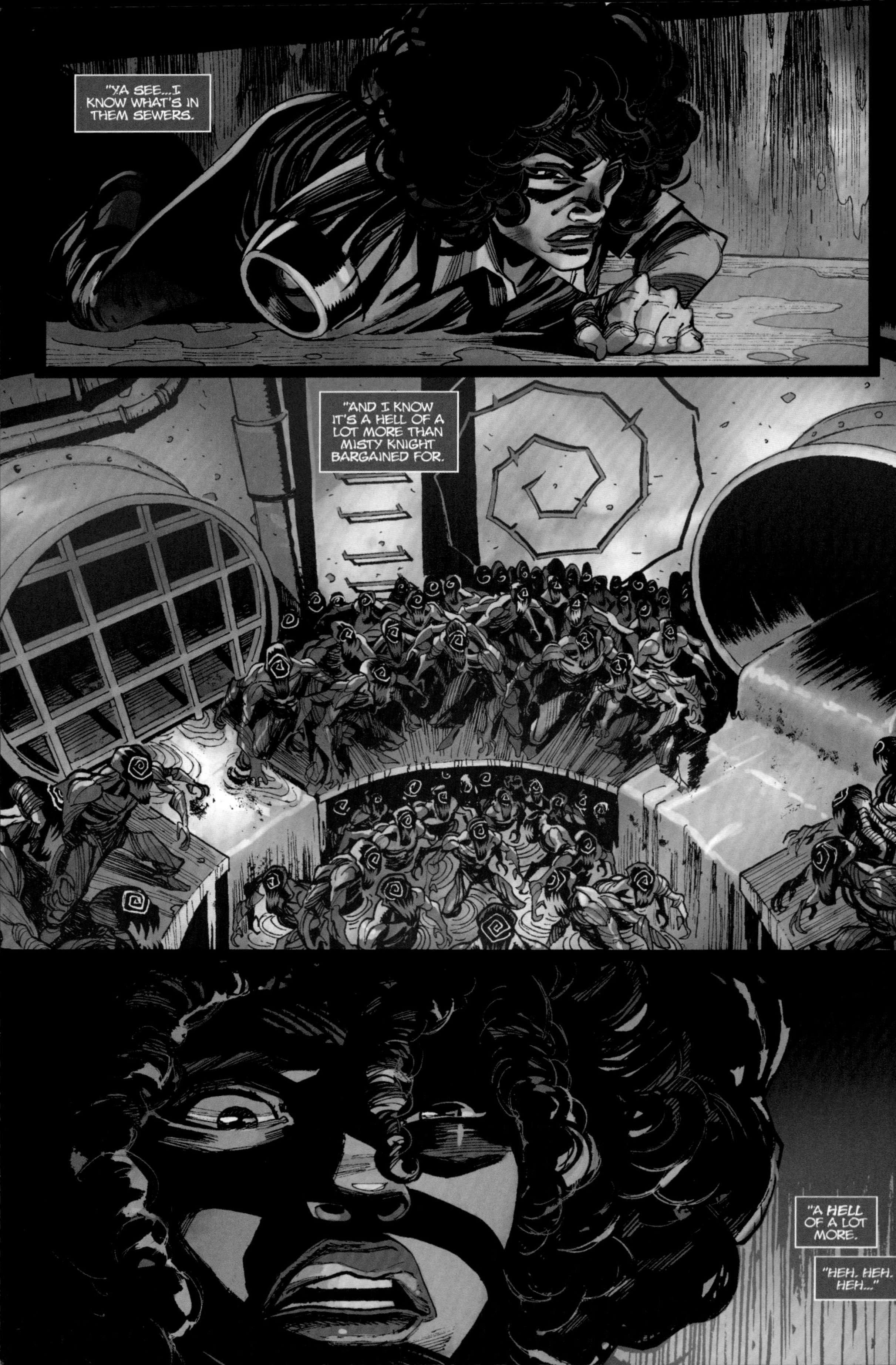
"Y'A SEE...I KNOW WHAT'S IN THEM SEWERS.
"AND I KNOW IT'S A HELL OF A LOT MORE THAN MISTY KNIGHT BARGAINED FOR.
"A HELL OF A LOT MORE.
"HEH. HEH. HEH..."

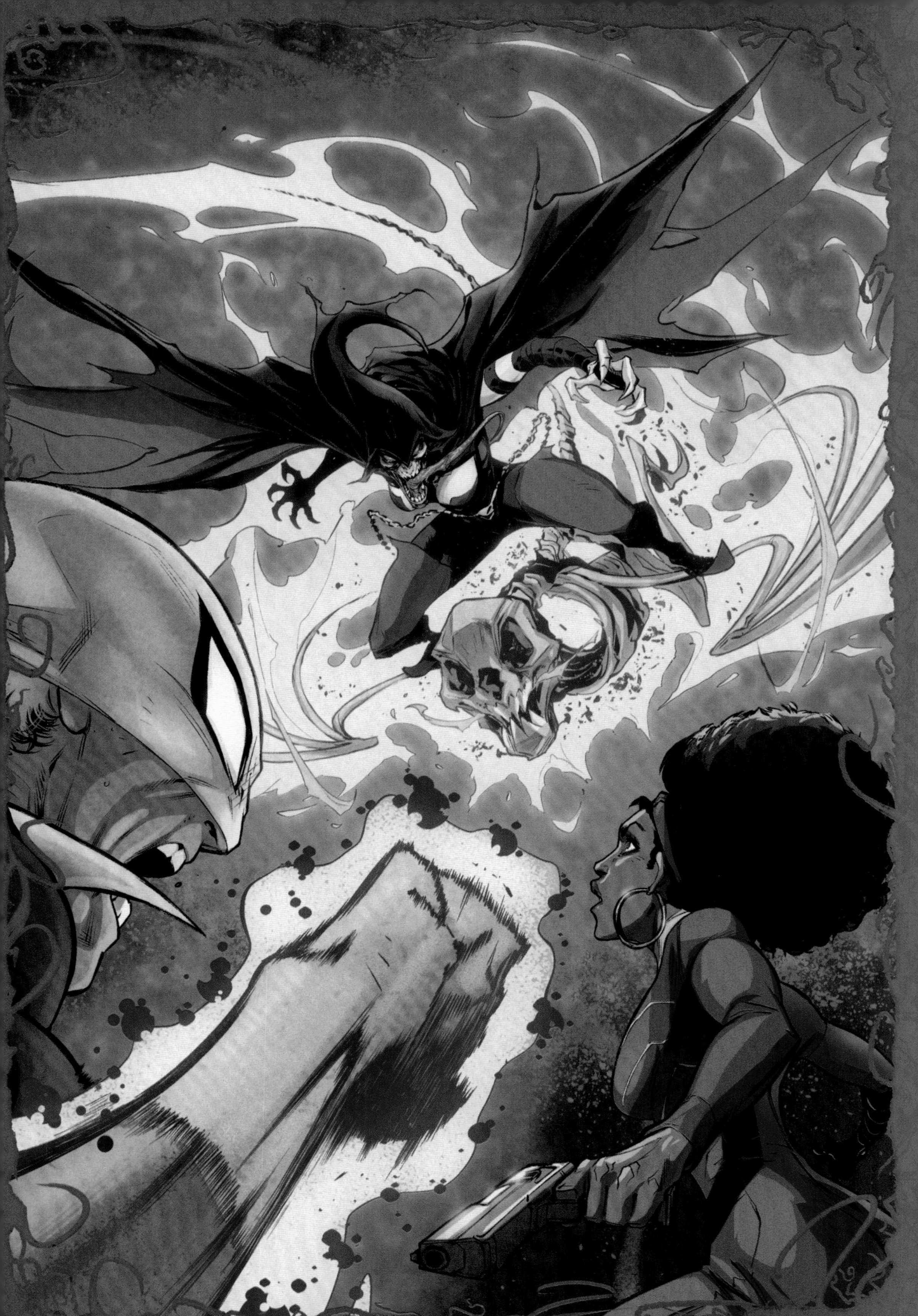

LETHAL PROTECTORS 2

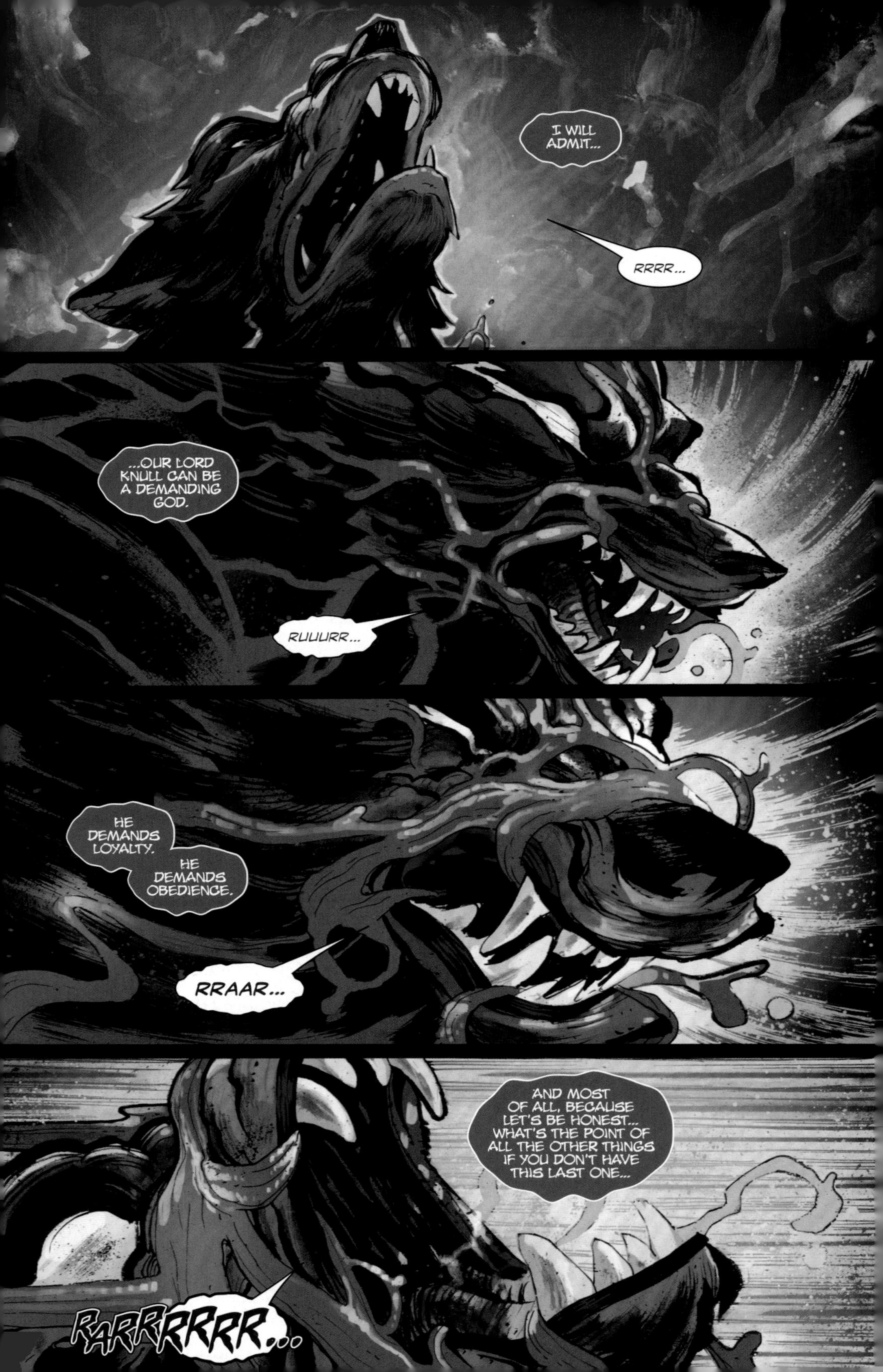

I WILL ADMIT...
RRRR...
...OUR LORD KNULL CAN BE A DEMANDING GOD.
RUUURR...
HE DEMANDS LOYALTY.
HE DEMANDS OBEDIENCE.
RRAAR...
AND MOST OF ALL, BECAUSE LET'S BE HONEST... WHAT'S THE POINT OF ALL THE OTHER THINGS IF YOU DON'T HAVE THIS LAST ONE...
RARRRRRR...

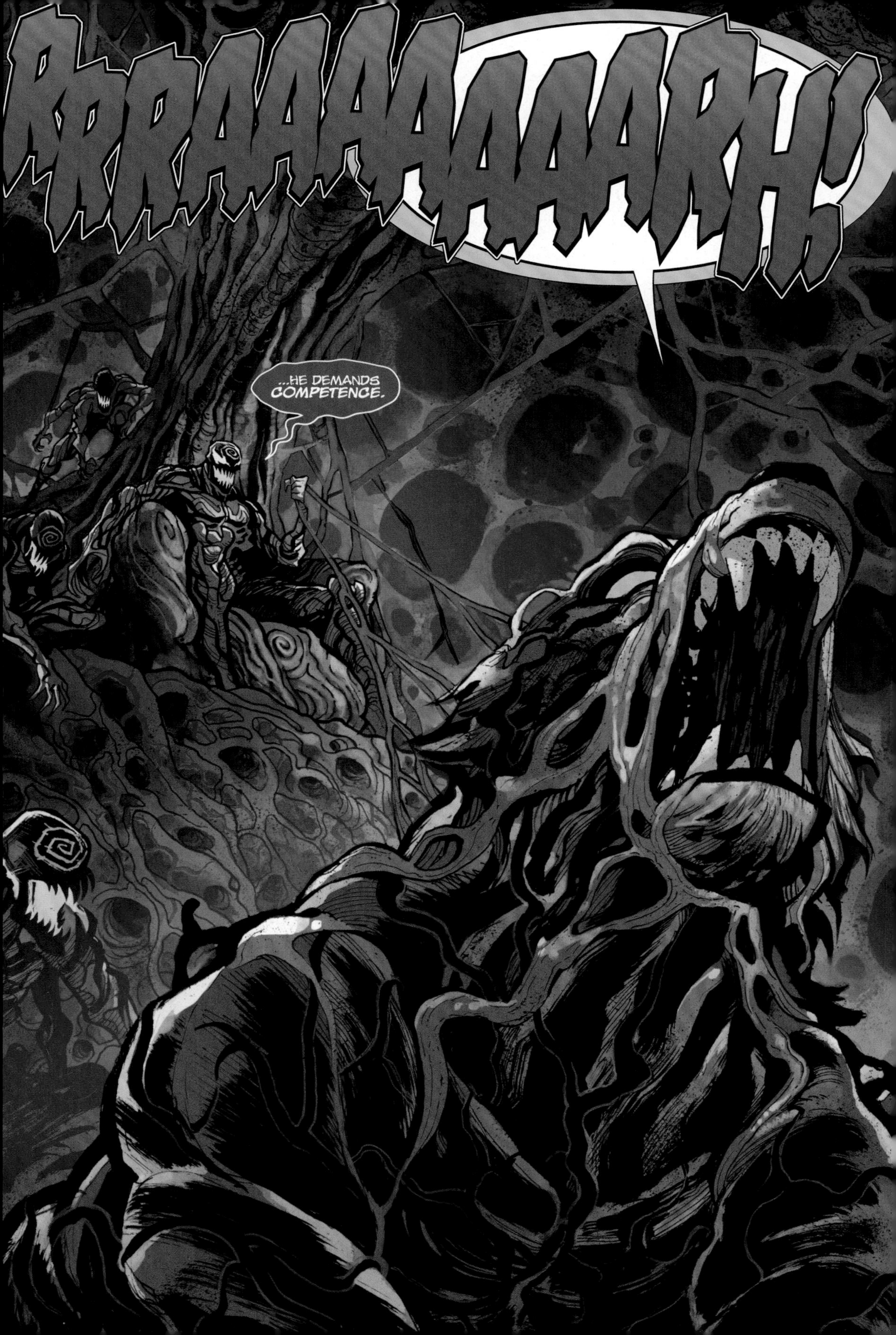
RRRAAAAAAARH!
...HE DEMANDS COMPETENCE.

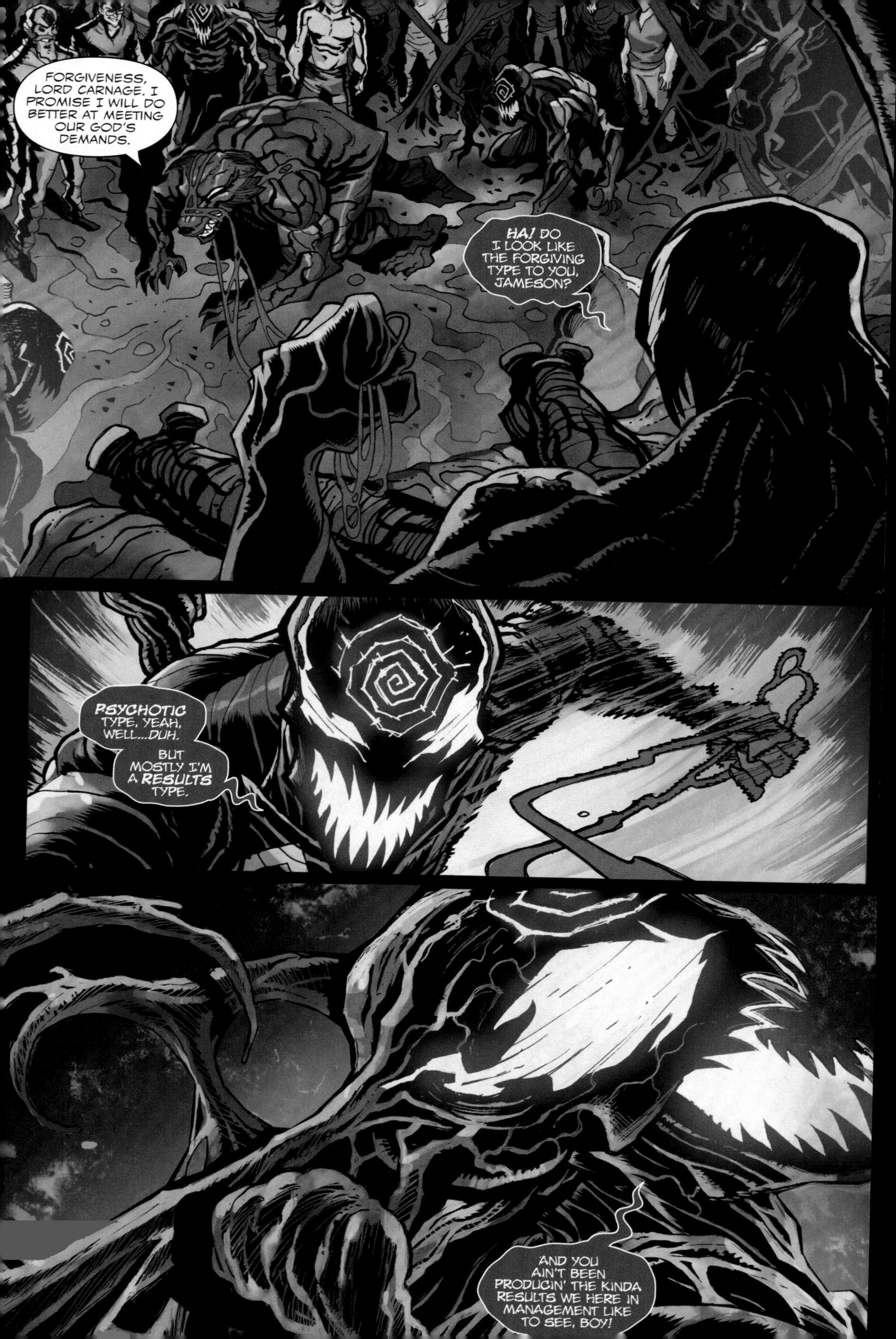
FORGIVENESS, LORD CARNAGE. I PROMISE I WILL DO BETTER AT MEETING OUR GOD'S DEMANDS.
HA! DO I LOOK LIKE THE FORGIVING TYPE TO YOU, JAMESON?
PSYCHOTIC TYPE, YEAH, WELL...DUH.
BUT MOSTLY I'M A RESULTS TYPE.
AND YOU AIN'T BEEN PRODUCIN' THE KINDA RESULTS WE HERE IN MANAGEMENT LIKE TO SEE, BOY!

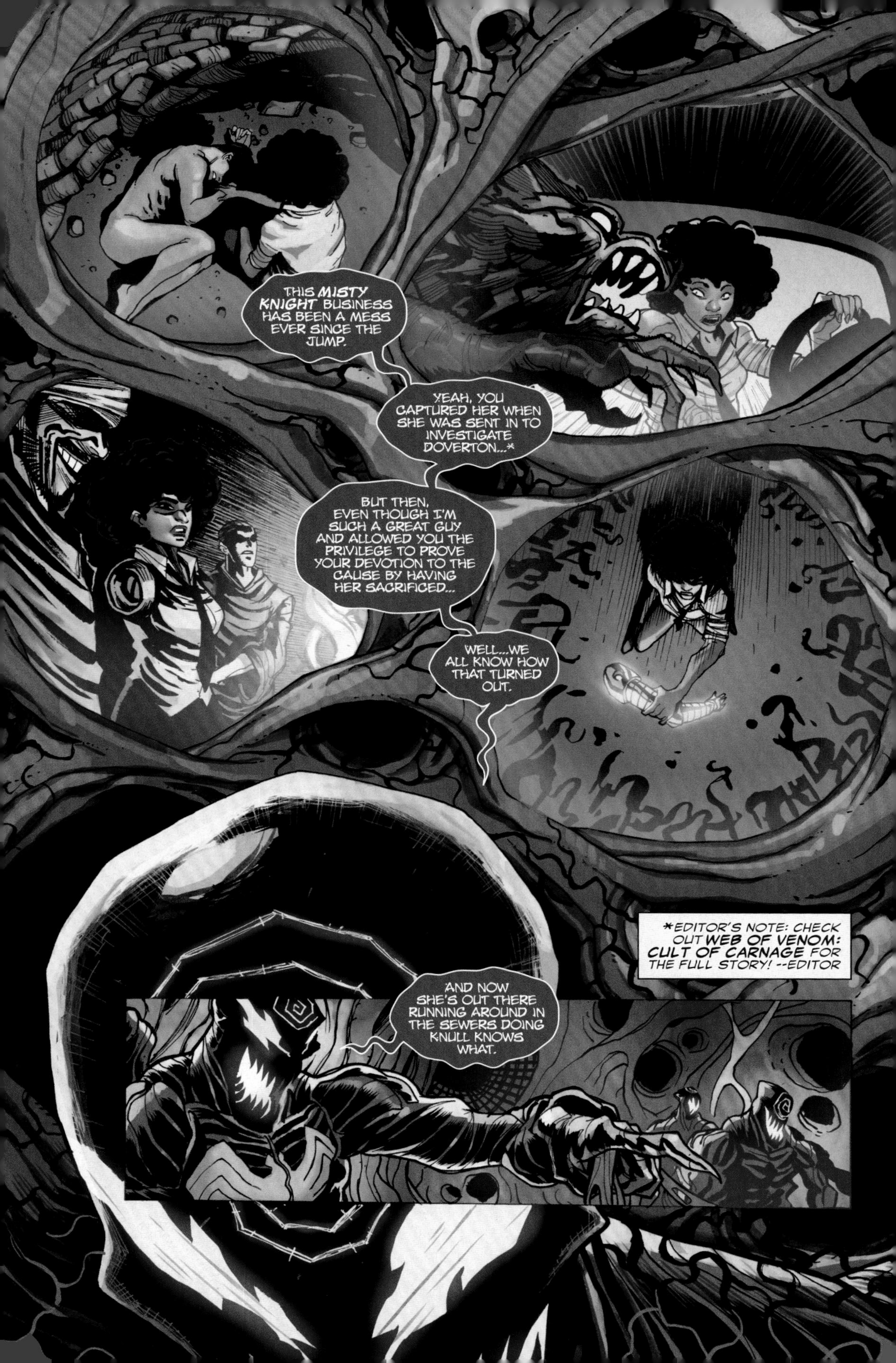
THIS MISTY KNIGHT BUSINESS HAS BEEN A MESS EVER SINCE THE JUMP.
YEAH, YOU CAPTURED HER WHEN SHE WAS SENT IN TO INVESTIGATE DOVERTON...*
BUT THEN, EVEN THOUGH I'M SUCH A GREAT GUY AND ALLOWED YOU THE PRIVILEGE TO PROVE YOUR DEVOTION TO THE CAUSE BY HAVING HER SACRIFICED...
WELL...WE ALL KNOW HOW THAT TURNED OUT.
*EDITOR'S NOTE: CHECK OUT WEB OF VENOM: CULT OF CARNAGE FOR THE FULL STORY! --EDITOR
AND NOW SHE'S OUT THERE RUNNING AROUND IN THE SEWERS DOING KNULL KNOWS WHAT.

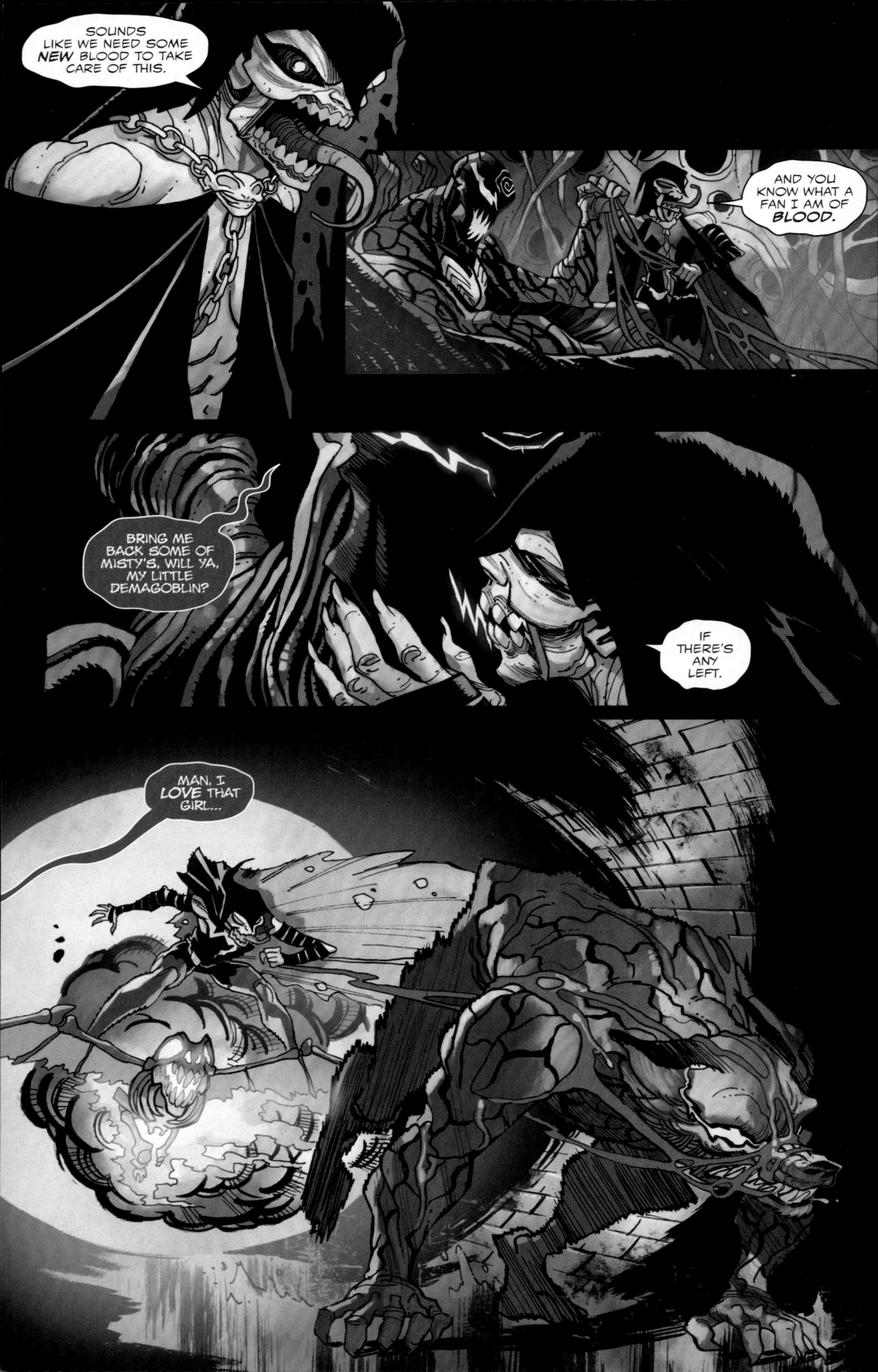
SOUNDS LIKE WE NEED SOME NEW BLOOD TO TAKE CARE OF THIS.
AND YOU KNOW WHAT A FAN I AM OF BLOOD.
BRING ME BACK SOME OF MISTY'S, WILL YA, MY LITTLE DEMAGOBLIN?
IF THERE'S ANY LEFT.
MAN, I LOVE THAT GIRL...

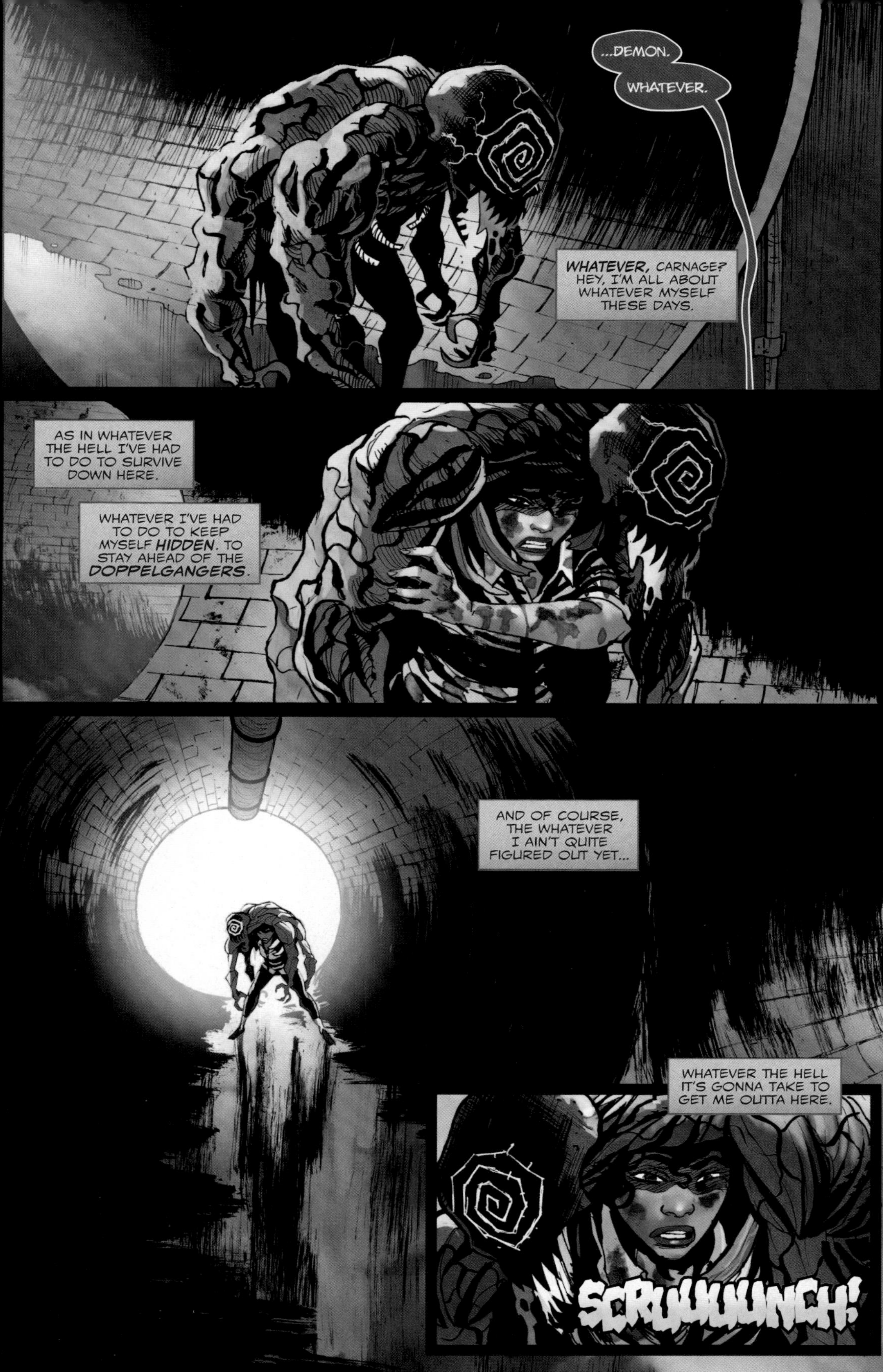
...DEMON.
WHATEVER.
WHATEVER, CARNAGE? HEY, I'M ALL ABOUT WHATEVER MYSELF THESE DAYS.
AS IN WHATEVER THE HELL I'VE HAD TO DO TO SURVIVE DOWN HERE.
WHATEVER I'VE HAD TO DO TO KEEP MYSELF HIDDEN. TO STAY AHEAD OF THE DOPPELGANGERS.
AND OF COURSE, THE WHATEVER I AIN'T QUITE FIGURED OUT YET...
WHATEVER THE HELL IT'S GONNA TAKE TO GET ME OUTTA HERE.
SCRUUUUUNCH!

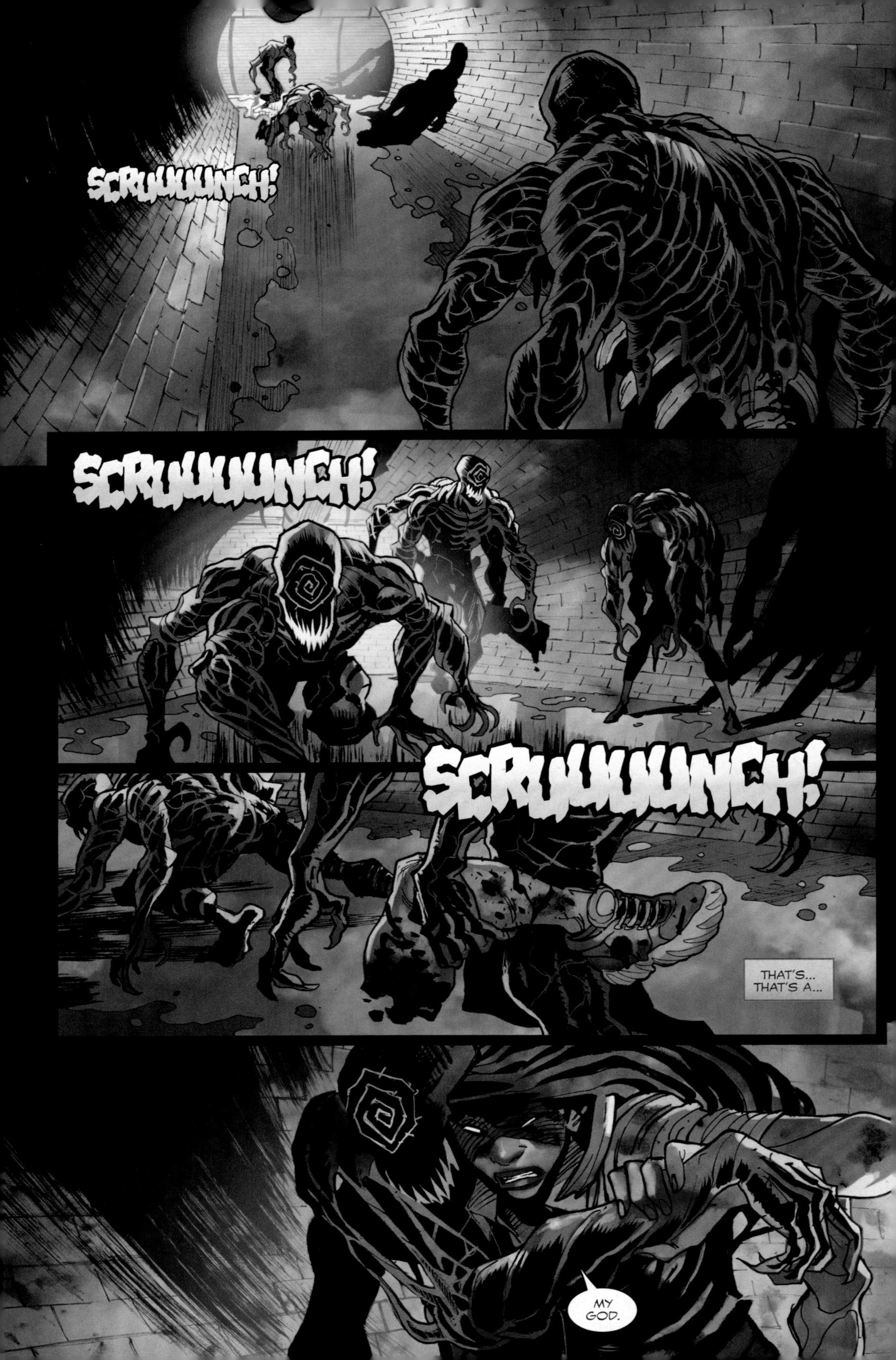
SCRUUUUNCH!
SCRUUUUUNCH!
SCRUUUUUNCH!
THAT'S... THAT'S A...
MY GOD.

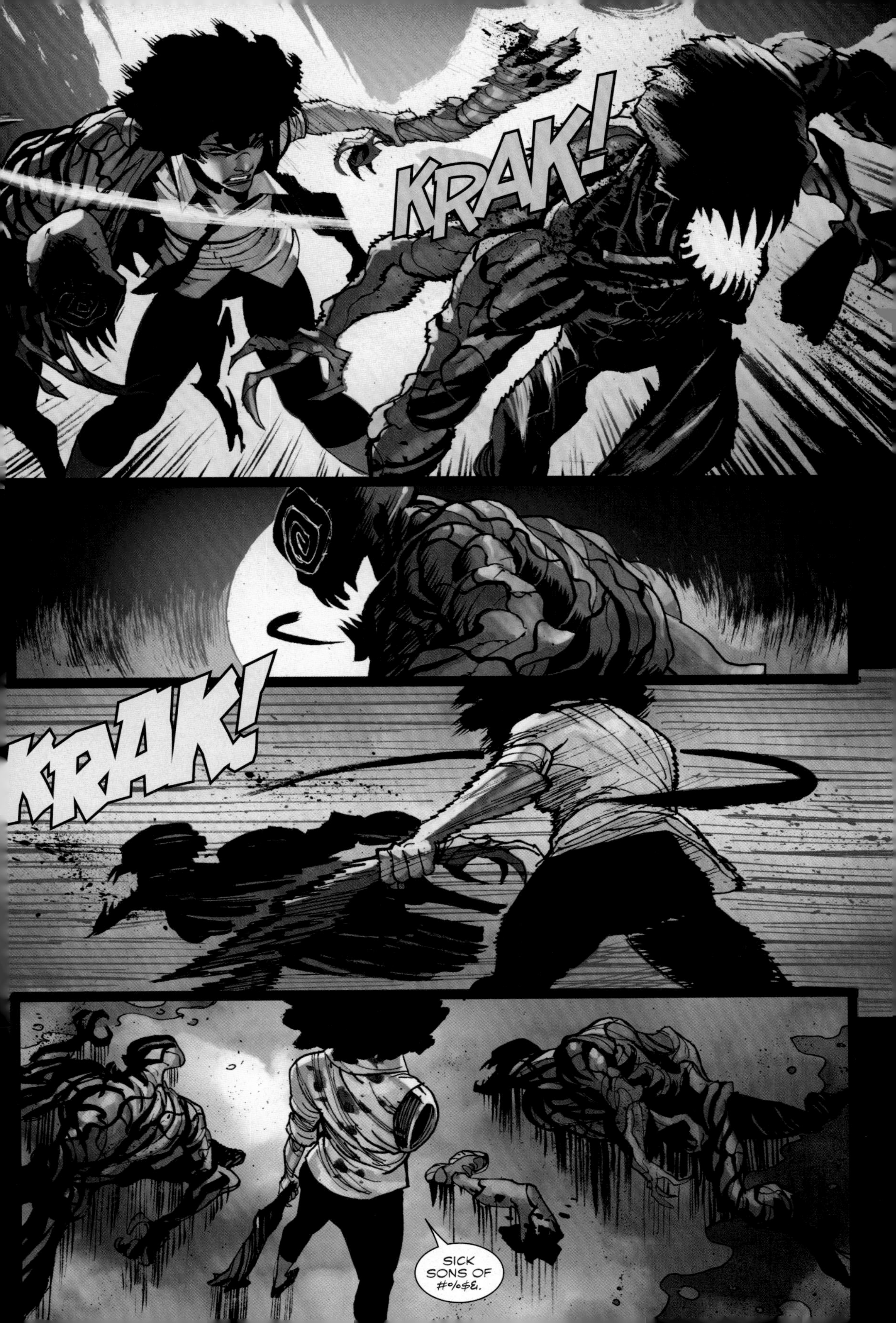
KRAK!
KRAK!
SICK SONS OF #%$&.

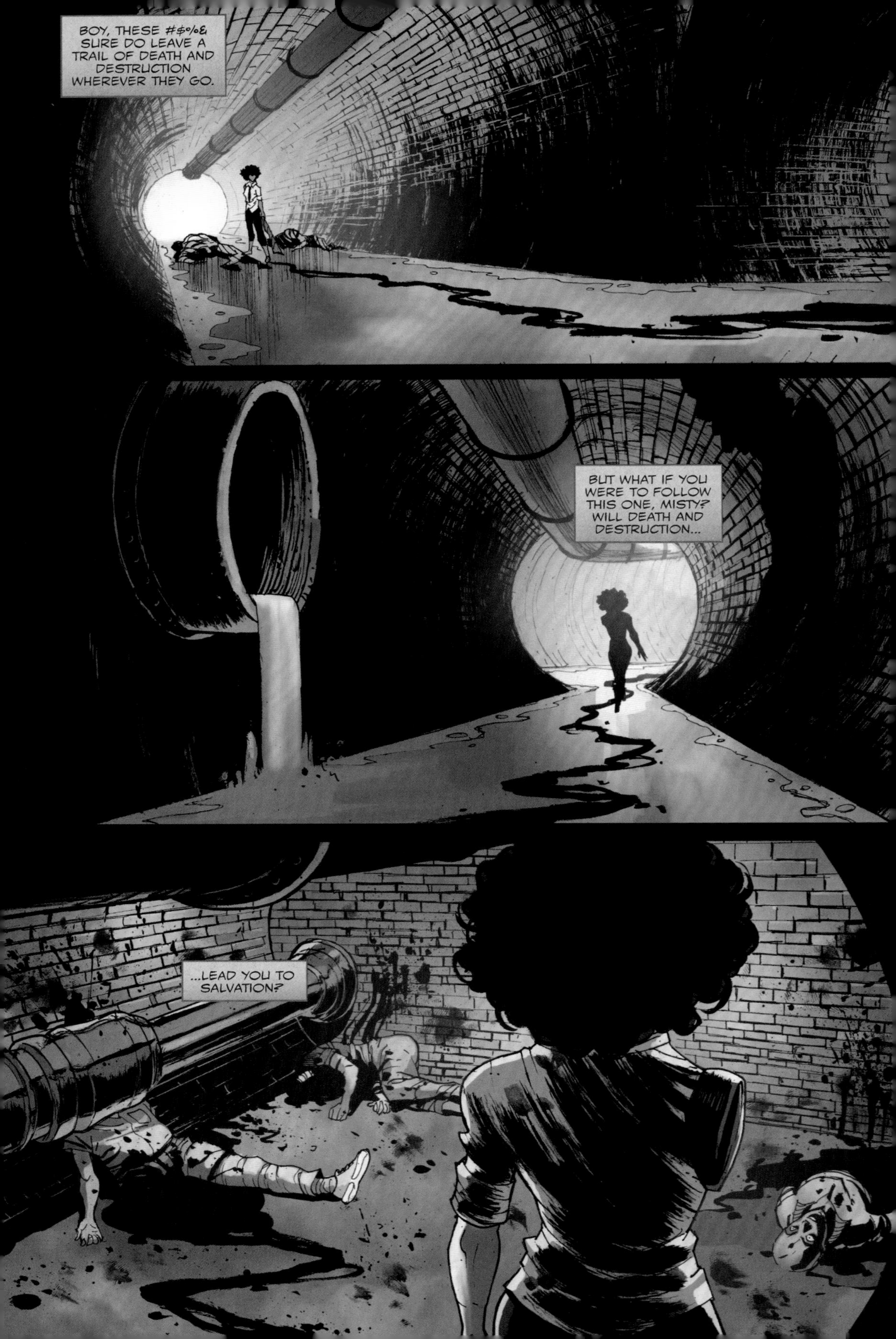
BOY, THESE #$%& SURE DO LEAVE A TRAIL OF DEATH AND DESTRUCTION WHEREVER THEY GO.
BUT WHAT IF YOU WERE TO FOLLOW THIS ONE, MISTY? WILL DEATH AND DESTRUCTION...
...LEAD YOU TO SALVATION?

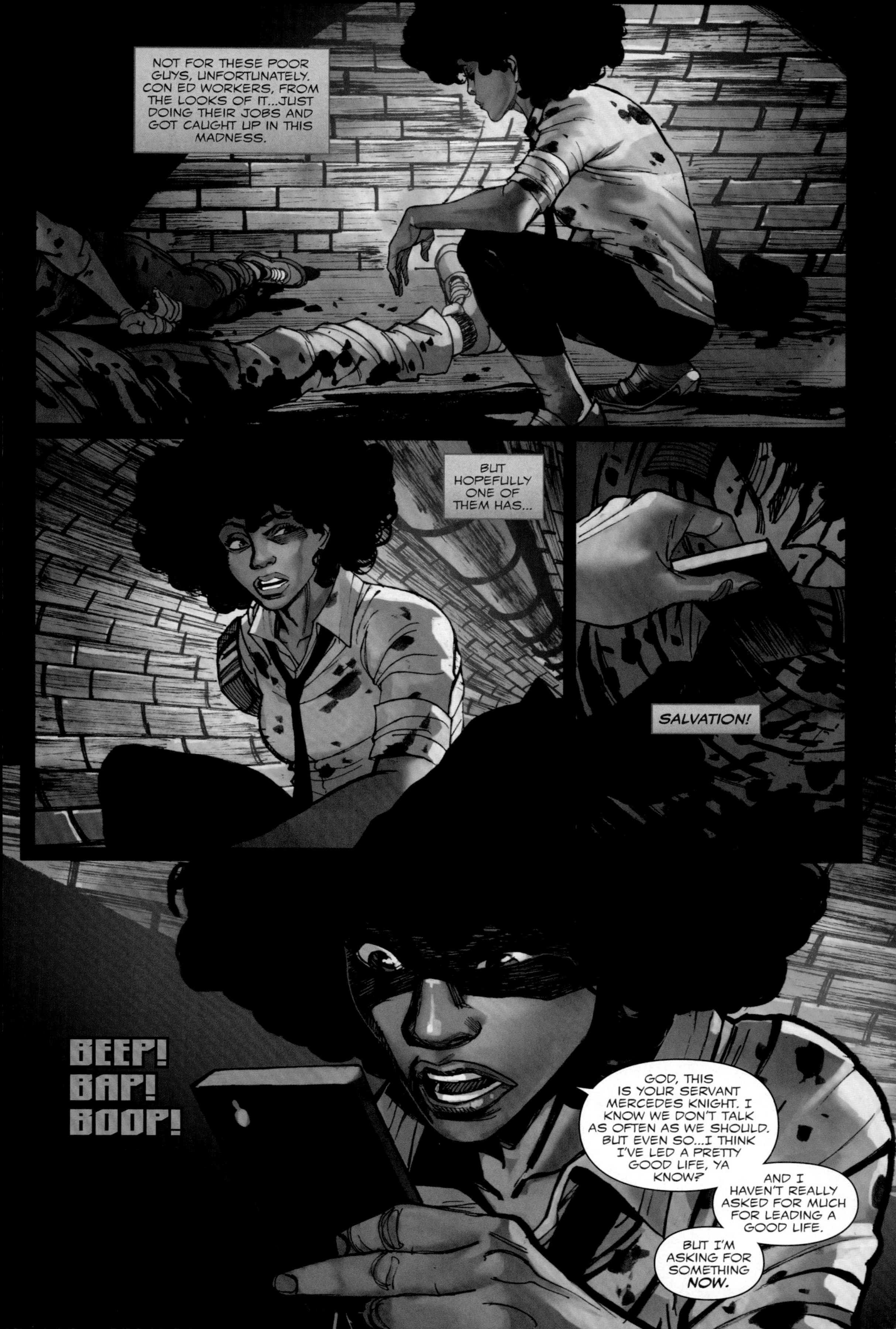
NOT FOR THESE POOR GUYS, UNFORTUNATELY. CON ED WORKERS, FROM THE LOOKS OF IT...JUST DOING THEIR JOBS AND GOT CAUGHT UP IN THIS MADNESS.
BUT HOPEFULLY ONE OF THEM HAS...
SALVATION!
BEEP! BAP! BOOP!
GOD, THIS IS YOUR SERVANT MERCEDES KNIGHT. I KNOW WE DON'T TALK AS OFTEN AS WE SHOULD. BUT EVEN SO...I THINK I'VE LED A PRETTY GOOD LIFE, YA KNOW?
AND I HAVEN'T REALLY ASKED FOR MUCH FOR LEADING A GOOD LIFE.
BUT I'M ASKING FOR SOMETHING *NOW.*

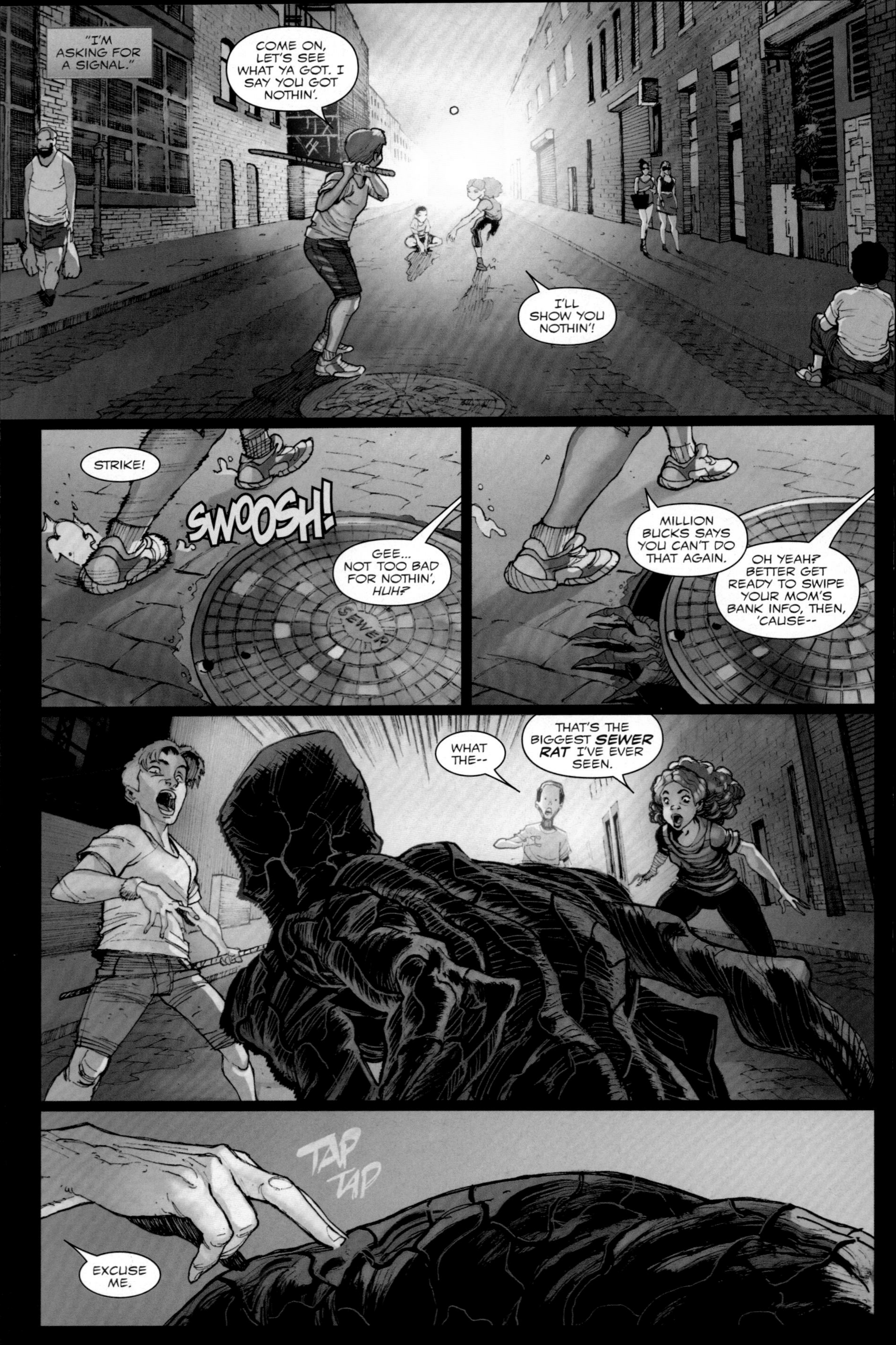
"I'M ASKING FOR A SIGNAL."
COME ON, LET'S SEE WHAT YA GOT. I SAY YOU GOT NOTHIN'.
I'LL SHOW YOU NOTHIN'!
STRIKE!
SWOOSH!
GEE... NOT TOO BAD FOR NOTHIN', HUH?
SEWER
MILLION BUCKS SAYS YOU CAN'T DO THAT AGAIN.
OH YEAH? BETTER GET READY TO SWIPE YOUR MOM'S BANK INFO, THEN, 'CAUSE--
WHAT THE--
THAT'S THE BIGGEST SEWER RAT I'VE EVER SEEN.
TAP TAP
EXCUSE ME.

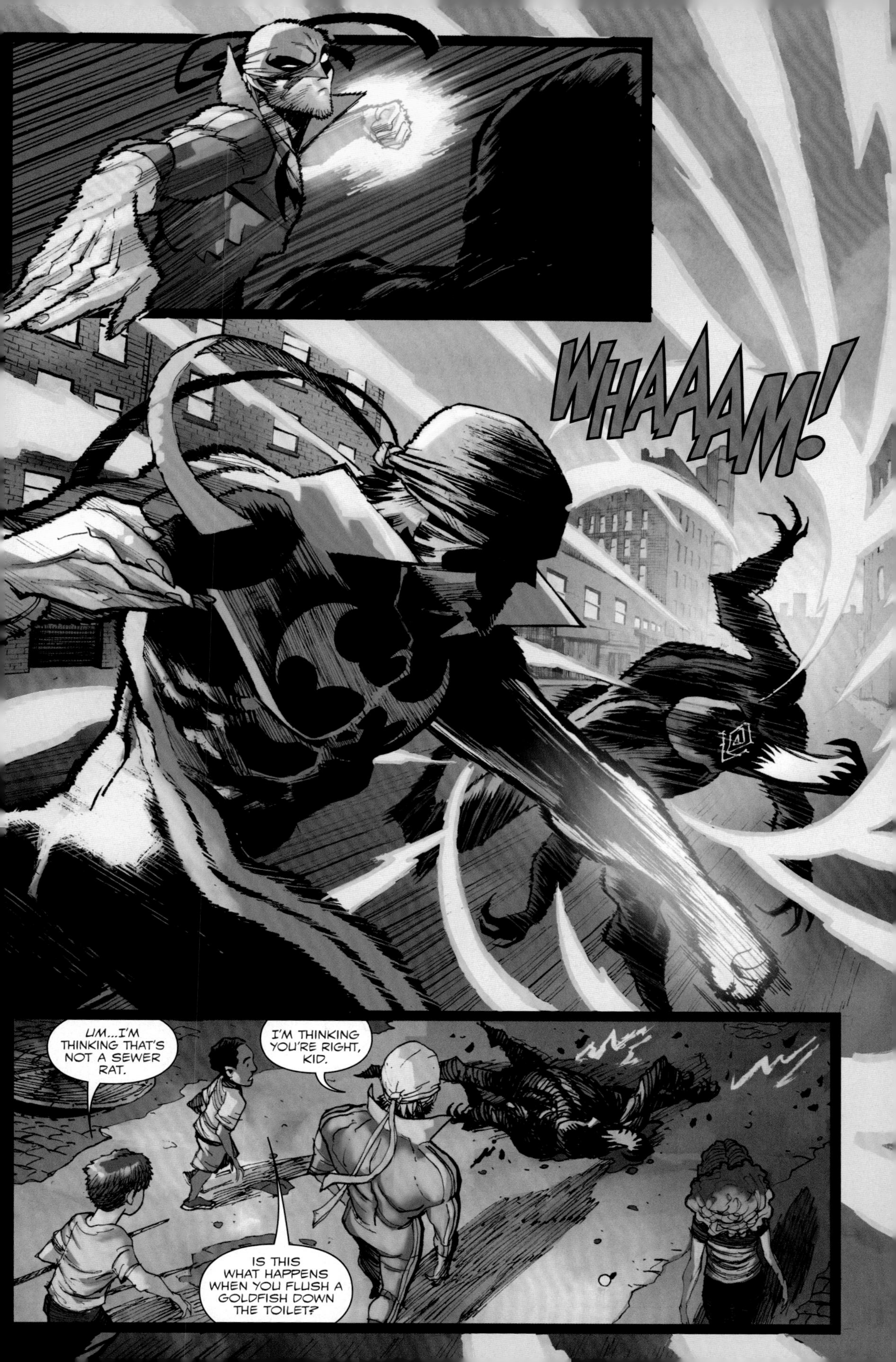
WHAAAM!
UM...I'M THINKING THAT'S NOT A SEWER RAT.
I'M THINKING YOU'RE RIGHT, KID.
IS THIS WHAT HAPPENS WHEN YOU FLUSH A GOLDFISH DOWN THE TOILET?

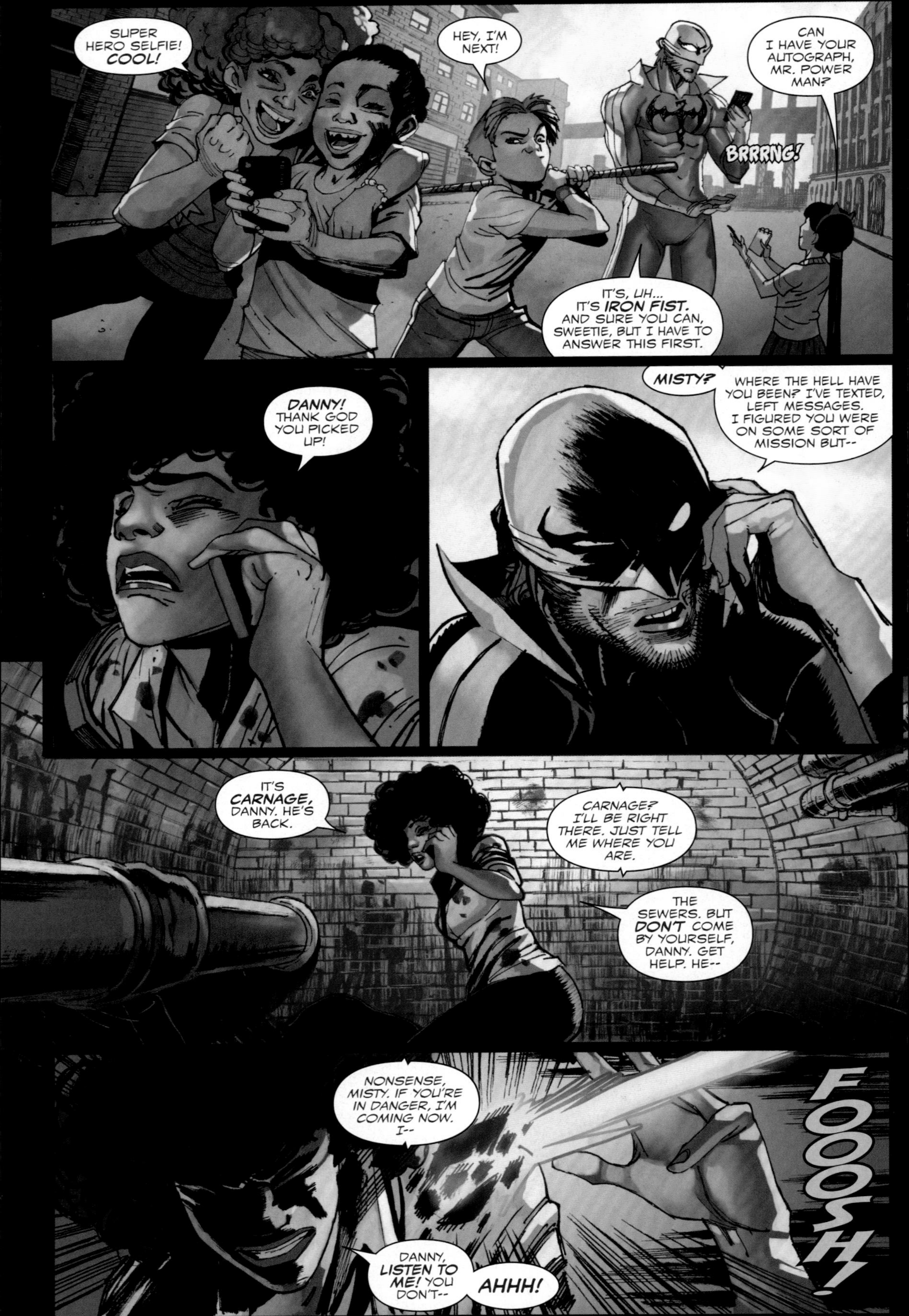
SUPER HERO SELFIE! **COOL!**
HEY, I'M NEXT!
CAN I HAVE YOUR AUTOGRAPH, MR. POWER MAN?
BRRRNG!
IT'S, UH... IT'S **IRON FIST.** AND SURE YOU CAN, SWEETIE, BUT I HAVE TO ANSWER THIS FIRST.
MISTY?
DANNY! THANK GOD YOU PICKED UP!
WHERE THE HELL HAVE YOU BEEN? I'VE TEXTED, LEFT MESSAGES. I FIGURED YOU WERE ON SOME SORT OF MISSION BUT--
IT'S **CARNAGE,** DANNY. HE'S BACK.
CARNAGE? I'LL BE RIGHT THERE. JUST TELL ME WHERE YOU ARE.
THE SEWERS. BUT **DON'T** COME BY YOURSELF, DANNY. GET HELP. HE--
NONSENSE, MISTY. IF YOU'RE IN DANGER, I'M COMING NOW. I--
FOOOSH!
DANNY, **LISTEN TO ME!** YOU DON'T--
AHHH!

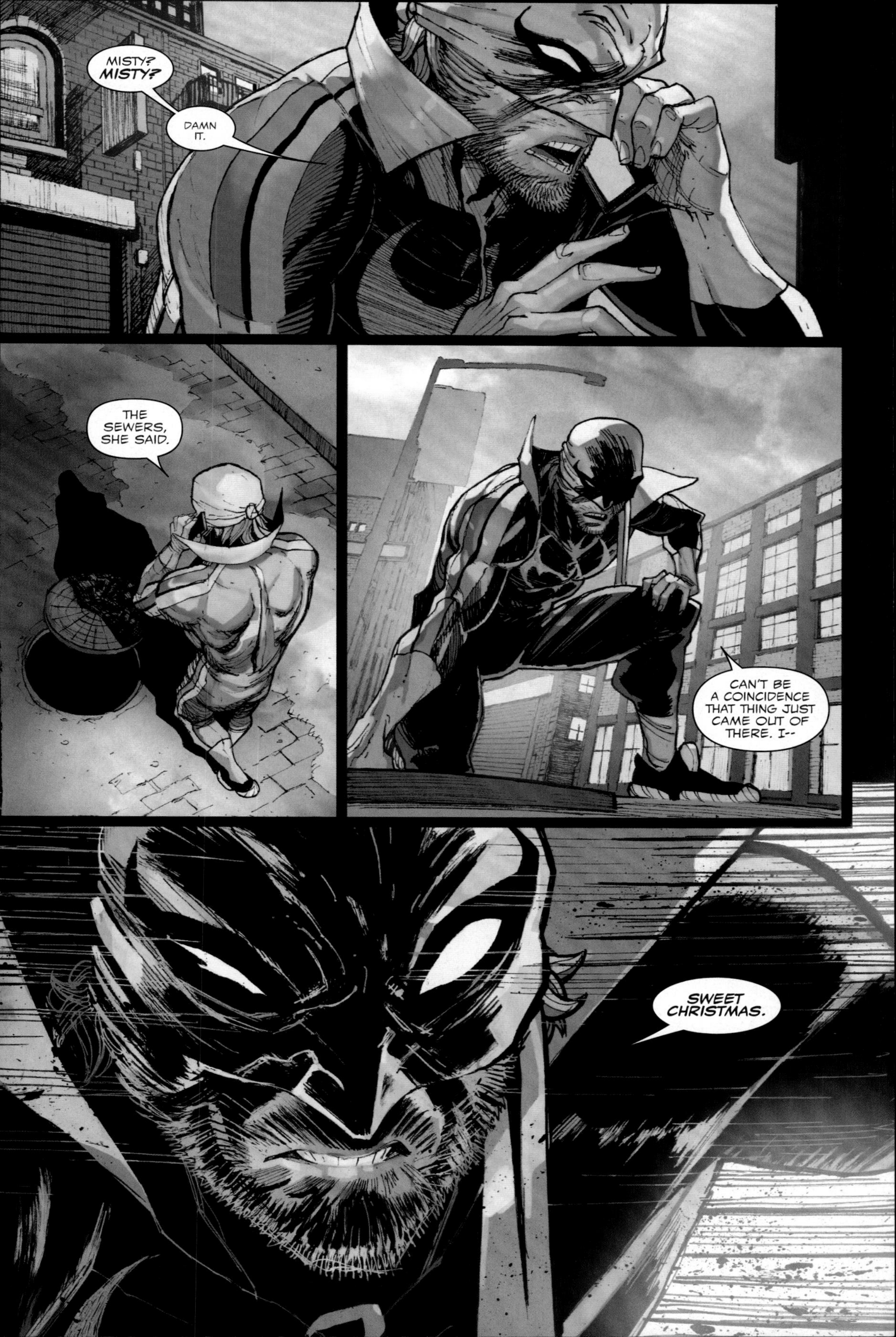
MISTY? MISTY?
DAMN IT.
THE SEWERS, SHE SAID.
CAN'T BE A COINCIDENCE THAT THING JUST CAME OUT OF THERE. I--
SWEET CHRISTMAS.

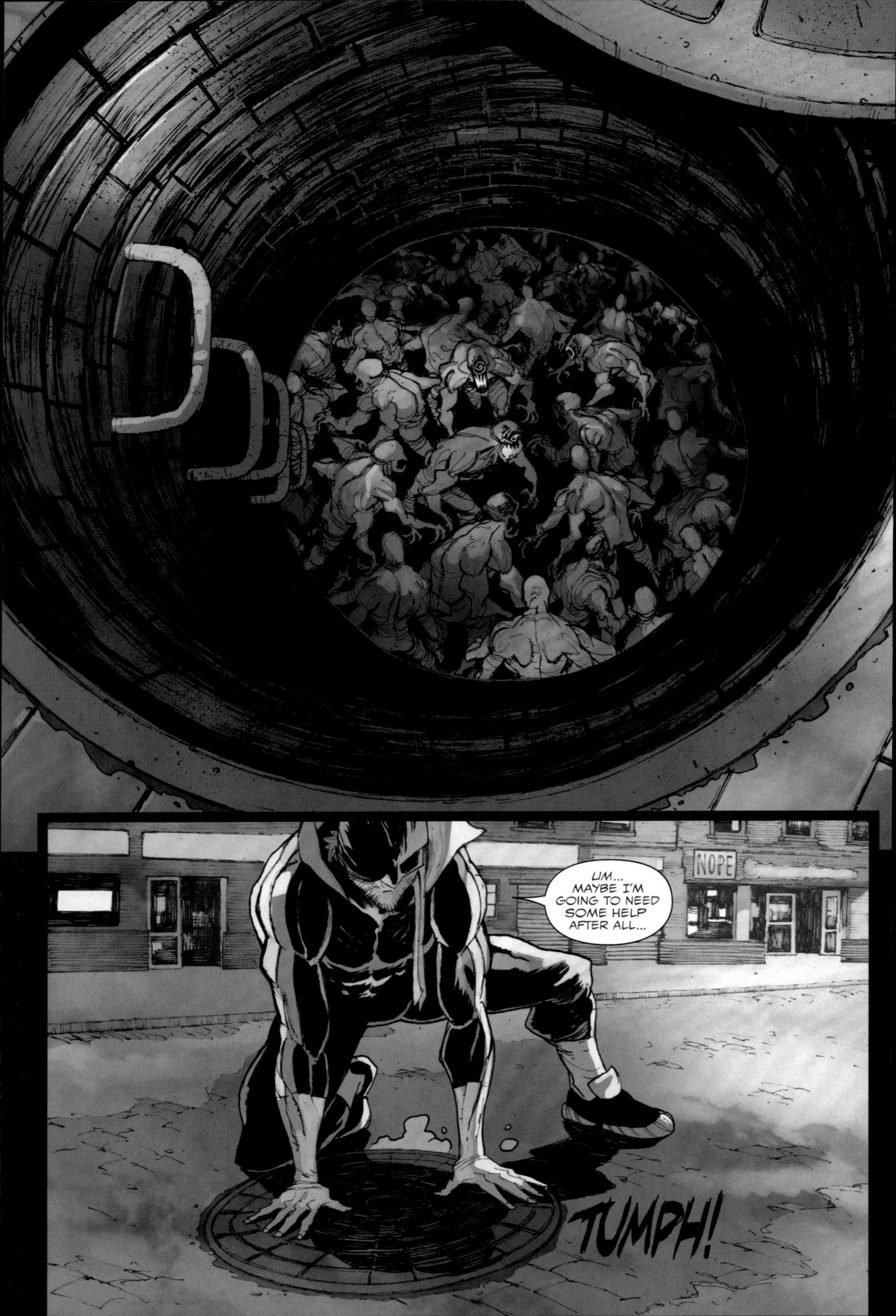
NOPE
UM... MAYBE I'M GOING TO NEED SOME HELP AFTER ALL...
TUMPH!

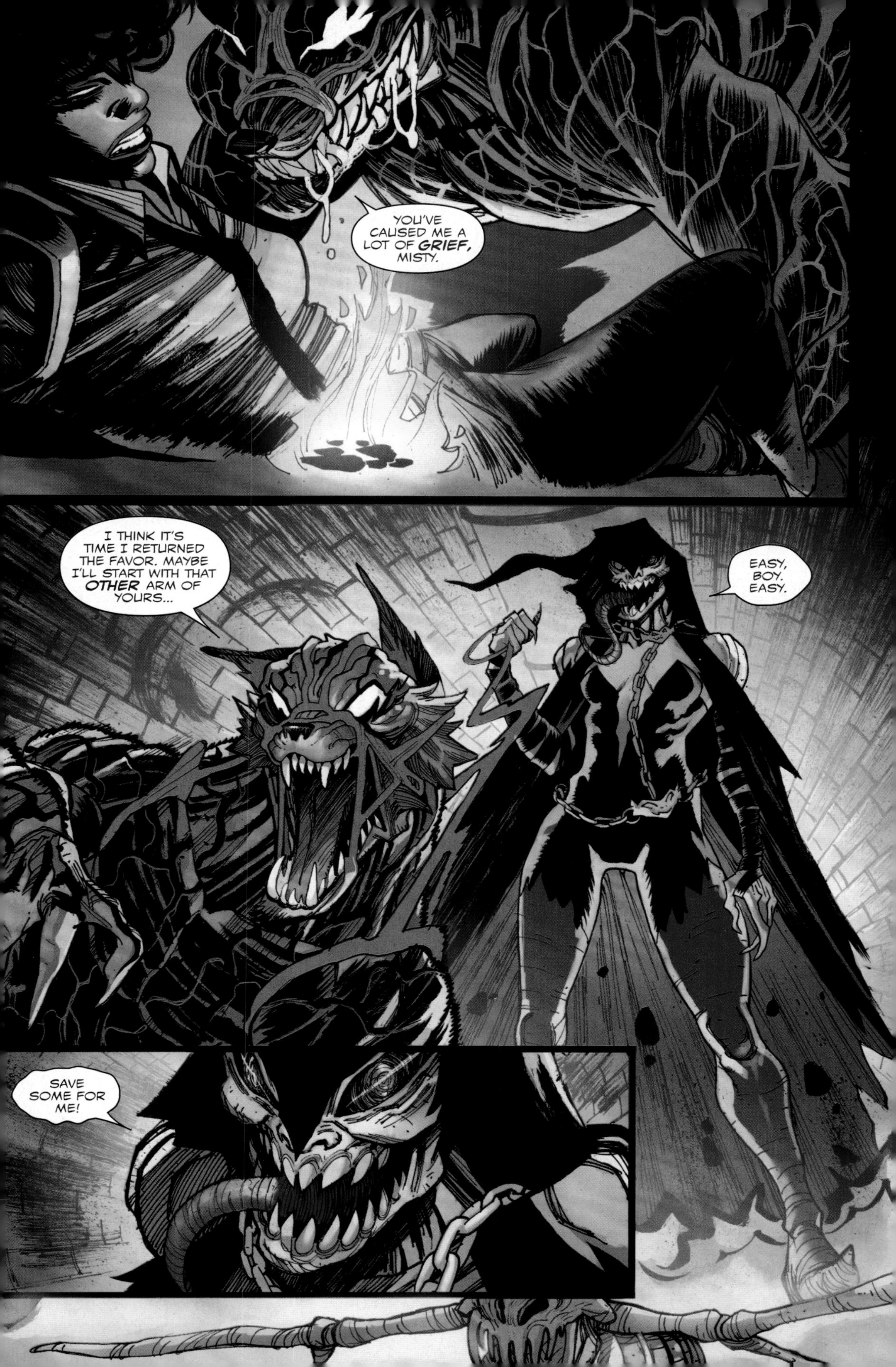
YOU'VE CAUSED ME A LOT OF GRIEF, MISTY.
I THINK IT'S TIME I RETURNED THE FAVOR. MAYBE I'LL START WITH THAT OTHER ARM OF YOURS...
EASY, BOY. EASY.
SAVE SOME FOR ME!

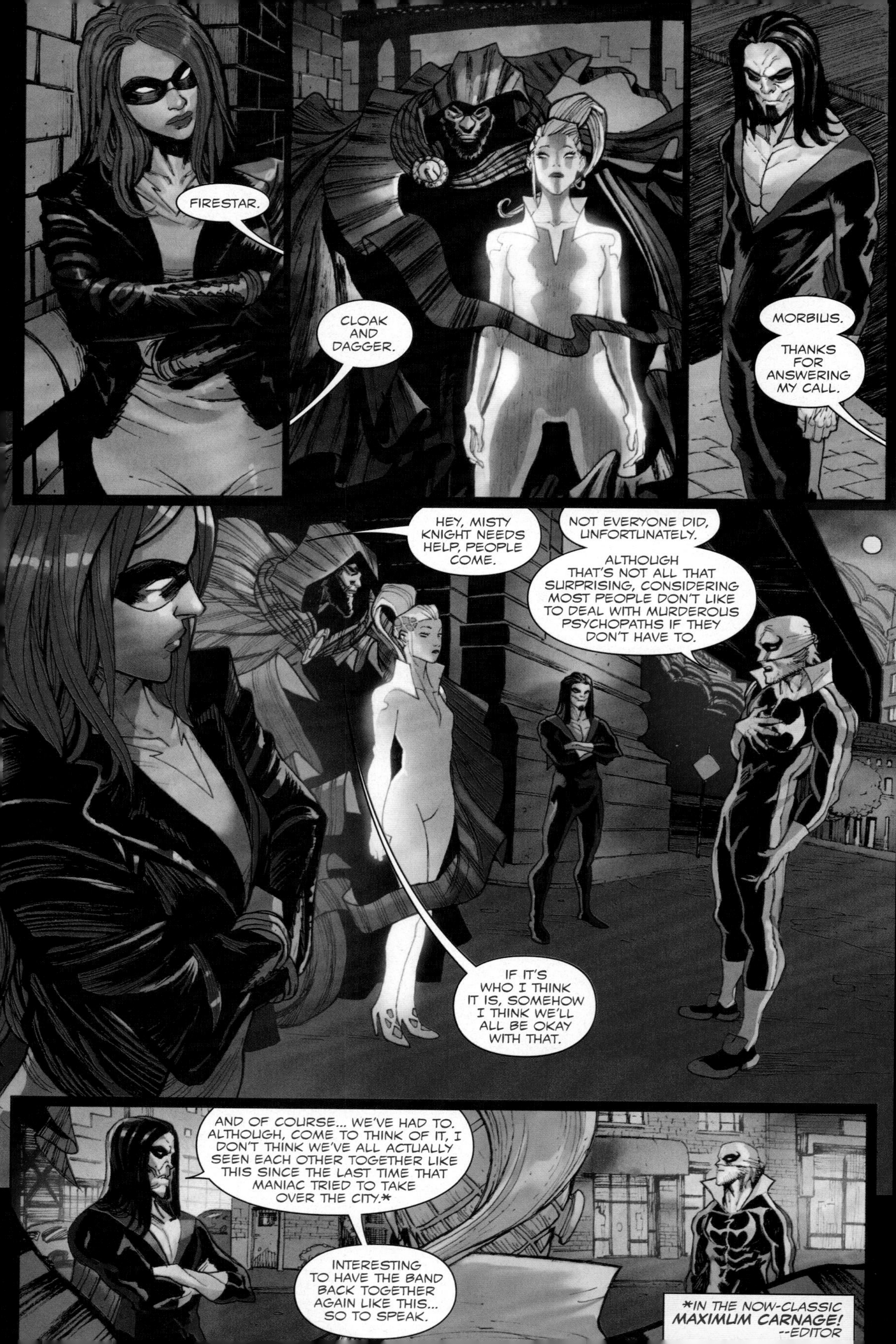
FIRESTAR.
CLOAK AND DAGGER.
MORBIUS.
THANKS FOR ANSWERING MY CALL.
HEY, MISTY KNIGHT NEEDS HELP, PEOPLE COME.
NOT EVERYONE DID, UNFORTUNATELY.
ALTHOUGH THAT'S NOT ALL THAT SURPRISING, CONSIDERING MOST PEOPLE DON'T LIKE TO DEAL WITH MURDEROUS PSYCHOPATHS IF THEY DON'T HAVE TO.
IF IT'S WHO I THINK IT IS, SOMEHOW I THINK WE'LL ALL BE OKAY WITH THAT.
AND OF COURSE... WE'VE HAD TO. ALTHOUGH, COME TO THINK OF IT, I DON'T THINK WE'VE ALL ACTUALLY SEEN EACH OTHER TOGETHER LIKE THIS SINCE THE LAST TIME THAT MANIAC TRIED TO TAKE OVER THE CITY.*
INTERESTING TO HAVE THE BAND BACK TOGETHER AGAIN LIKE THIS... SO TO SPEAK.
*IN THE NOW-CLASSIC ***MAXIMUM CARNAGE!*** --EDITOR

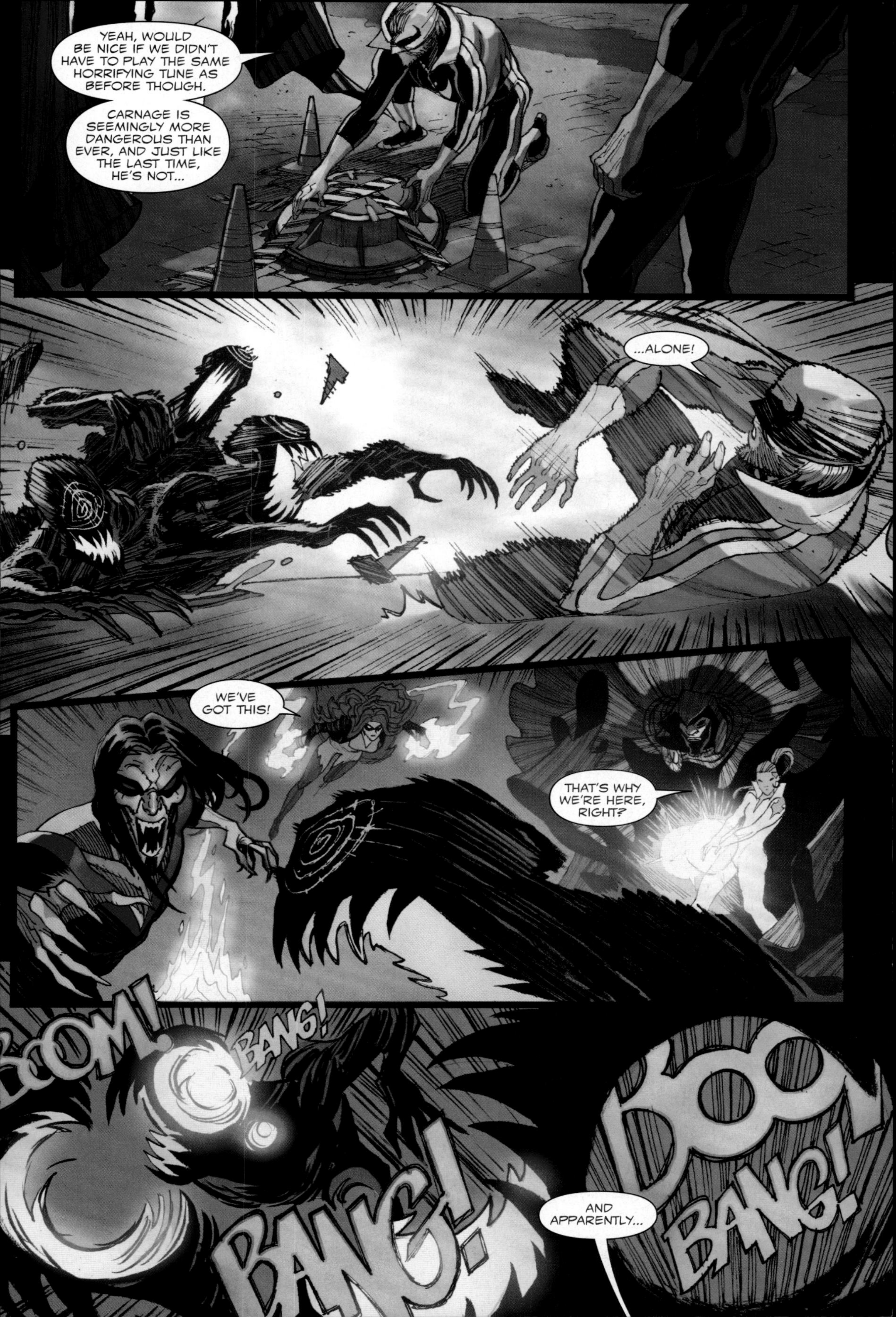

YEAH, WOULD BE NICE IF WE DIDN'T HAVE TO PLAY THE SAME HORRIFYING TUNE AS BEFORE THOUGH.
CARNAGE IS SEEMINGLY MORE DANGEROUS THAN EVER, AND JUST LIKE THE LAST TIME, HE'S NOT...
...ALONE!
WE'VE GOT THIS!
THAT'S WHY WE'RE HERE, RIGHT?
BANG!
BANG!
BANG!
BANG!
AND APPARENTLY...

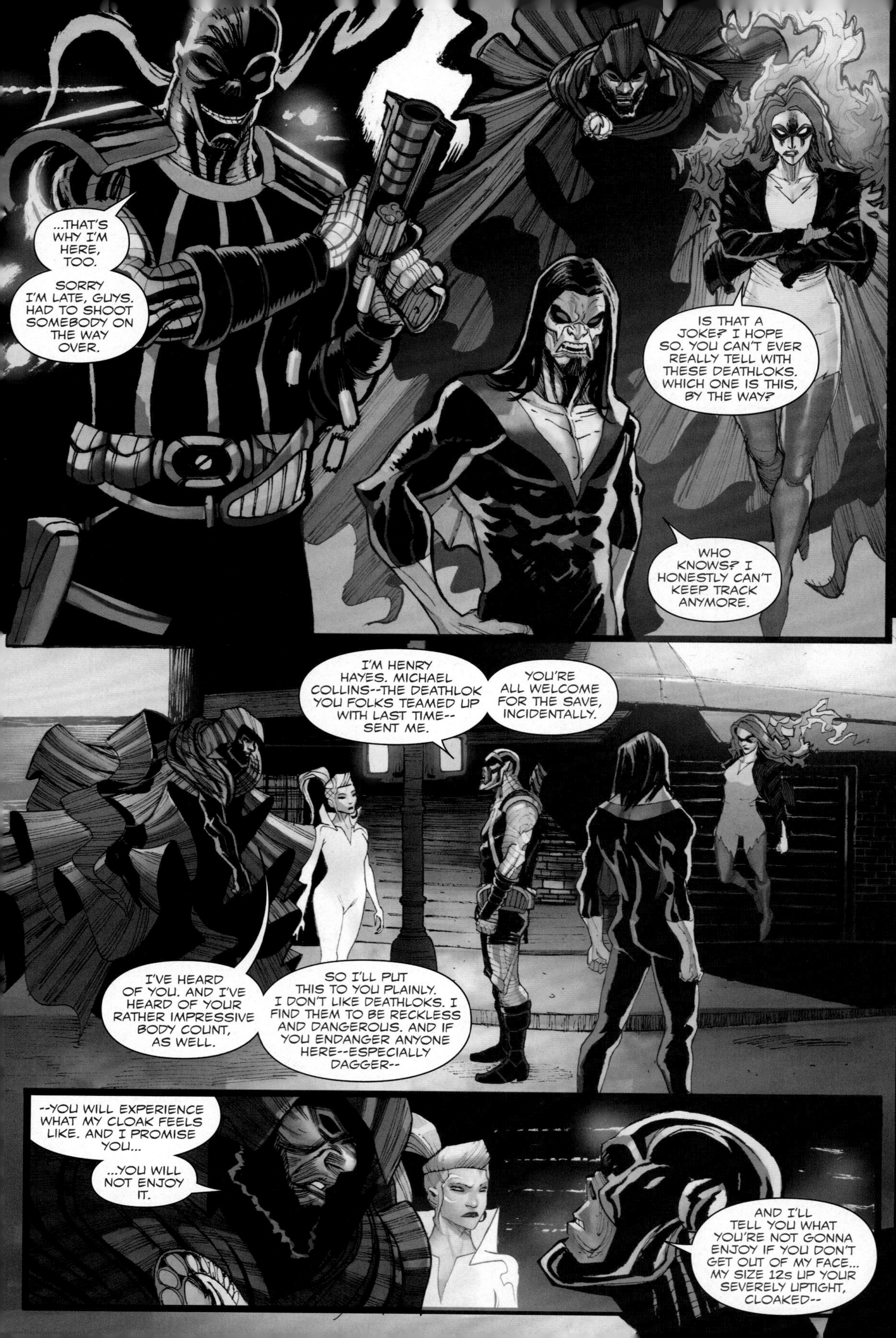
...THAT'S WHY I'M HERE, TOO.
SORRY I'M LATE, GUYS. HAD TO SHOOT SOMEBODY ON THE WAY OVER.
IS THAT A JOKE? I HOPE SO. YOU CAN'T EVER REALLY TELL WITH THESE DEATHLOKS. WHICH ONE IS THIS, BY THE WAY?
WHO KNOWS? I HONESTLY CAN'T KEEP TRACK ANYMORE.
I'M HENRY HAYES. MICHAEL COLLINS--THE DEATHLOK YOU FOLKS TEAMED UP WITH LAST TIME--SENT ME.
YOU'RE ALL WELCOME FOR THE SAVE, INCIDENTALLY.
I'VE HEARD OF YOU. AND I'VE HEARD OF YOUR RATHER IMPRESSIVE BODY COUNT, AS WELL.
SO I'LL PUT THIS TO YOU PLAINLY. I DON'T LIKE DEATHLOKS. I FIND THEM TO BE RECKLESS AND DANGEROUS. AND IF YOU ENDANGER ANYONE HERE--ESPECIALLY DAGGER--
--YOU WILL EXPERIENCE WHAT MY CLOAK FEELS LIKE. AND I PROMISE YOU...
...YOU WILL NOT ENJOY IT.
AND I'LL TELL YOU WHAT YOU'RE NOT GONNA ENJOY IF YOU DON'T GET OUT OF MY FACE... MY SIZE 12s UP YOUR SEVERELY UPTIGHT, CLOAKED--

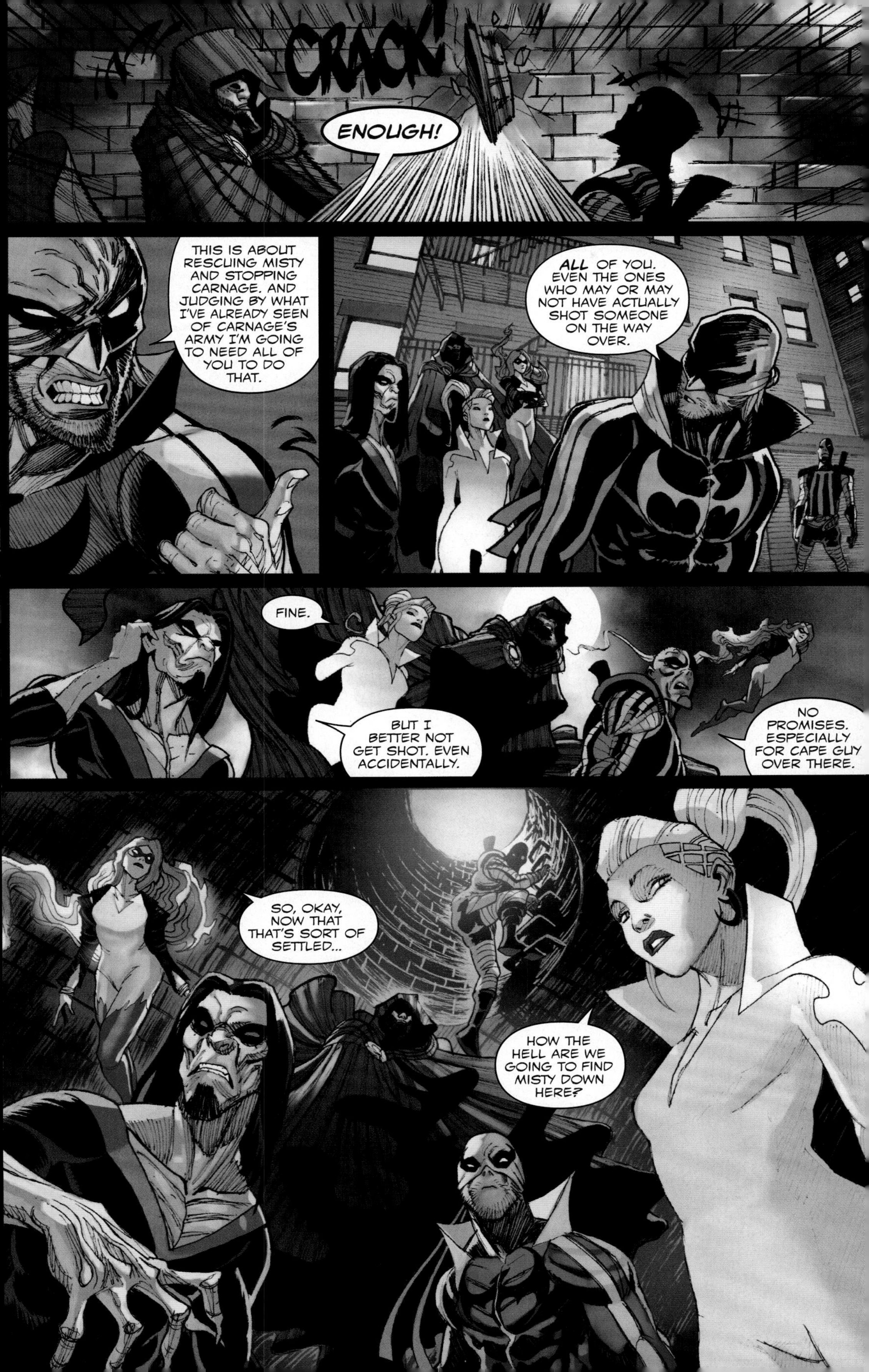
CRACK!
ENOUGH!
THIS IS ABOUT RESCUING MISTY AND STOPPING CARNAGE. AND JUDGING BY WHAT I'VE ALREADY SEEN OF CARNAGE'S ARMY I'M GOING TO NEED ALL OF YOU TO DO THAT.
ALL OF YOU. EVEN THE ONES WHO MAY OR MAY NOT HAVE ACTUALLY SHOT SOMEONE ON THE WAY OVER.
FINE.
BUT I BETTER NOT GET SHOT. EVEN ACCIDENTALLY.
NO PROMISES. ESPECIALLY FOR CAPE GUY OVER THERE.
SO, OKAY, NOW THAT THAT'S SORT OF SETTLED...
HOW THE HELL ARE WE GOING TO FIND MISTY DOWN HERE?

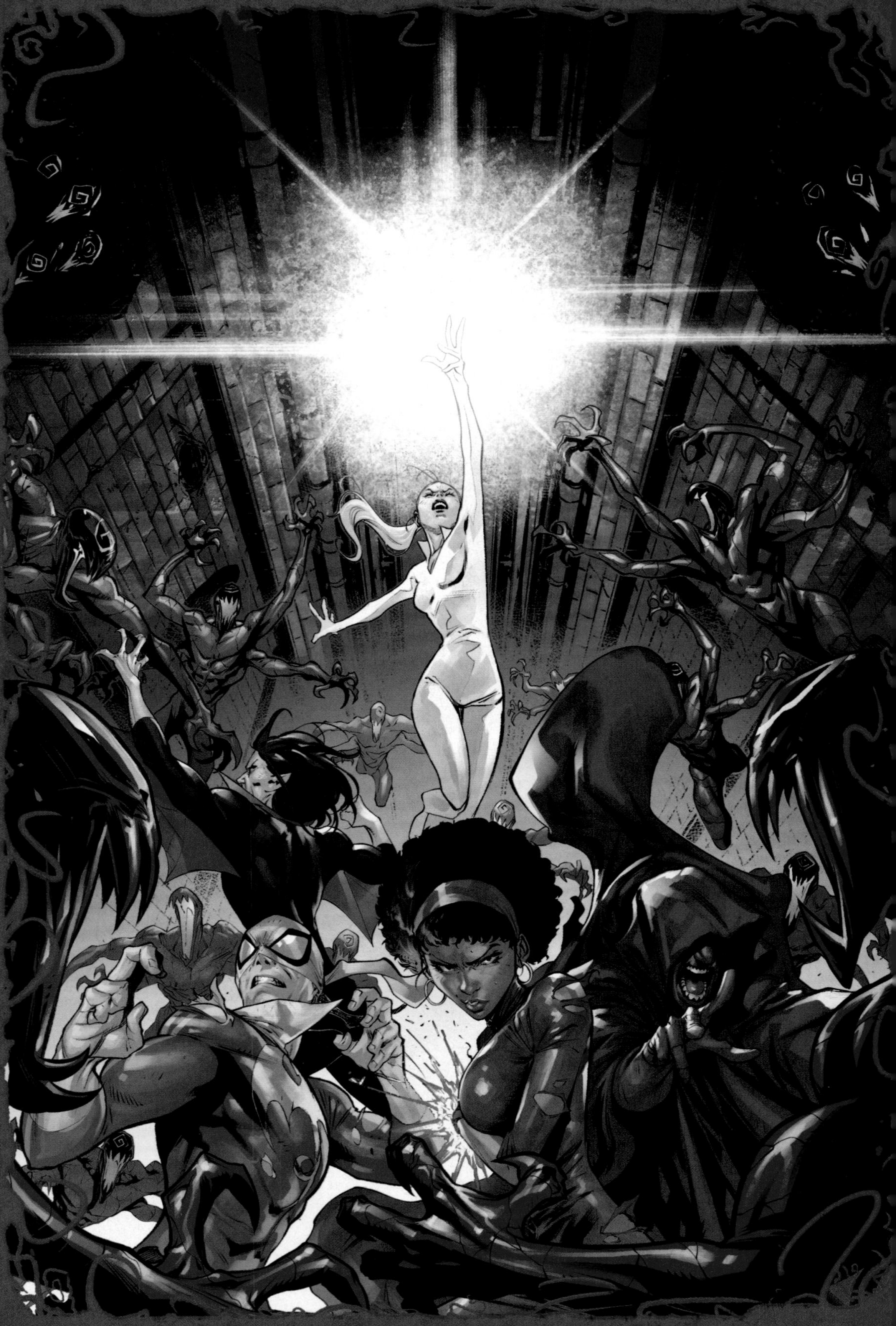

LETHAL PROTECTORS 3

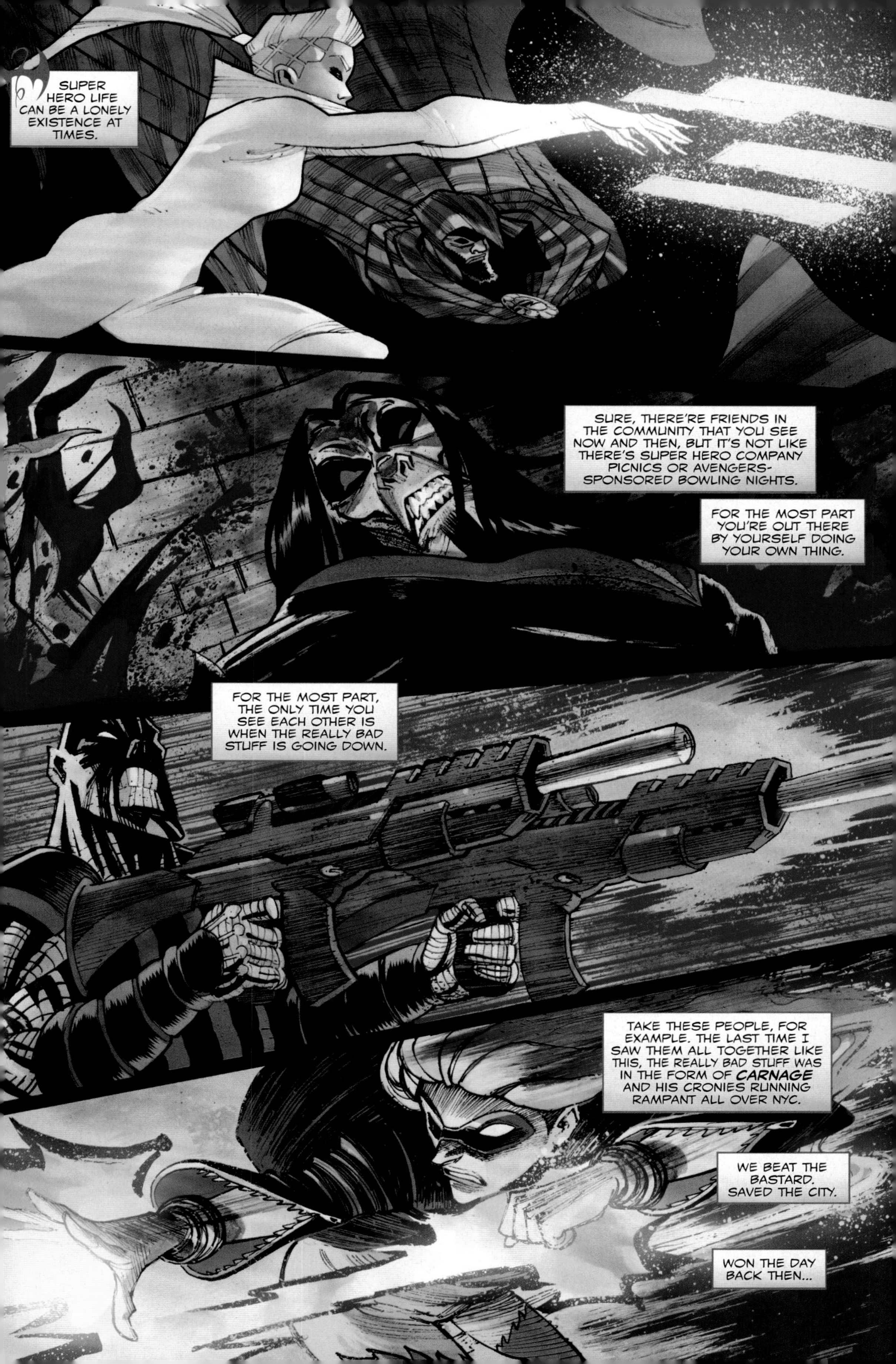
SUPER HERO LIFE CAN BE A LONELY EXISTENCE AT TIMES.
SURE, THERE'RE FRIENDS IN THE COMMUNITY THAT YOU SEE NOW AND THEN, BUT IT'S NOT LIKE THERE'S SUPER HERO COMPANY PICNICS OR AVENGERS-SPONSORED BOWLING NIGHTS.
FOR THE MOST PART YOU'RE OUT THERE BY YOURSELF DOING YOUR OWN THING.
FOR THE MOST PART, THE ONLY TIME YOU SEE EACH OTHER IS WHEN THE REALLY BAD STUFF IS GOING DOWN.
TAKE THESE PEOPLE, FOR EXAMPLE. THE LAST TIME I SAW THEM ALL TOGETHER LIKE THIS, THE REALLY BAD STUFF WAS IN THE FORM OF ***CARNAGE*** AND HIS CRONIES RUNNING RAMPANT ALL OVER NYC.
WE BEAT THE BASTARD. SAVED THE CITY.
WON THE DAY BACK THEN...

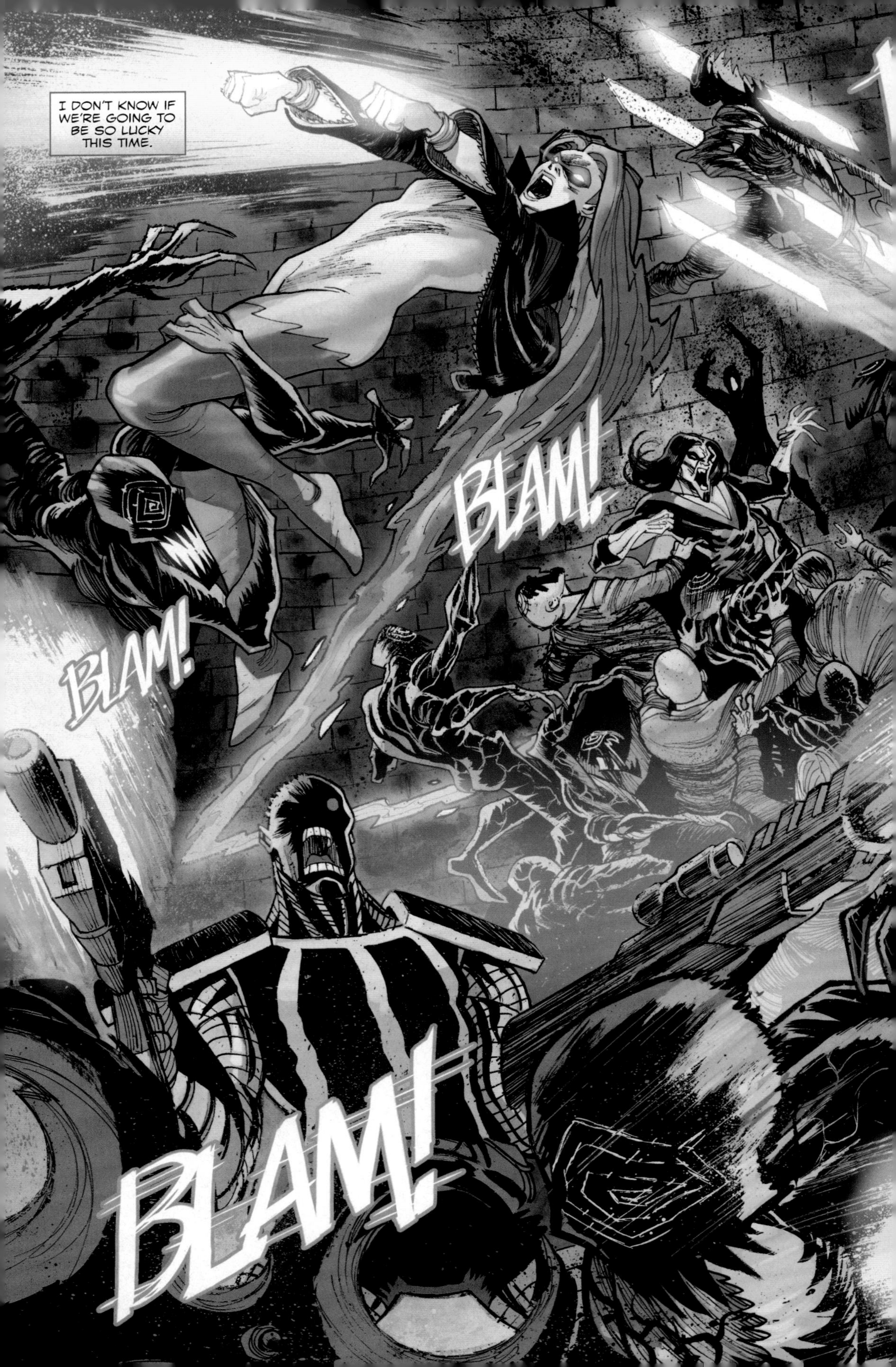
I DON'T KNOW IF WE'RE GOING TO BE SO LUCKY THIS TIME.
BLAM!
BLAM!
BLAM!

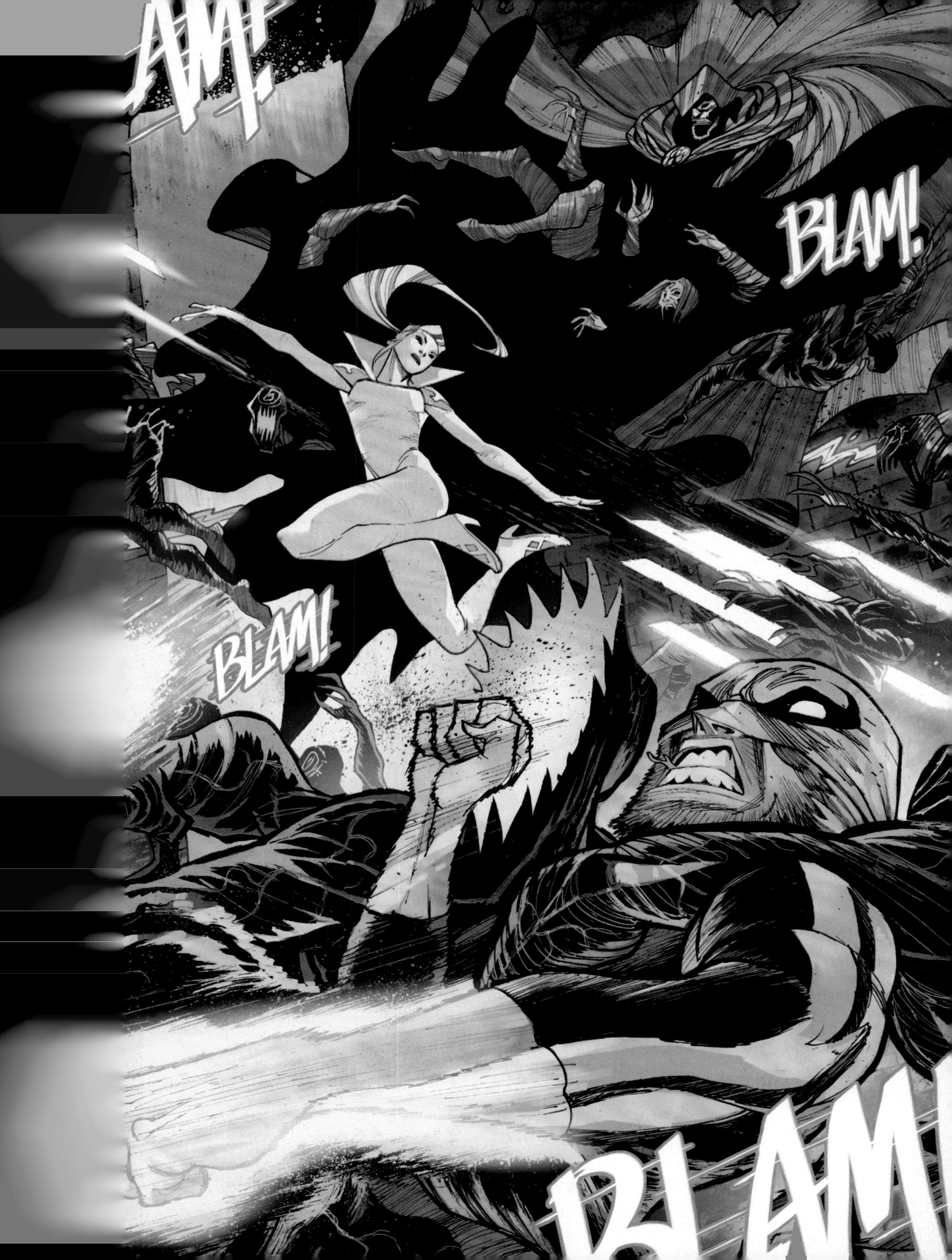
AM!
BLAM!
BLAM!
BLAM!

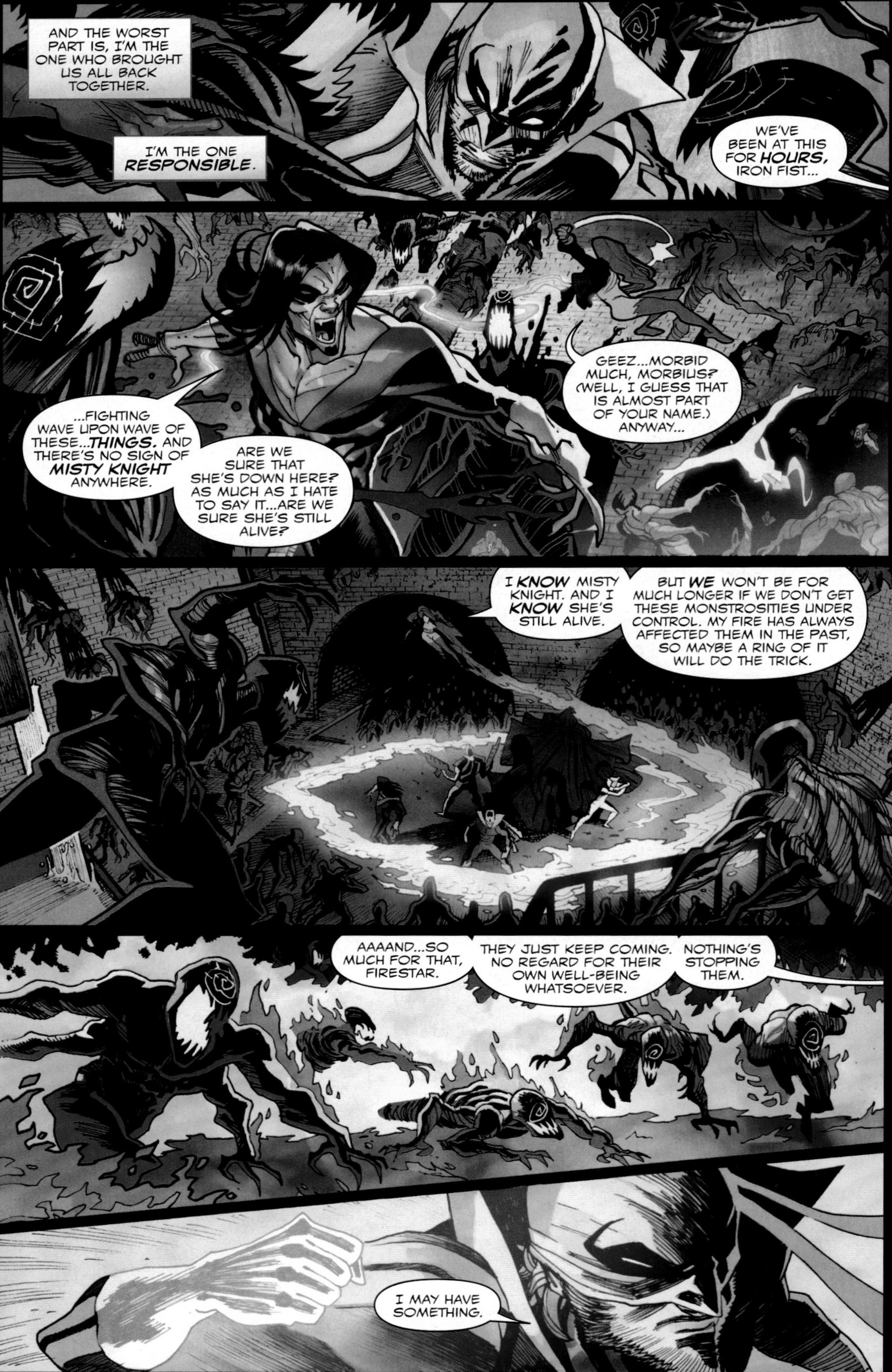
AND THE WORST PART IS, I'M THE ONE WHO BROUGHT US ALL BACK TOGETHER.
I'M THE ONE ***RESPONSIBLE***.
WE'VE BEEN AT THIS FOR ***HOURS***, IRON FIST...
...FIGHTING WAVE UPON WAVE OF THESE...***THINGS***. AND THERE'S NO SIGN OF ***MISTY KNIGHT*** ANYWHERE.
ARE WE SURE THAT SHE'S DOWN HERE? AS MUCH AS I HATE TO SAY IT...ARE WE SURE SHE'S STILL ALIVE?
GEEZ...MORBID MUCH, MORBIUS? (WELL, I GUESS THAT IS ALMOST PART OF YOUR NAME.) ANYWAY...
I ***KNOW*** MISTY KNIGHT. AND I ***KNOW*** SHE'S STILL ALIVE.
BUT ***WE*** WON'T BE FOR MUCH LONGER IF WE DON'T GET THESE MONSTROSITIES UNDER CONTROL. MY FIRE HAS ALWAYS AFFECTED THEM IN THE PAST, SO MAYBE A RING OF IT WILL DO THE TRICK.
AAAAND...SO MUCH FOR THAT, FIRESTAR.
THEY JUST KEEP COMING. NO REGARD FOR THEIR OWN WELL-BEING WHATSOEVER.
NOTHING'S STOPPING THEM.
I MAY HAVE SOMETHING.

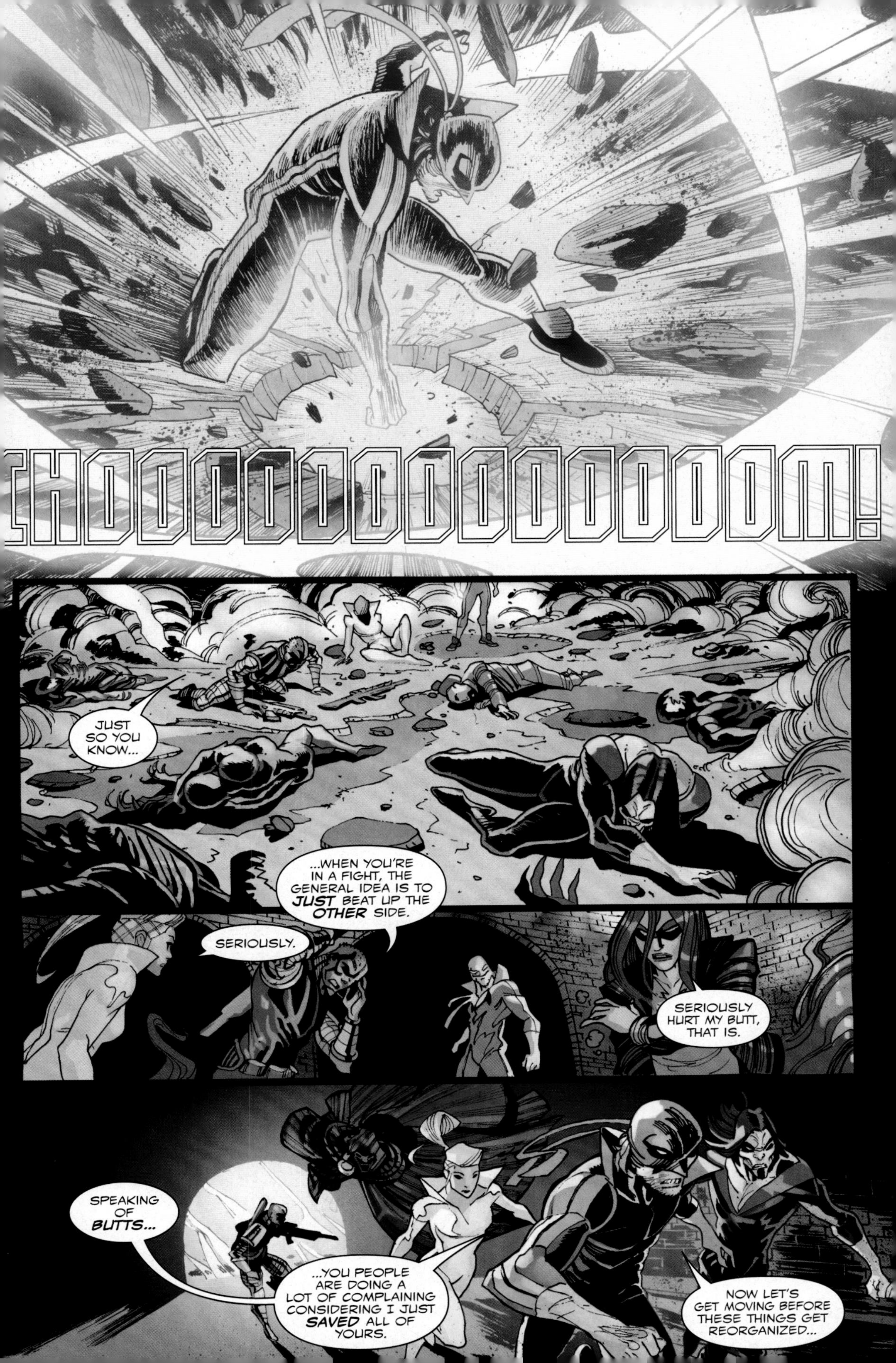
CHOOOOOOOOOOOOOOM!
JUST SO YOU KNOW...
...WHEN YOU'RE IN A FIGHT, THE GENERAL IDEA IS TO JUST BEAT UP THE OTHER SIDE.
SERIOUSLY.
SERIOUSLY HURT MY BUTT, THAT IS.
SPEAKING OF BUTTS...
...YOU PEOPLE ARE DOING A LOT OF COMPLAINING CONSIDERING I JUST SAVED ALL OF YOURS.
NOW LET'S GET MOVING BEFORE THESE THINGS GET REORGANIZED...

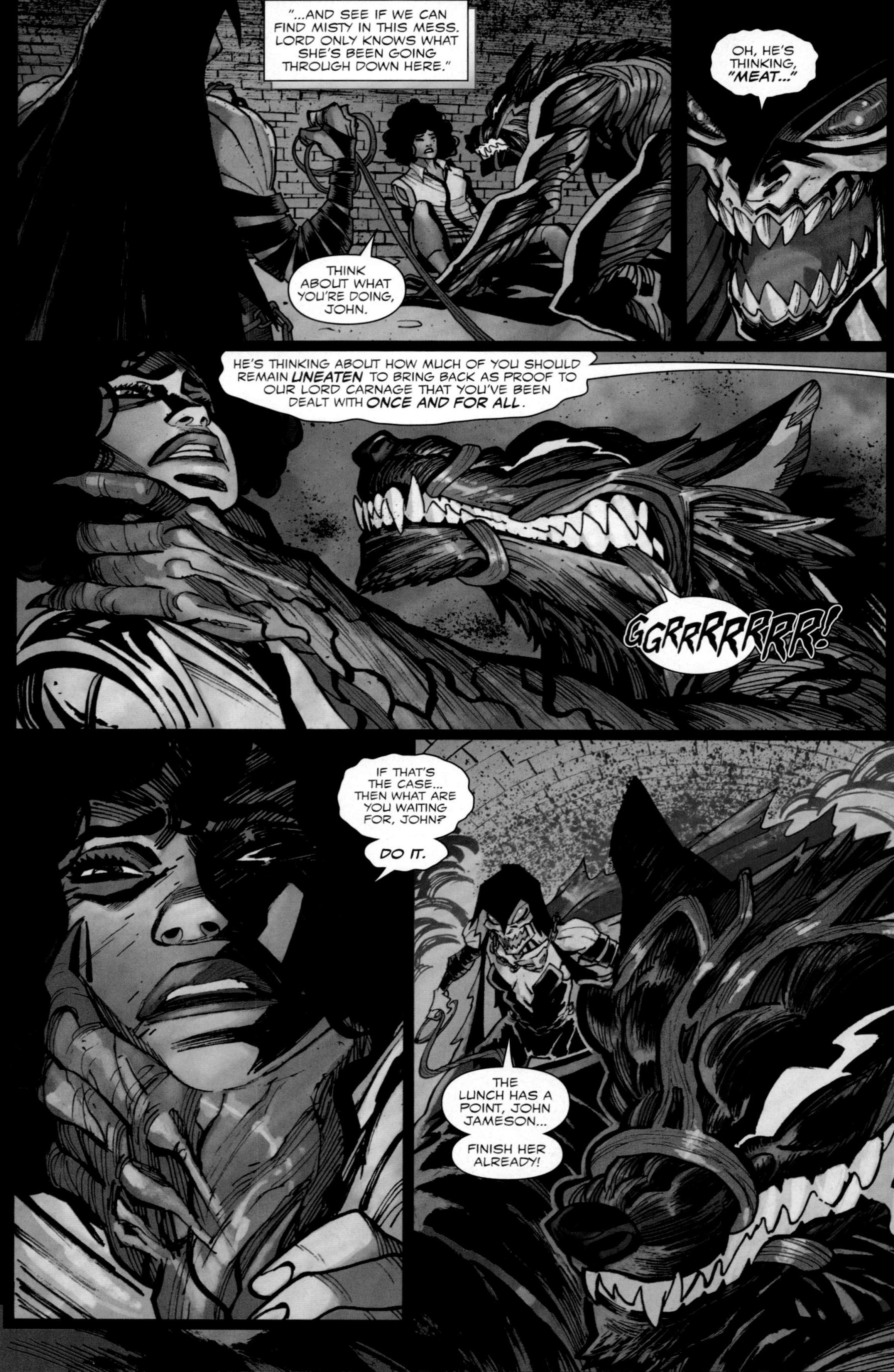
"...AND SEE IF WE CAN FIND MISTY IN THIS MESS. LORD ONLY KNOWS WHAT SHE'S BEEN GOING THROUGH DOWN HERE."
THINK ABOUT WHAT YOU'RE DOING, JOHN.
OH, HE'S THINKING, "MEAT..."
HE'S THINKING ABOUT HOW MUCH OF YOU SHOULD REMAIN UNEATEN TO BRING BACK AS PROOF TO OUR LORD CARNAGE THAT YOU'VE BEEN DEALT WITH ONCE AND FOR ALL.
GGRRRRRRRR!
IF THAT'S THE CASE... THEN WHAT ARE YOU WAITING FOR, JOHN?
DO IT.
THE LUNCH HAS A POINT, JOHN JAMESON...
FINISH HER ALREADY!

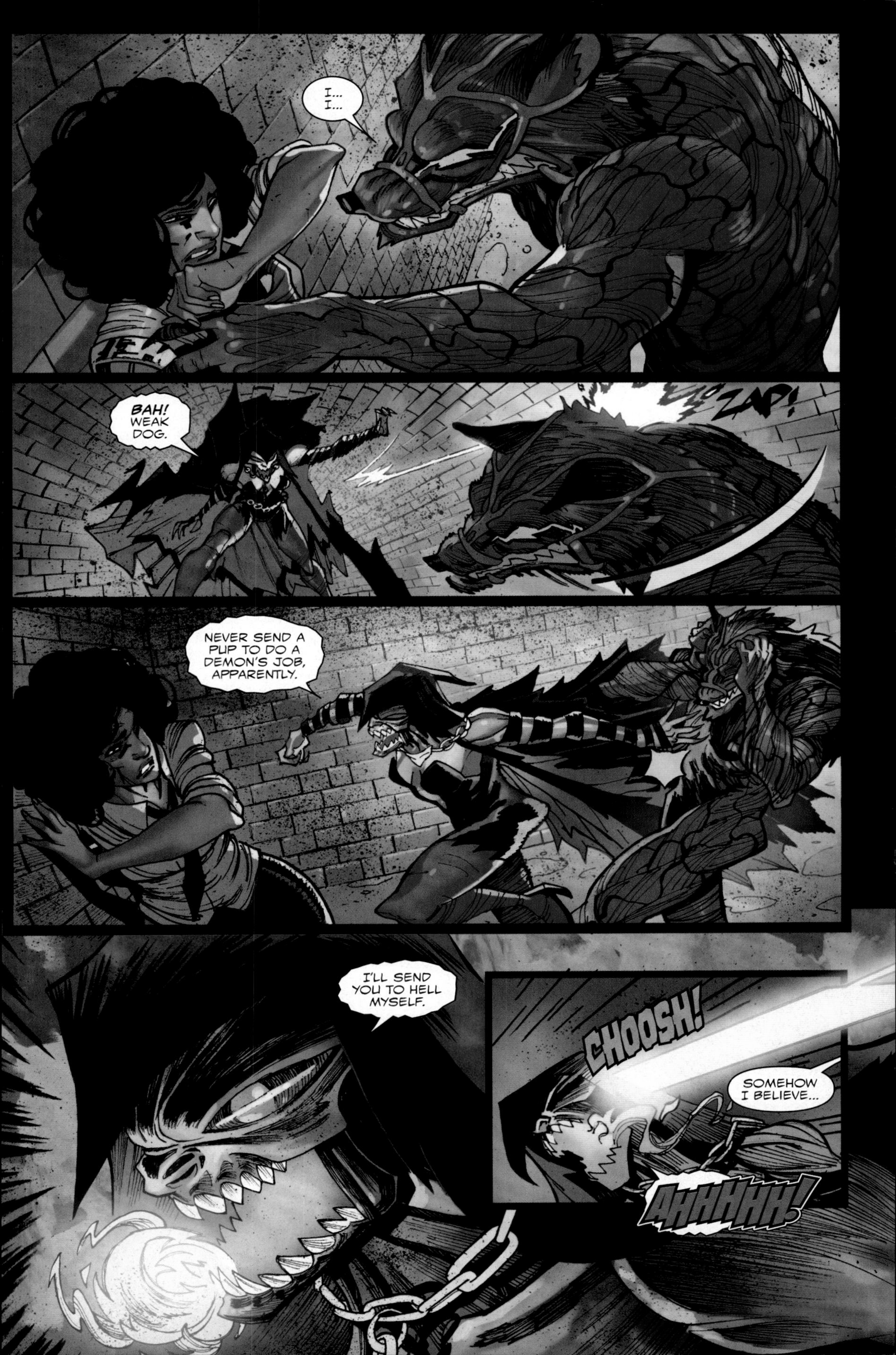
I...
I...
BAH! WEAK DOG.
ZAP!
NEVER SEND A PUP TO DO A DEMON'S JOB, APPARENTLY.
I'LL SEND YOU TO HELL MYSELF.
CHOOSH!
SOMEHOW I BELIEVE...
AHHHHH!

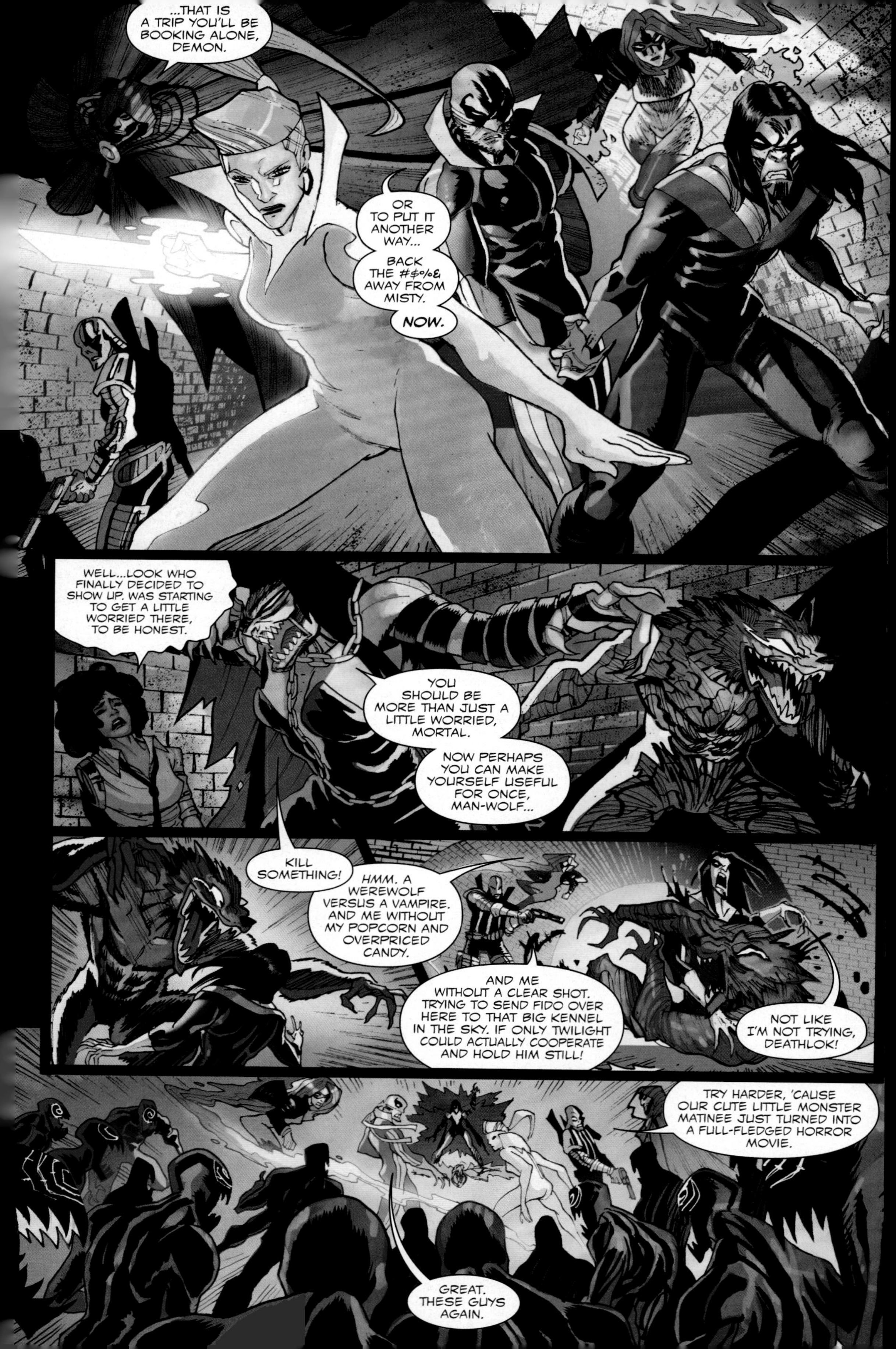
...THAT IS A TRIP YOU'LL BE BOOKING ALONE, DEMON.
OR TO PUT IT ANOTHER WAY... BACK THE #$%& AWAY FROM MISTY.
NOW.
WELL...LOOK WHO FINALLY DECIDED TO SHOW UP. WAS STARTING TO GET A LITTLE WORRIED THERE, TO BE HONEST.
YOU SHOULD BE MORE THAN JUST A LITTLE WORRIED, MORTAL.
NOW PERHAPS YOU CAN MAKE YOURSELF USEFUL FOR ONCE, MAN-WOLF...
KILL SOMETHING!
HMM. A WEREWOLF VERSUS A VAMPIRE. AND ME WITHOUT MY POPCORN AND OVERPRICED CANDY.
AND ME WITHOUT A CLEAR SHOT. TRYING TO SEND FIDO OVER HERE TO THAT BIG KENNEL IN THE SKY. IF ONLY TWILIGHT COULD ACTUALLY COOPERATE AND HOLD HIM STILL!
NOT LIKE I'M NOT TRYING, DEATHLOK!
TRY HARDER, 'CAUSE OUR CUTE LITTLE MONSTER MATINEE JUST TURNED INTO A FULL-FLEDGED HORROR MOVIE.
GREAT. THESE GUYS AGAIN.

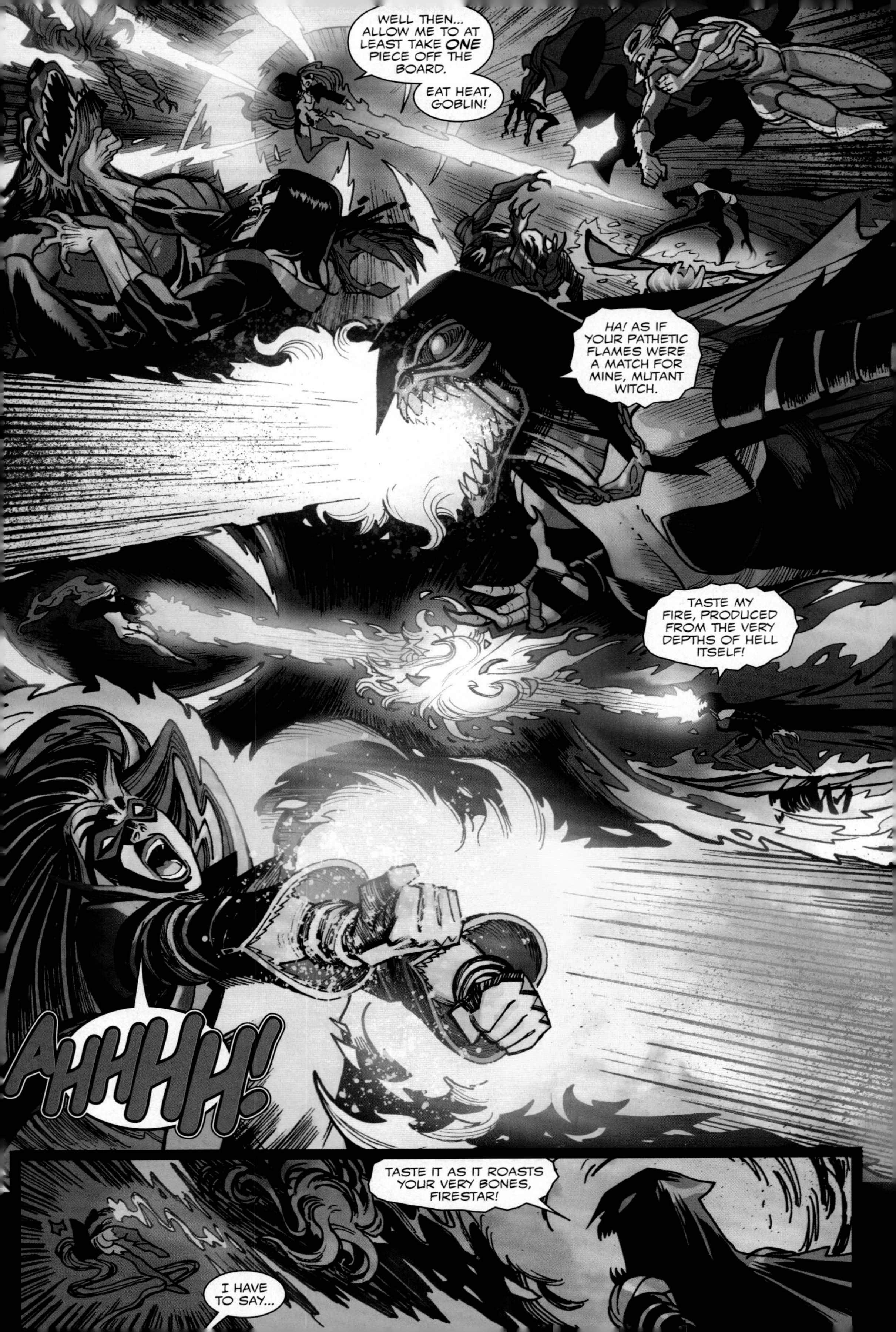

WELL THEN... ALLOW ME TO AT LEAST TAKE ONE PIECE OFF THE BOARD.
EAT HEAT, GOBLIN!
HA! AS IF YOUR PATHETIC FLAMES WERE A MATCH FOR MINE, MUTANT WITCH.
TASTE MY FIRE, PRODUCED FROM THE VERY DEPTHS OF HELL ITSELF!
AHHHH!
TASTE IT AS IT ROASTS YOUR VERY BONES, FIRESTAR!
I HAVE TO SAY...

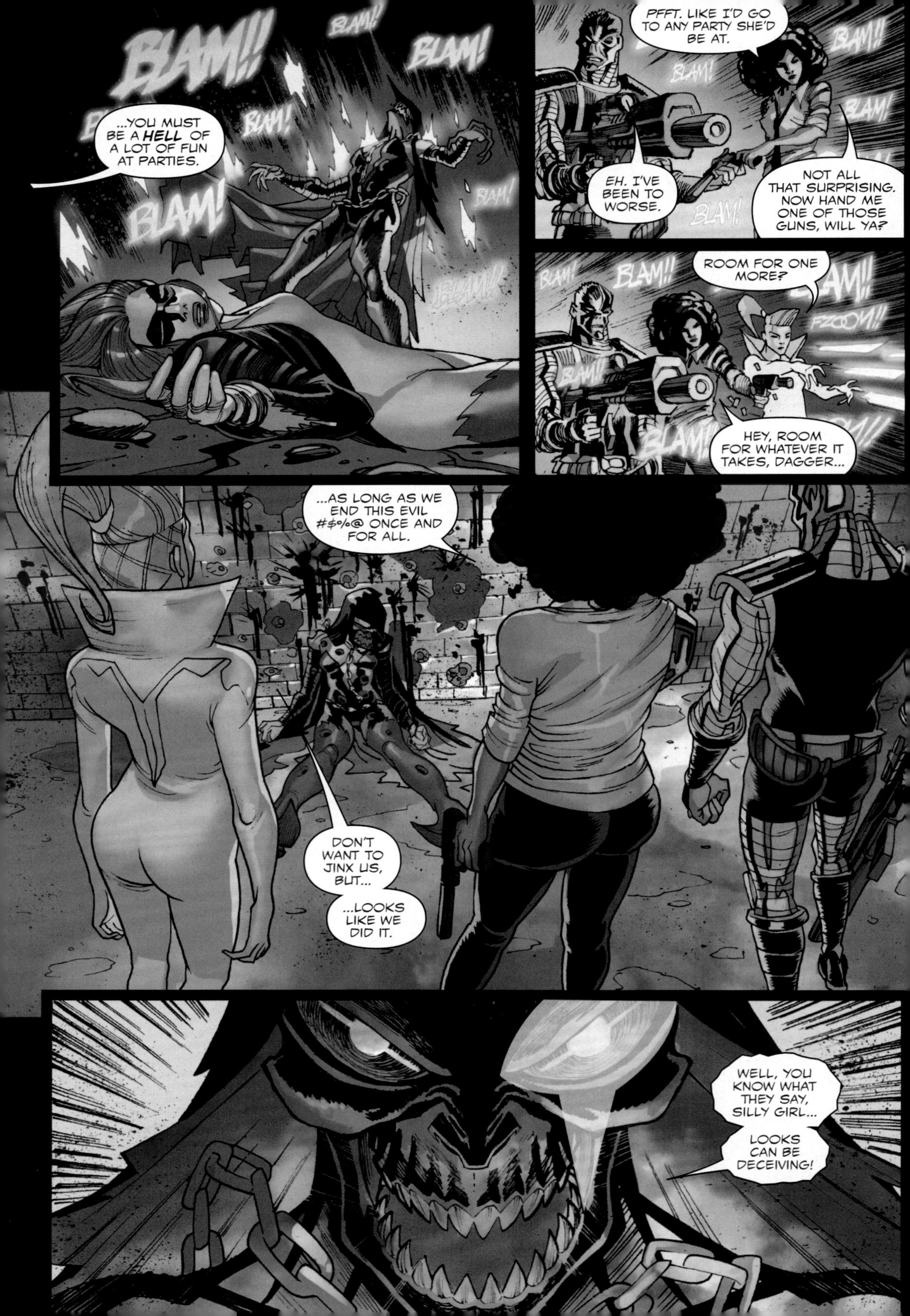
BLAM!!
BLAM!!
BLAM!
BLAM!
...YOU MUST BE A ***HELL*** OF A LOT OF FUN AT PARTIES.
BLAM!
BLAM!
BLAM!!
PFFT. LIKE I'D GO TO ANY PARTY SHE'D BE AT.
BLAM!!
BLAM!
BLAM!
EH. I'VE BEEN TO WORSE.
NOT ALL THAT SURPRISING. NOW HAND ME ONE OF THOSE GUNS, WILL YA?
BLAM!
BLAM!
BLAM!!
ROOM FOR ONE MORE?
BLAM!!
FZOOM!!
BLAM!!
BLAM!!
HEY, ROOM FOR WHATEVER IT TAKES, DAGGER...
...AS LONG AS WE END THIS EVIL #$%@ ONCE AND FOR ALL.
DON'T WANT TO JINX US, BUT...
...LOOKS LIKE WE DID IT.
WELL, YOU KNOW WHAT THEY SAY, SILLY GIRL...
LOOKS CAN BE DECEIVING!

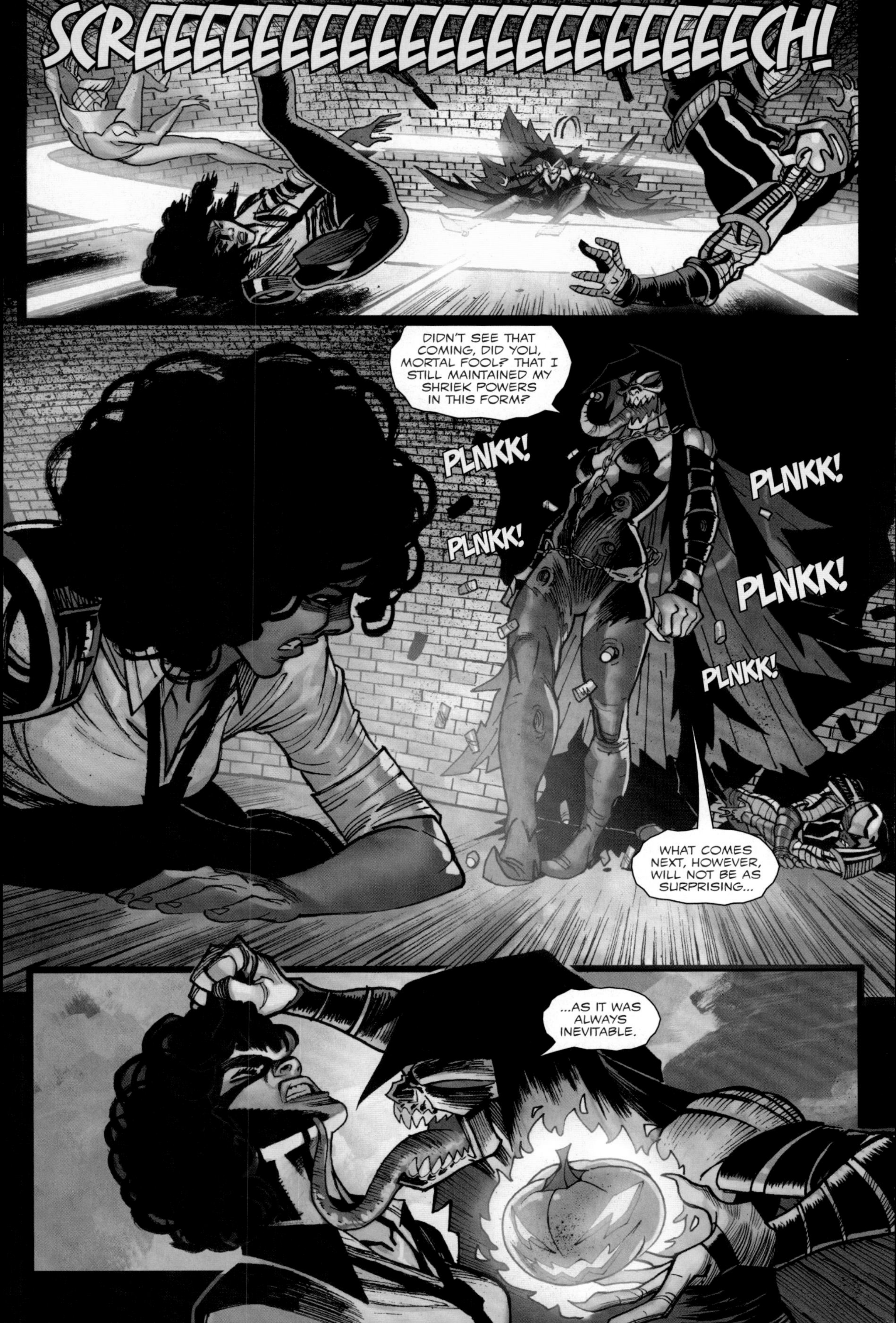
SCREEEEEEEEEEEEEEEEEEEEEEEEEECH!
DIDN'T SEE THAT COMING, DID YOU, MORTAL FOOL? THAT I STILL MAINTAINED MY SHRIEK POWERS IN THIS FORM?
PLNKK!
PLNKK!
PLNKK!
PLNKK!
PLNKK!
WHAT COMES NEXT, HOWEVER, WILL NOT BE AS SURPRISING...
...AS IT WAS ALWAYS INEVITABLE.

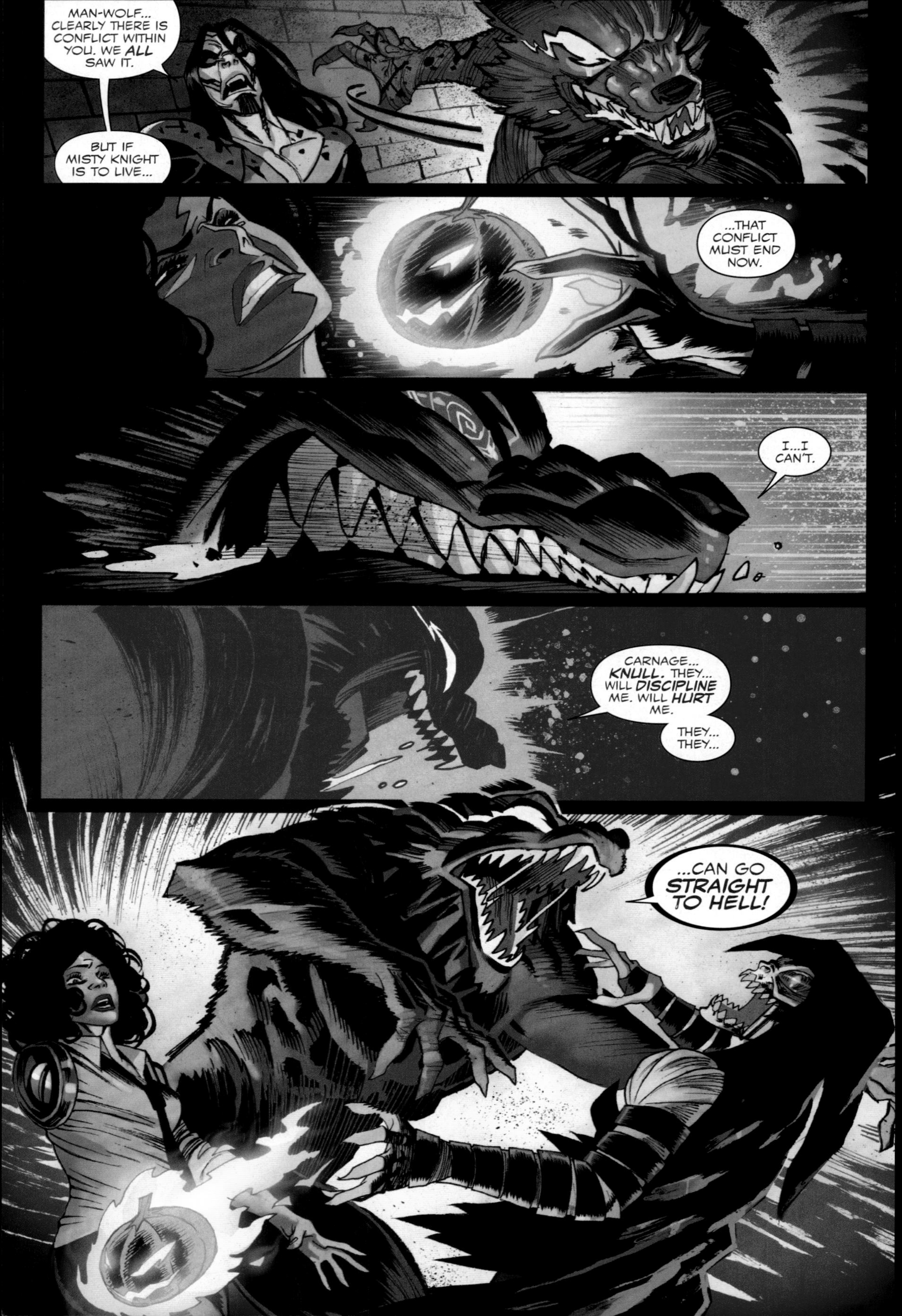
MAN-WOLF... CLEARLY THERE IS CONFLICT WITHIN YOU. WE ALL SAW IT.
BUT IF MISTY KNIGHT IS TO LIVE...
...THAT CONFLICT MUST END NOW.
I...I CAN'T.
CARNAGE... KNULL. THEY... WILL DISCIPLINE ME. WILL HURT ME.
THEY... THEY...
...CAN GO STRAIGHT TO HELL!

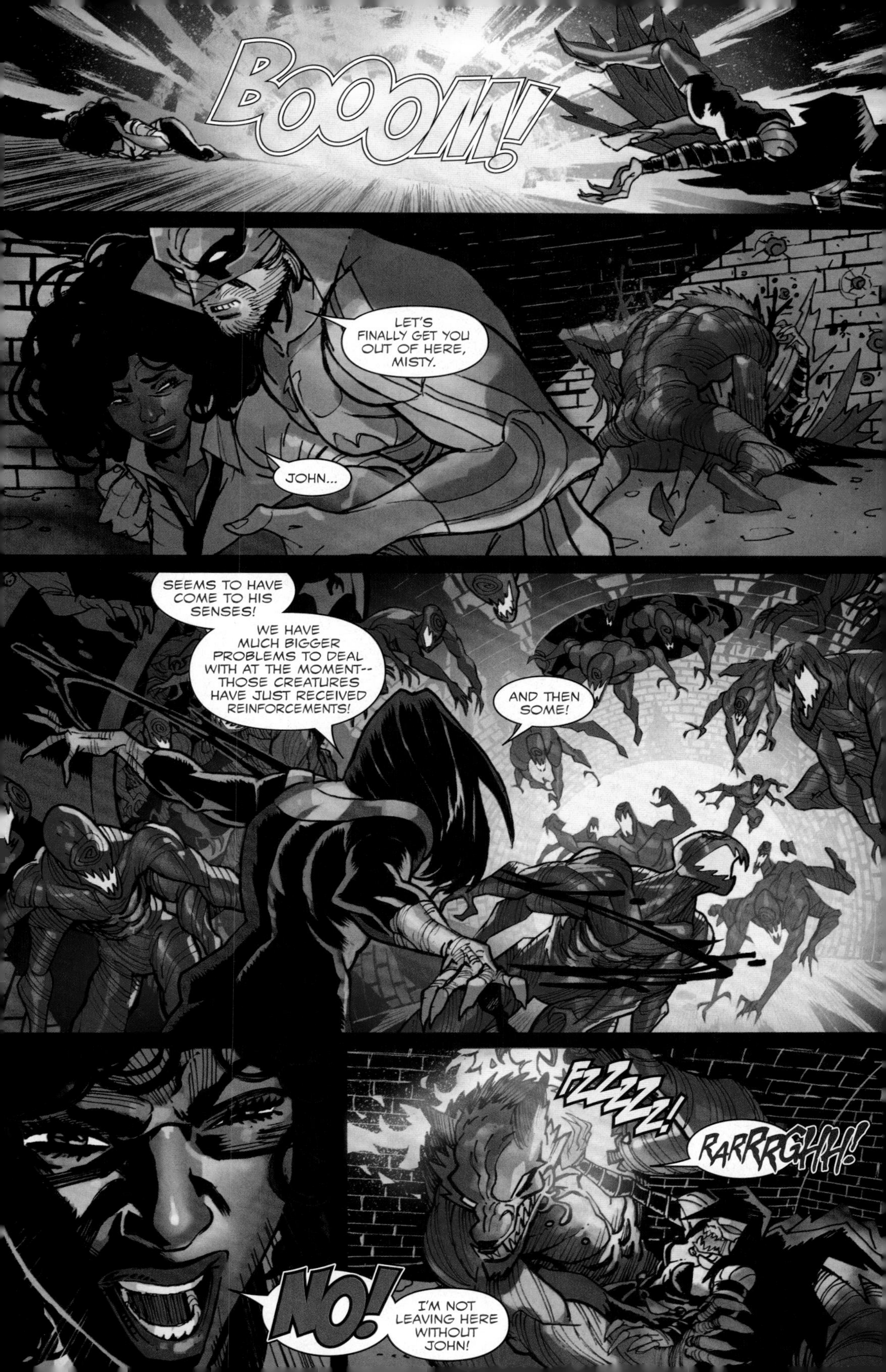
BOOOOM!
LET'S FINALLY GET YOU OUT OF HERE, MISTY.
JOHN...
SEEMS TO HAVE COME TO HIS SENSES!
WE HAVE MUCH BIGGER PROBLEMS TO DEAL WITH AT THE MOMENT-- THOSE CREATURES HAVE JUST RECEIVED REINFORCEMENTS!
AND THEN SOME!
FZZZZZ!
RARRRGHH!
NO!
I'M NOT LEAVING HERE WITHOUT JOHN!

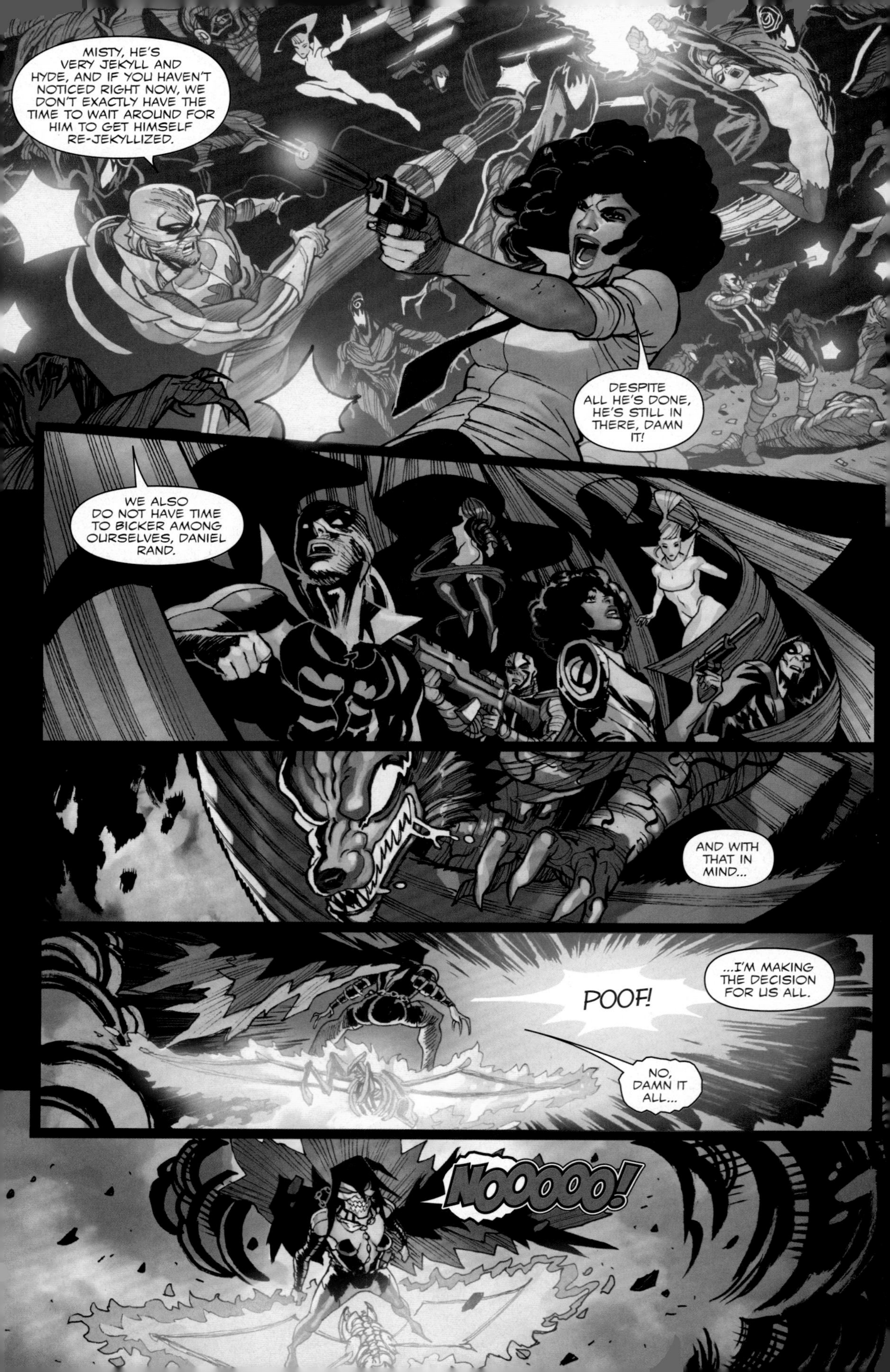
MISTY, HE'S VERY JEKYLL AND HYDE, AND IF YOU HAVEN'T NOTICED RIGHT NOW, WE DON'T EXACTLY HAVE THE TIME TO WAIT AROUND FOR HIM TO GET HIMSELF RE-JEKYLLIZED.
DESPITE ALL HE'S DONE, HE'S STILL IN THERE, DAMN IT!
WE ALSO DO NOT HAVE TIME TO BICKER AMONG OURSELVES, DANIEL RAND.
AND WITH THAT IN MIND...
...I'M MAKING THE DECISION FOR US ALL.
POOF!
NO, DAMN IT ALL...
NOOOOO!

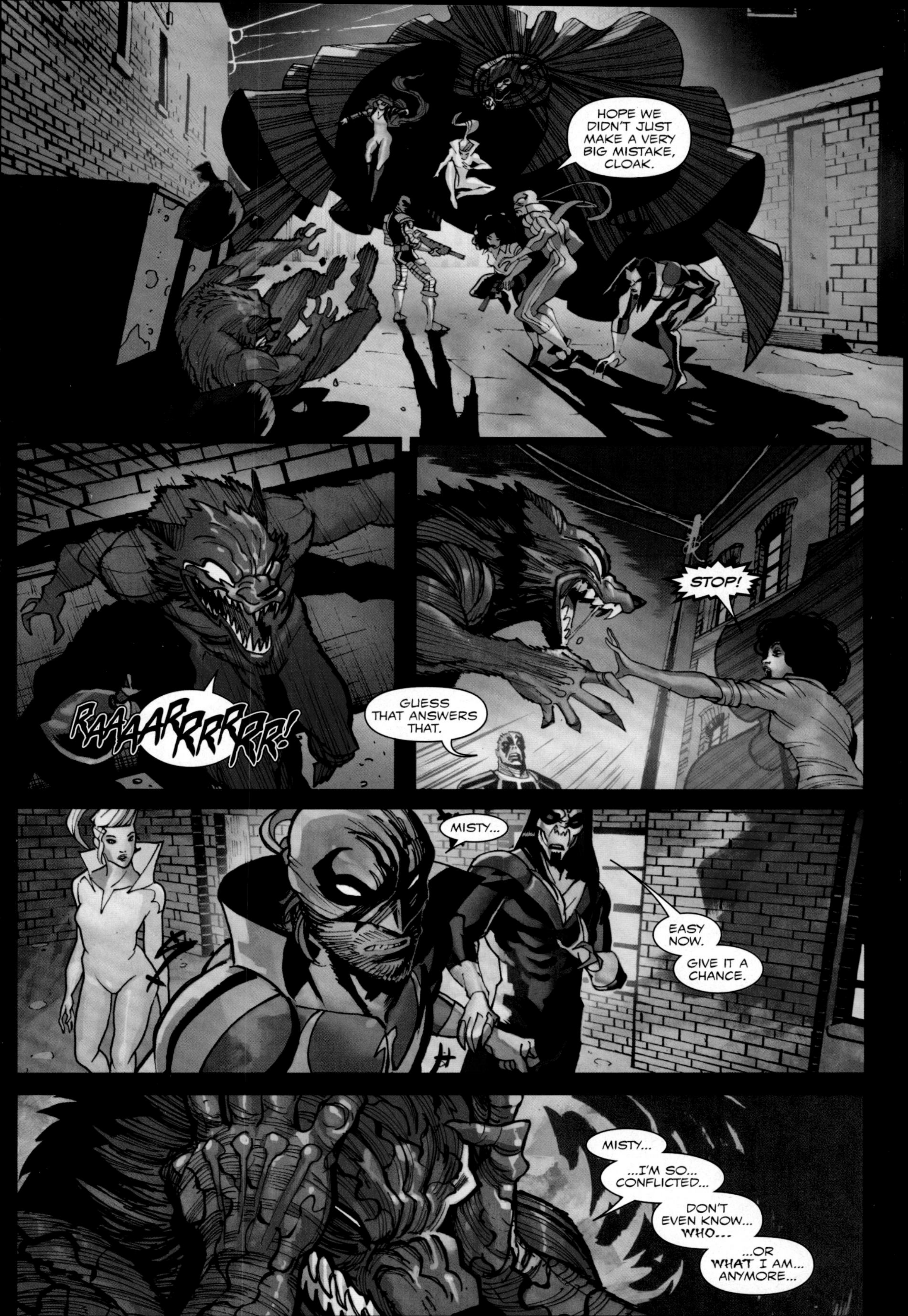
HOPE WE DIDN'T JUST MAKE A VERY BIG MISTAKE, CLOAK.
RAAAARRRRRR!
GUESS THAT ANSWERS THAT.
STOP!
MISTY...
EASY NOW.
GIVE IT A CHANCE.
MISTY...
...I'M SO... CONFLICTED...
DON'T EVEN KNOW... WHO...
...OR WHAT I AM... ANYMORE...

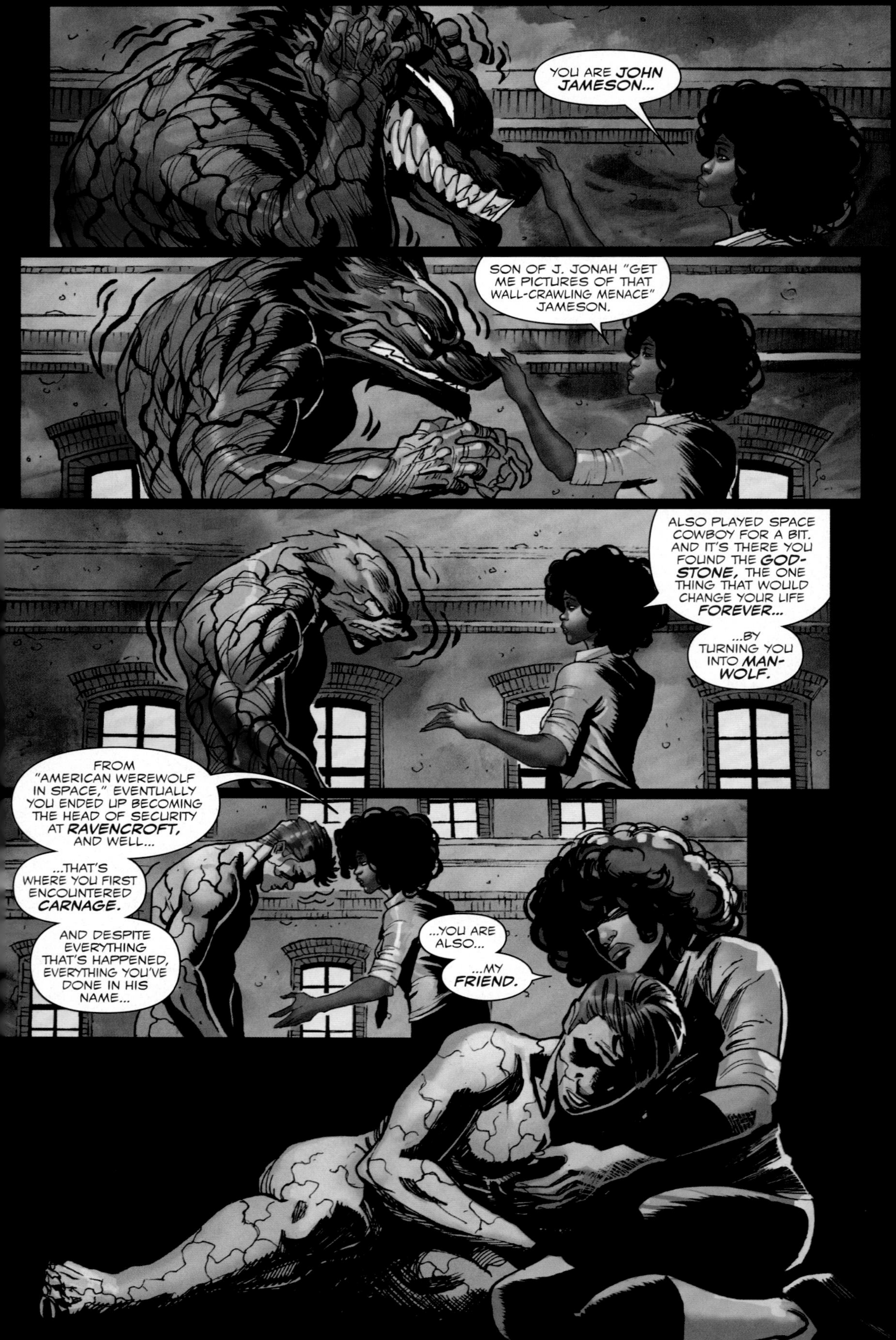
YOU ARE JOHN JAMESON...
SON OF J. JONAH "GET ME PICTURES OF THAT WALL-CRAWLING MENACE" JAMESON.
ALSO PLAYED SPACE COWBOY FOR A BIT. AND IT'S THERE YOU FOUND THE GOD-STONE, THE ONE THING THAT WOULD CHANGE YOUR LIFE FOREVER...
...BY TURNING YOU INTO MAN-WOLF.
FROM "AMERICAN WEREWOLF IN SPACE," EVENTUALLY YOU ENDED UP BECOMING THE HEAD OF SECURITY AT RAVENCROFT, AND WELL...
...THAT'S WHERE YOU FIRST ENCOUNTERED CARNAGE.
AND DESPITE EVERYTHING THAT'S HAPPENED, EVERYTHING YOU'VE DONE IN HIS NAME...
...YOU ARE ALSO...
...MY FRIEND.

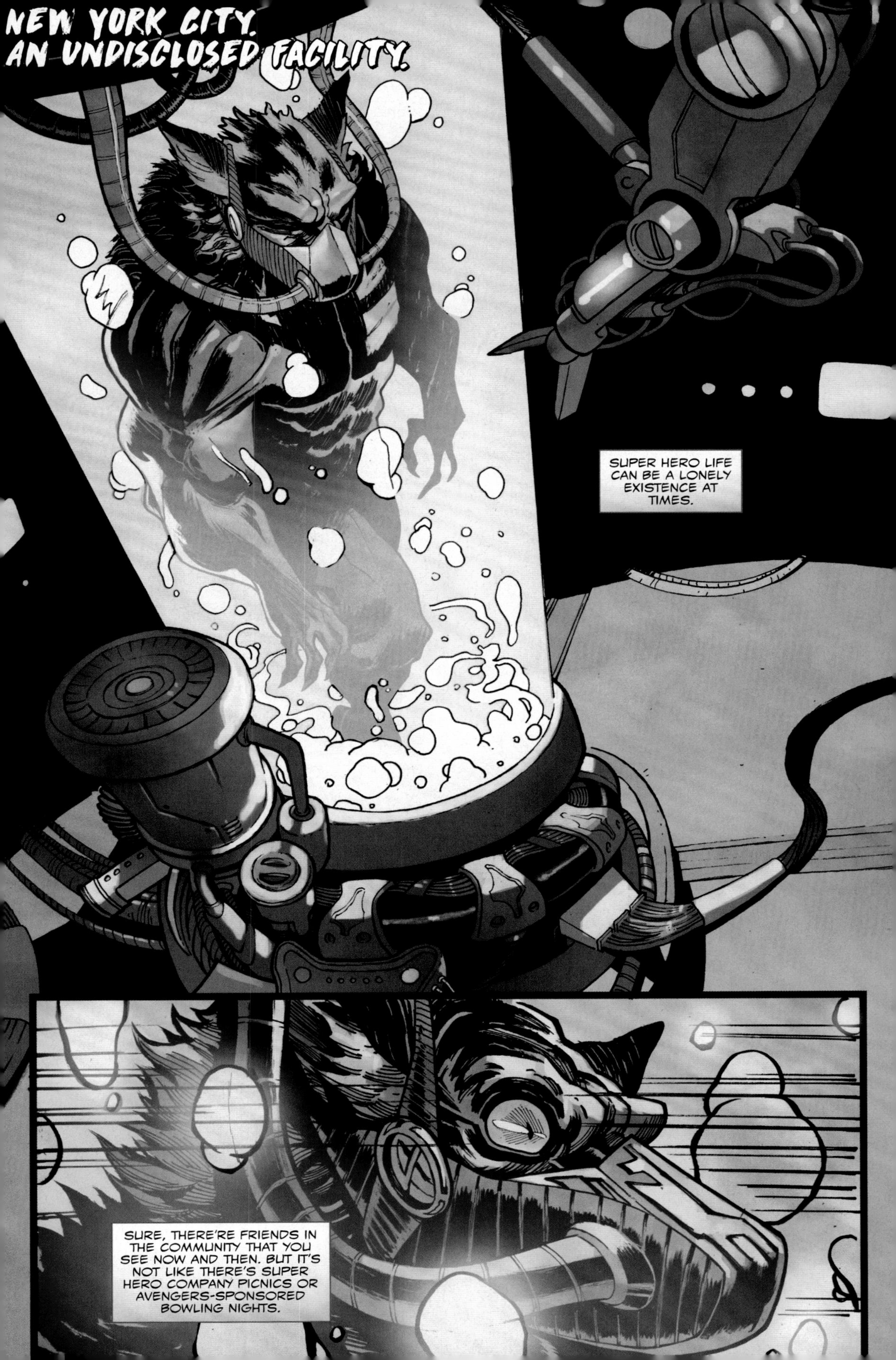
NEW YORK CITY.
AN UNDISCLOSED FACILITY.
SUPER HERO LIFE CAN BE A LONELY EXISTENCE AT TIMES.
SURE, THERE'RE FRIENDS IN THE COMMUNITY THAT YOU SEE NOW AND THEN. BUT IT'S NOT LIKE THERE'S SUPER HERO COMPANY PICNICS OR AVENGERS-SPONSORED BOWLING NIGHTS.

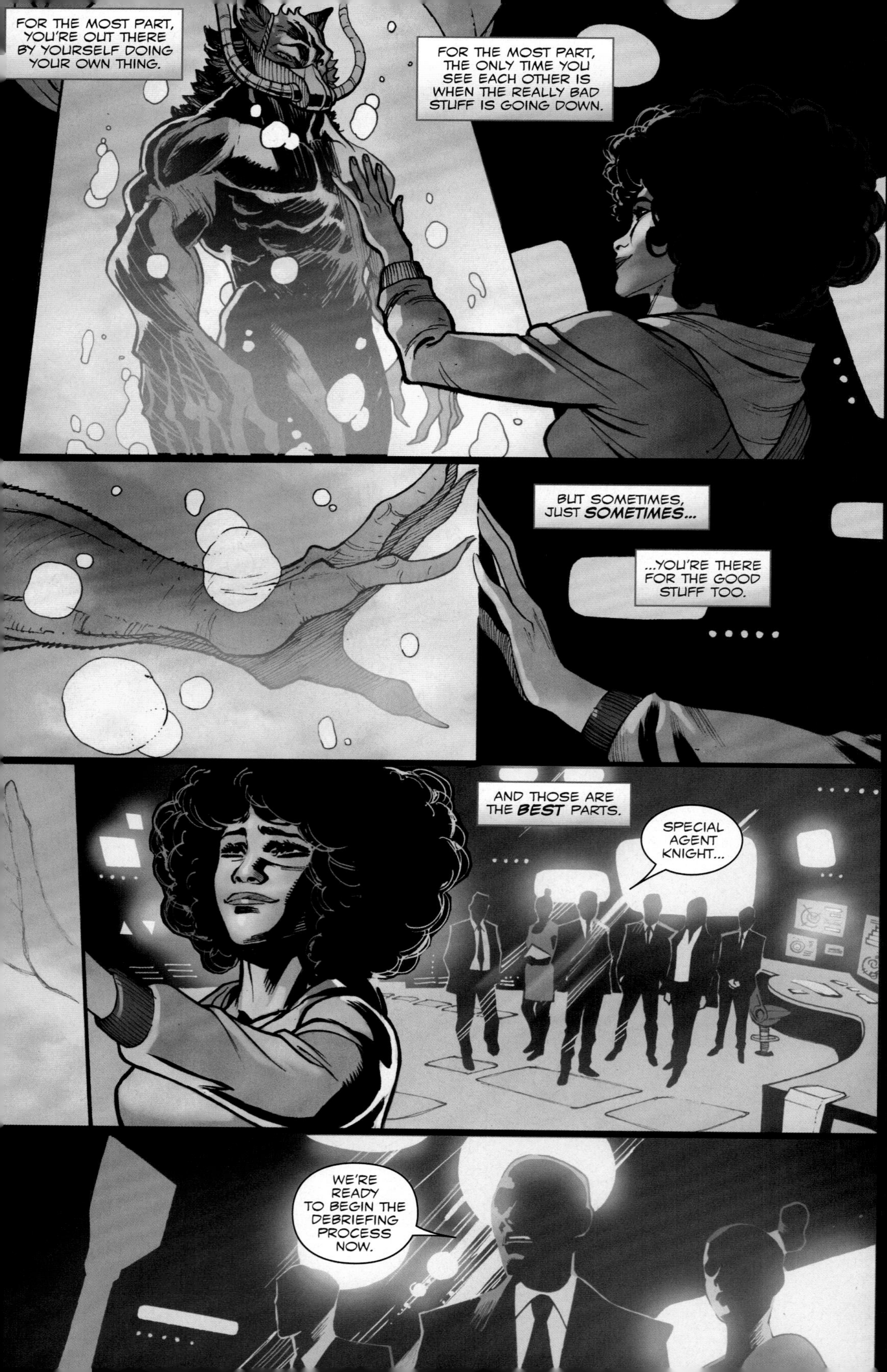
FOR THE MOST PART, YOU'RE OUT THERE BY YOURSELF DOING YOUR OWN THING.
FOR THE MOST PART, THE ONLY TIME YOU SEE EACH OTHER IS WHEN THE REALLY BAD STUFF IS GOING DOWN.
BUT SOMETIMES, JUST SOMETIMES...
...YOU'RE THERE FOR THE GOOD STUFF TOO.
AND THOSE ARE THE BEST PARTS.
SPECIAL AGENT KNIGHT...
WE'RE READY TO BEGIN THE DEBRIEFING PROCESS NOW.

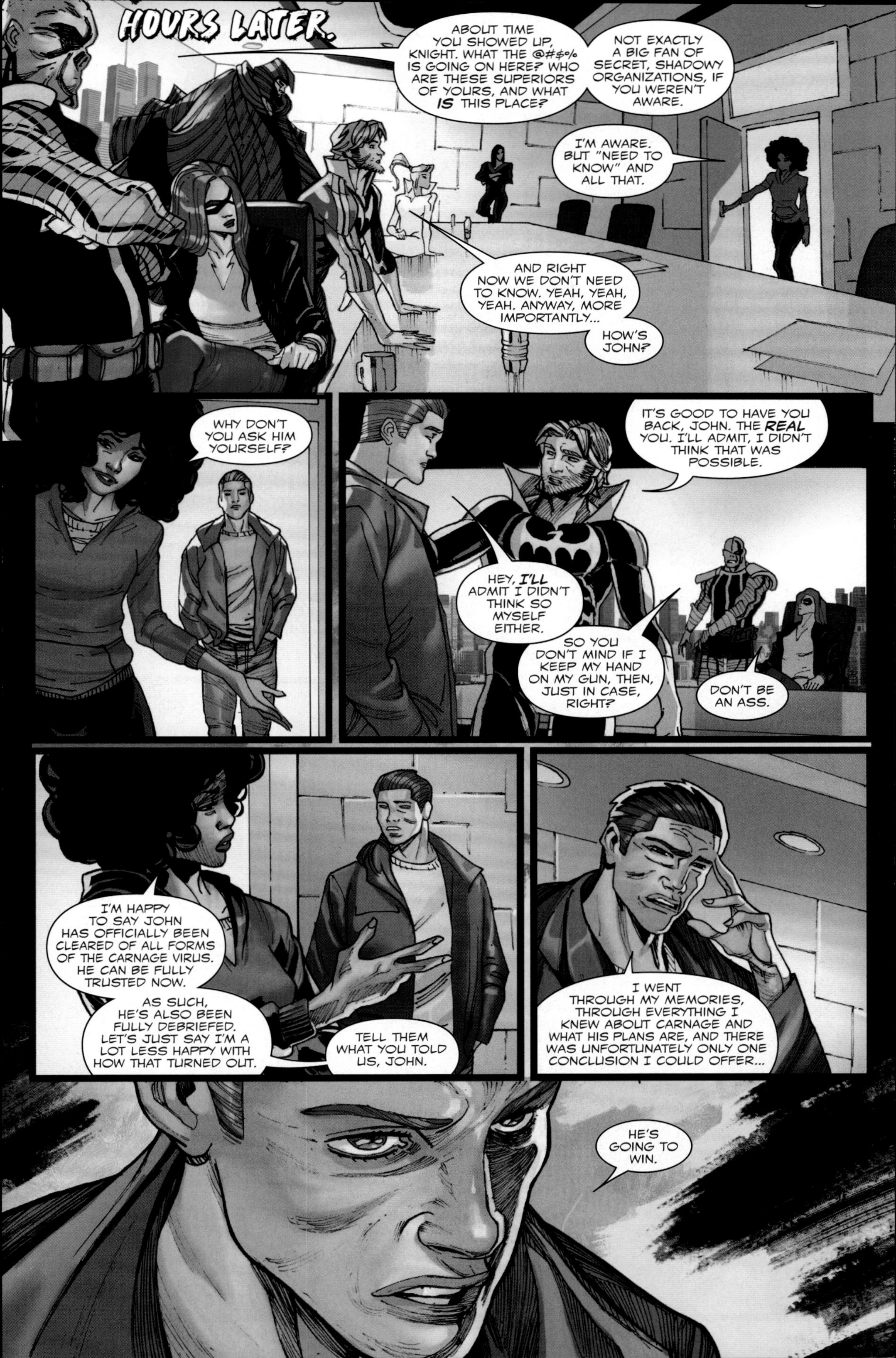
HOURS LATER.
ABOUT TIME YOU SHOWED UP, KNIGHT. WHAT THE @#$% IS GOING ON HERE? WHO ARE THESE SUPERIORS OF YOURS, AND WHAT IS THIS PLACE?
NOT EXACTLY A BIG FAN OF SECRET, SHADOWY ORGANIZATIONS, IF YOU WEREN'T AWARE.
I'M AWARE. BUT "NEED TO KNOW" AND ALL THAT.
AND RIGHT NOW WE DON'T NEED TO KNOW. YEAH, YEAH, YEAH. ANYWAY, MORE IMPORTANTLY...
HOW'S JOHN?
WHY DON'T YOU ASK HIM YOURSELF?
IT'S GOOD TO HAVE YOU BACK, JOHN. THE REAL YOU. I'LL ADMIT, I DIDN'T THINK THAT WAS POSSIBLE.
HEY, I'LL ADMIT I DIDN'T THINK SO MYSELF EITHER.
SO YOU DON'T MIND IF I KEEP MY HAND ON MY GUN, THEN, JUST IN CASE, RIGHT?
DON'T BE AN ASS.
I'M HAPPY TO SAY JOHN HAS OFFICIALLY BEEN CLEARED OF ALL FORMS OF THE CARNAGE VIRUS. HE CAN BE FULLY TRUSTED NOW.
AS SUCH, HE'S ALSO BEEN FULLY DEBRIEFED. LET'S JUST SAY I'M A LOT LESS HAPPY WITH HOW THAT TURNED OUT.
TELL THEM WHAT YOU TOLD US, JOHN.
I WENT THROUGH MY MEMORIES, THROUGH EVERYTHING I KNEW ABOUT CARNAGE AND WHAT HIS PLANS ARE, AND THERE WAS UNFORTUNATELY ONLY ONE CONCLUSION I COULD OFFER...
HE'S GOING TO WIN.

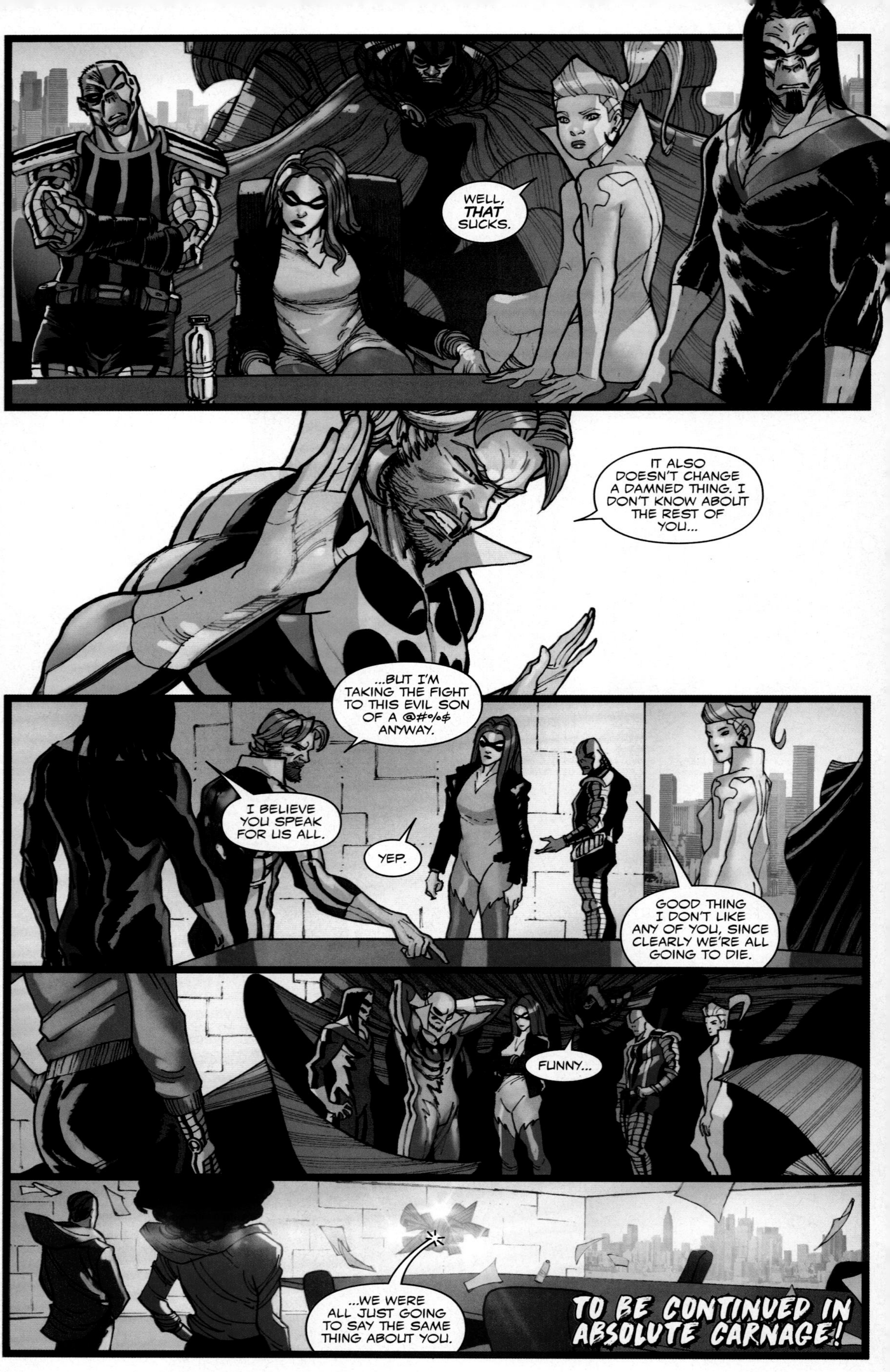
WELL, THAT SUCKS.
IT ALSO DOESN'T CHANGE A DAMNED THING. I DON'T KNOW ABOUT THE REST OF YOU...
...BUT I'M TAKING THE FIGHT TO THIS EVIL SON OF A @#%$ ANYWAY.
I BELIEVE YOU SPEAK FOR US ALL.
YEP.
GOOD THING I DON'T LIKE ANY OF YOU, SINCE CLEARLY WE'RE ALL GOING TO DIE.
FUNNY...
...WE WERE ALL JUST GOING TO SAY THE SAME THING ABOUT YOU.
TO BE CONTINUED IN ABSOLUTE CARNAGE!

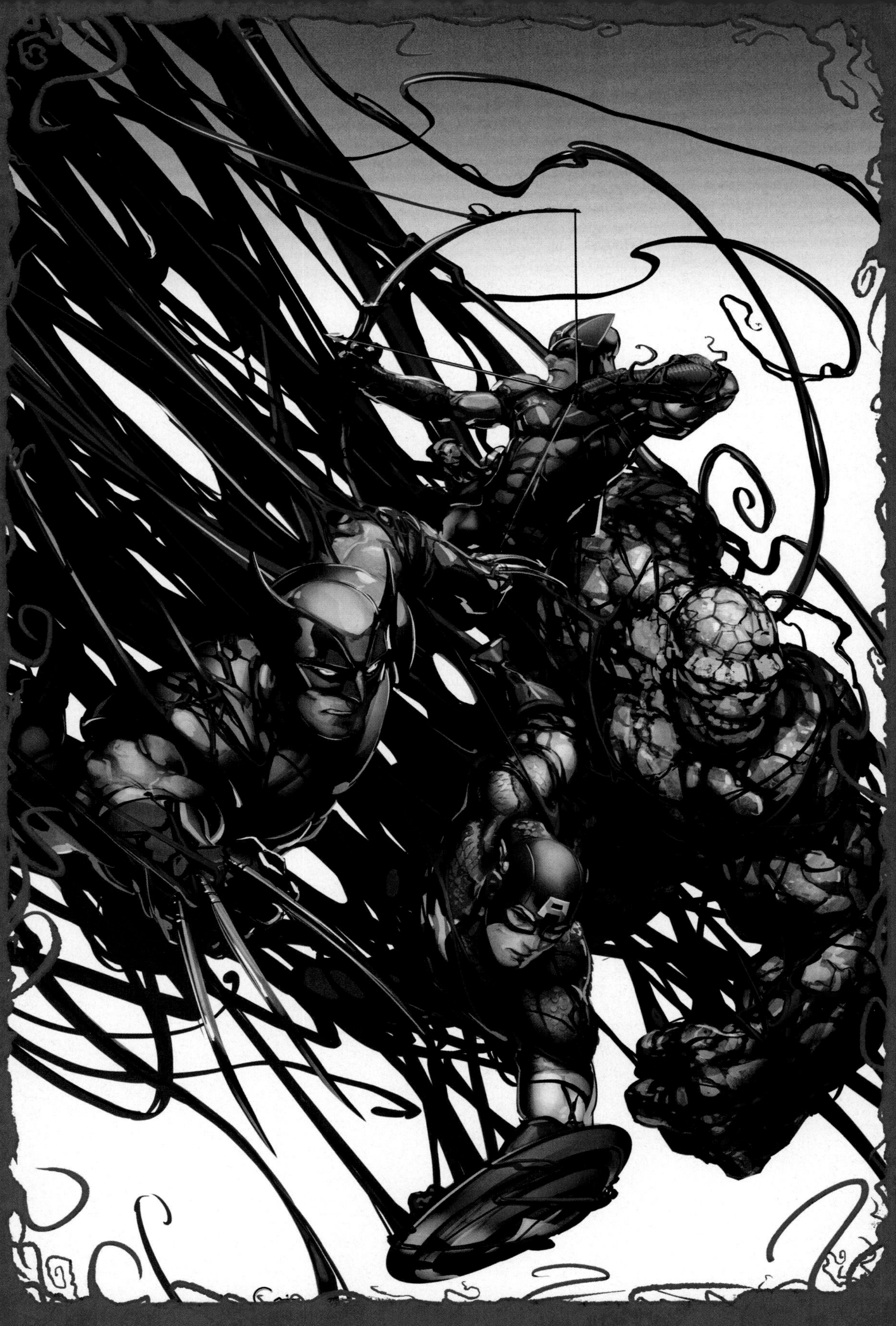

ABSOLUTE CARNAGE: AVENGERS

THE AVENGERS

Cletus Kasady was a serial killer sharing a cell in Ryker's Island with a man named Eddie Brock, better known as Venom. When the Venom symbiote broke Eddie out of prison, it spawned a new symbiote that bonded with Kasady, turning him into the blood-crazed Carnage.

Months ago, Carnage took over the small town of Doverton, Colorado, prompting an immediate intervention by some of the Avengers at the time: Captain America, Hawkeye, Wolverine, the Thing and Spider-Man. During the fight, Carnage took control of the Avengers members, except for Spider-Man. With help from the people of Doverton, Spider-Man freed the town and the Avengers from Carnage's control.

Now empowered by the symbiote god, Knull, Carnage is setting his sights on collecting the codices — little pieces of DNA left in former hosts — to unlock Knull from his prison. Across the country, Carnage and his horde are hunting down anyone who has ever worn a symbiote, including the Doverton Avengers team…

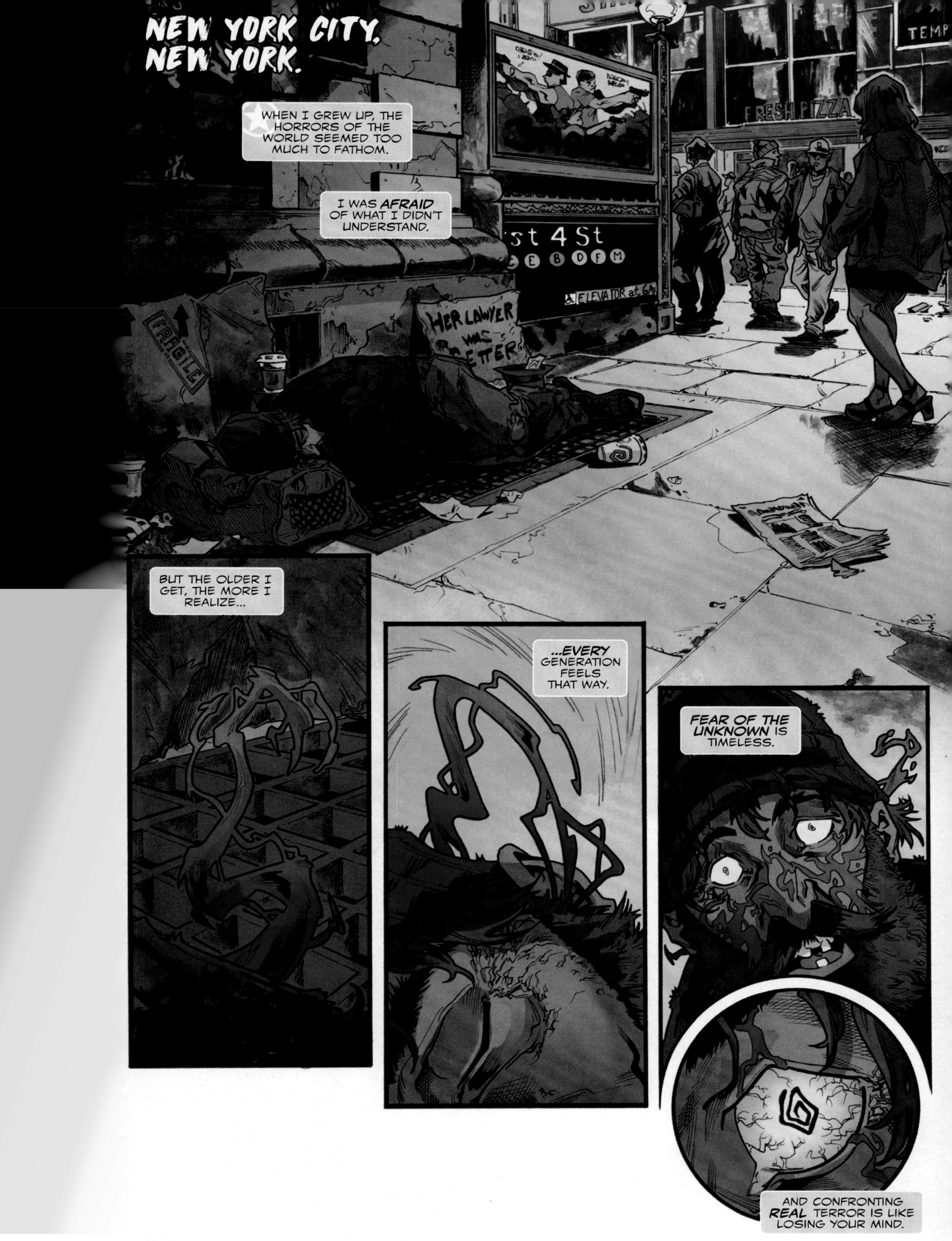
NEW YORK CITY, NEW YORK.
WHEN I GREW UP, THE HORRORS OF THE WORLD SEEMED TOO MUCH TO FATHOM.
I WAS AFRAID OF WHAT I DIDN'T UNDERSTAND.
FRESH PIZZA
st 4 St
ELEVATOR at 6Av
HER LAWYER WAS BETTER
FRAGILE
BUT THE OLDER I GET, THE MORE I REALIZE...
...EVERY GENERATION FEELS THAT WAY.
FEAR OF THE UNKNOWN IS TIMELESS.
AND CONFRONTING REAL TERROR IS LIKE LOSING YOUR MIND.

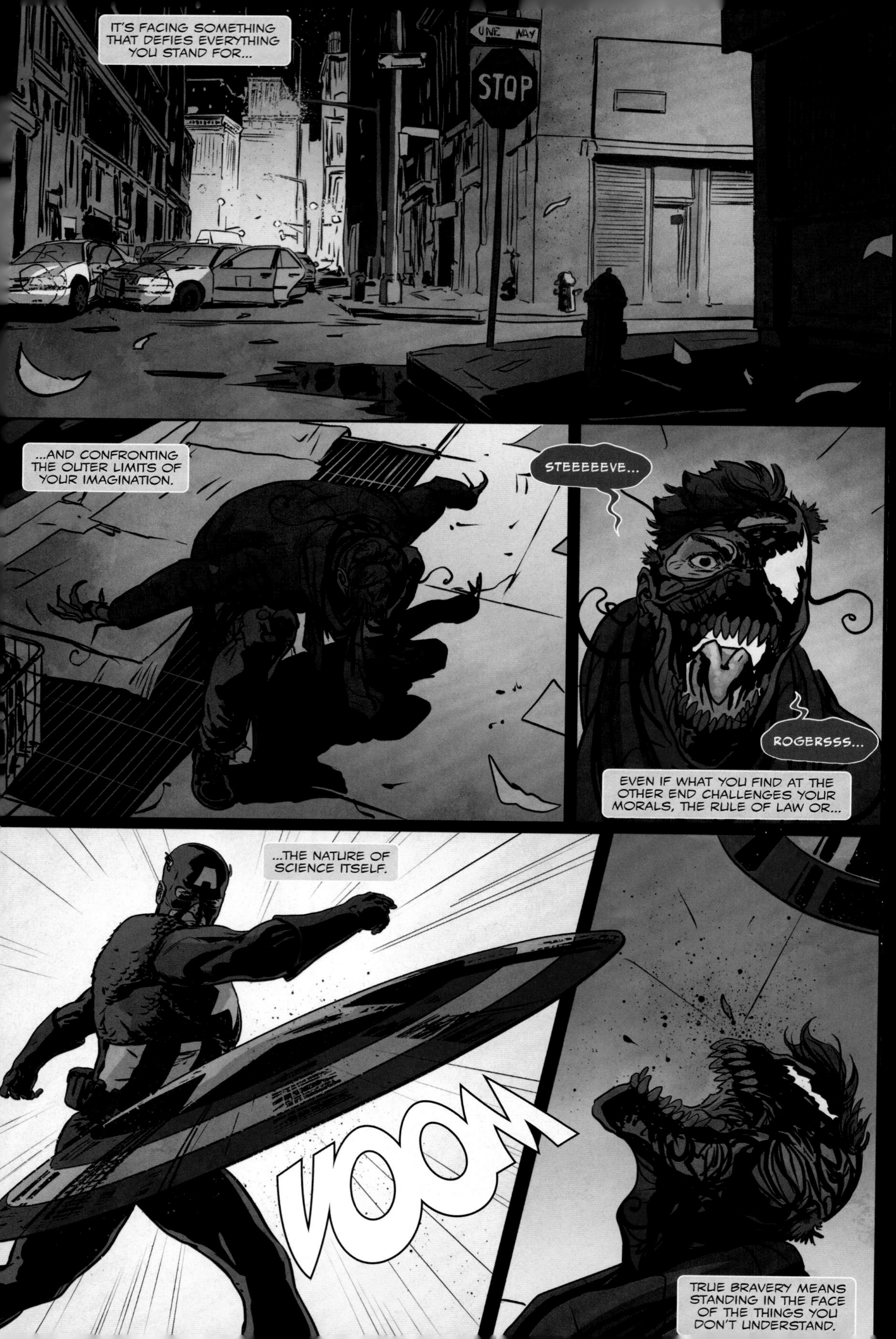
IT'S FACING SOMETHING THAT DEFIES EVERYTHING YOU STAND FOR...
ONE WAY
STOP
...AND CONFRONTING THE OUTER LIMITS OF YOUR IMAGINATION.
STEEEEEVE...
ROGERSSS...
EVEN IF WHAT YOU FIND AT THE OTHER END CHALLENGES YOUR MORALS, THE RULE OF LAW OR...
...THE NATURE OF SCIENCE ITSELF.
VOOM
TRUE BRAVERY MEANS STANDING IN THE FACE OF THE THINGS YOU DON'T UNDERSTAND.

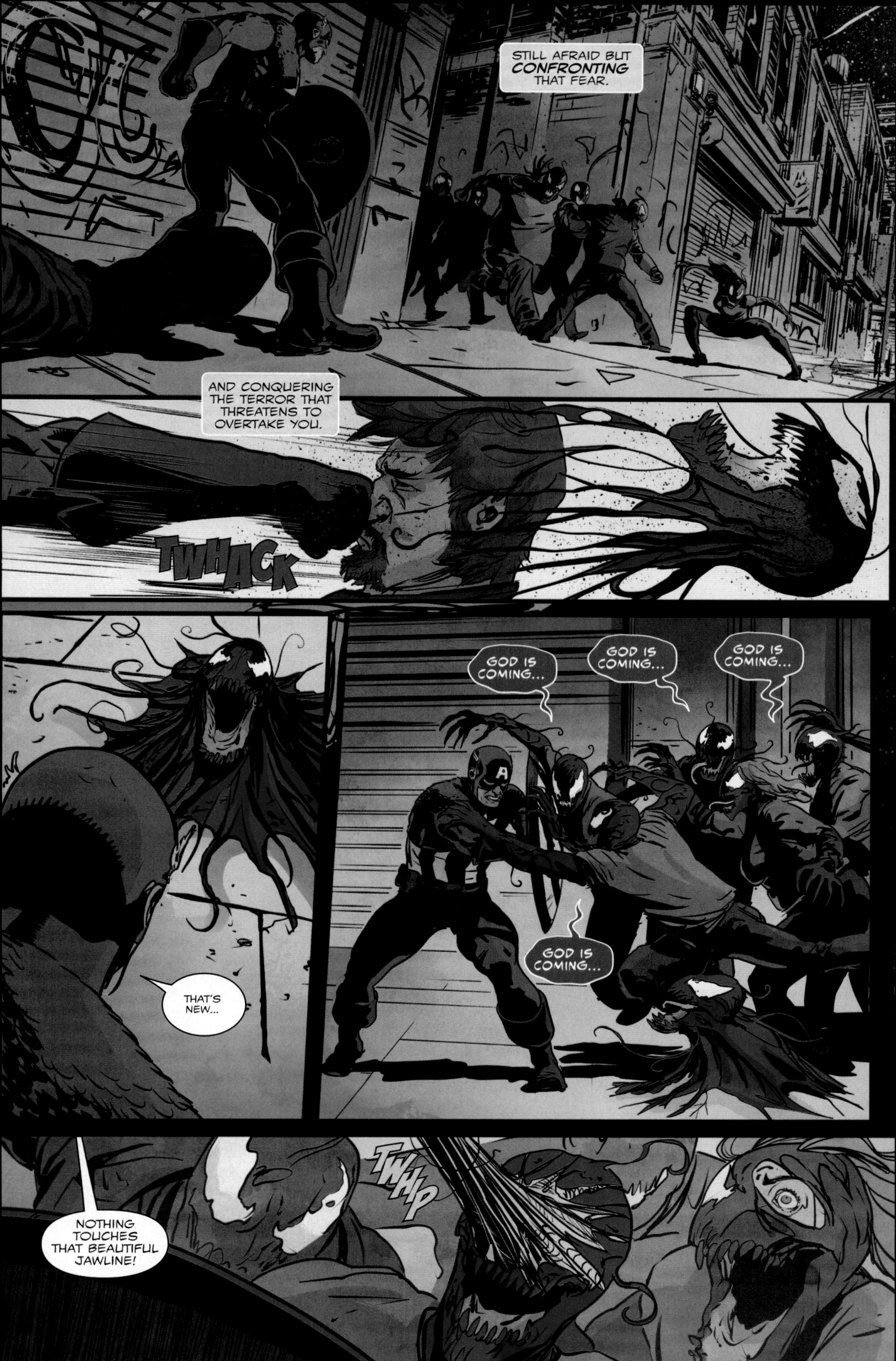
STILL AFRAID BUT CONFRONTING THAT FEAR.
AND CONQUERING THE TERROR THAT THREATENS TO OVERTAKE YOU.
TWHACK
THAT'S NEW...
GOD IS COMING...
GOD IS COMING...
GOD IS COMING...
GOD IS COMING...
NOTHING TOUCHES THAT BEAUTIFUL JAWLINE!
TWHIP

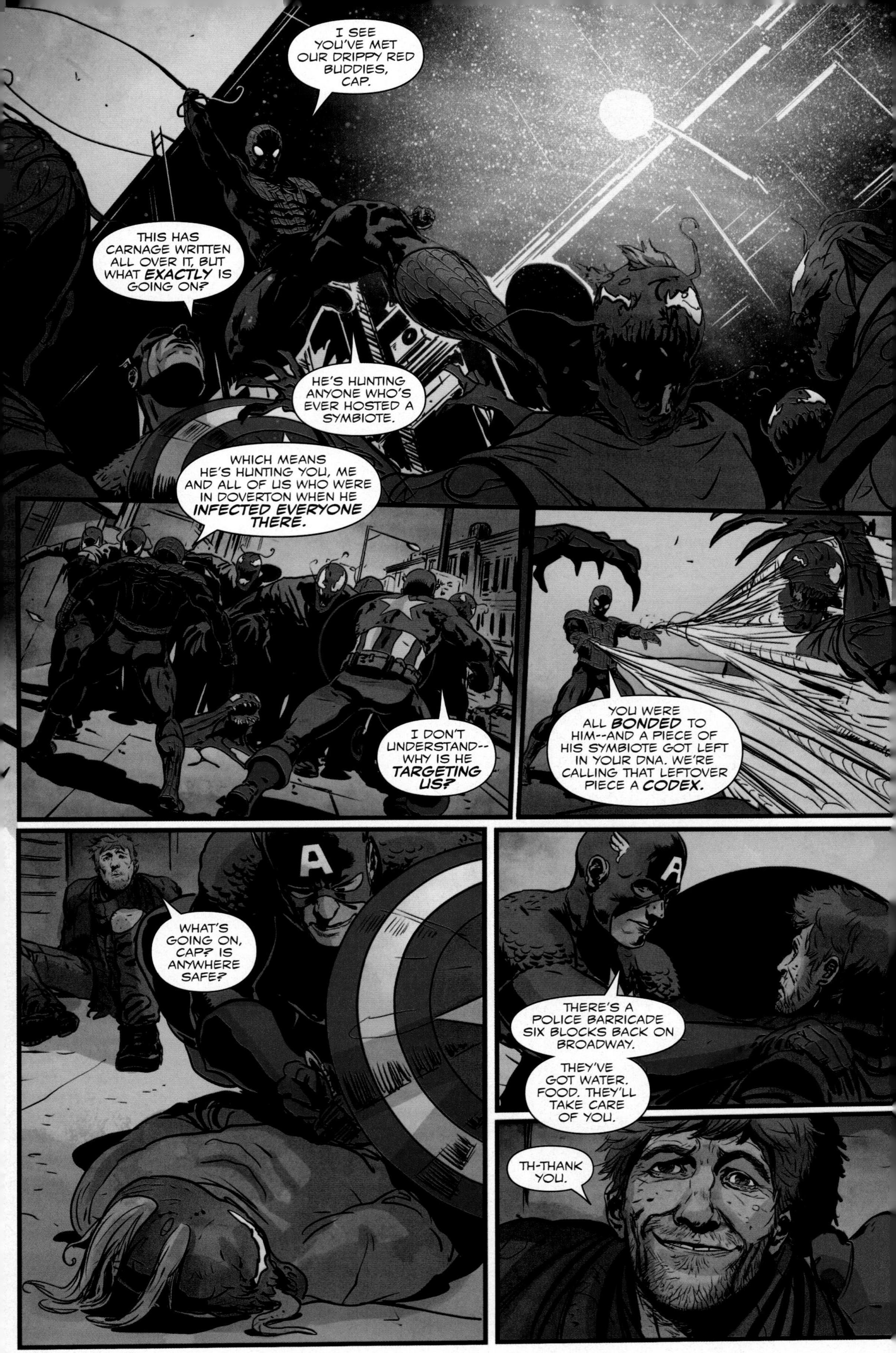
I SEE YOU'VE MET OUR DRIPPY RED BUDDIES, CAP.
THIS HAS CARNAGE WRITTEN ALL OVER IT, BUT WHAT EXACTLY IS GOING ON?
HE'S HUNTING ANYONE WHO'S EVER HOSTED A SYMBIOTE.
WHICH MEANS HE'S HUNTING YOU, ME AND ALL OF US WHO WERE IN DOVERTON WHEN HE INFECTED EVERYONE THERE.
I DON'T UNDERSTAND-- WHY IS HE TARGETING US?
YOU WERE ALL BONDED TO HIM--AND A PIECE OF HIS SYMBIOTE GOT LEFT IN YOUR DNA. WE'RE CALLING THAT LEFTOVER PIECE A CODEX.
WHAT'S GOING ON, CAP? IS ANYWHERE SAFE?
THERE'S A POLICE BARRICADE SIX BLOCKS BACK ON BROADWAY.
THEY'VE GOT WATER. FOOD. THEY'LL TAKE CARE OF YOU.
TH-THANK YOU.

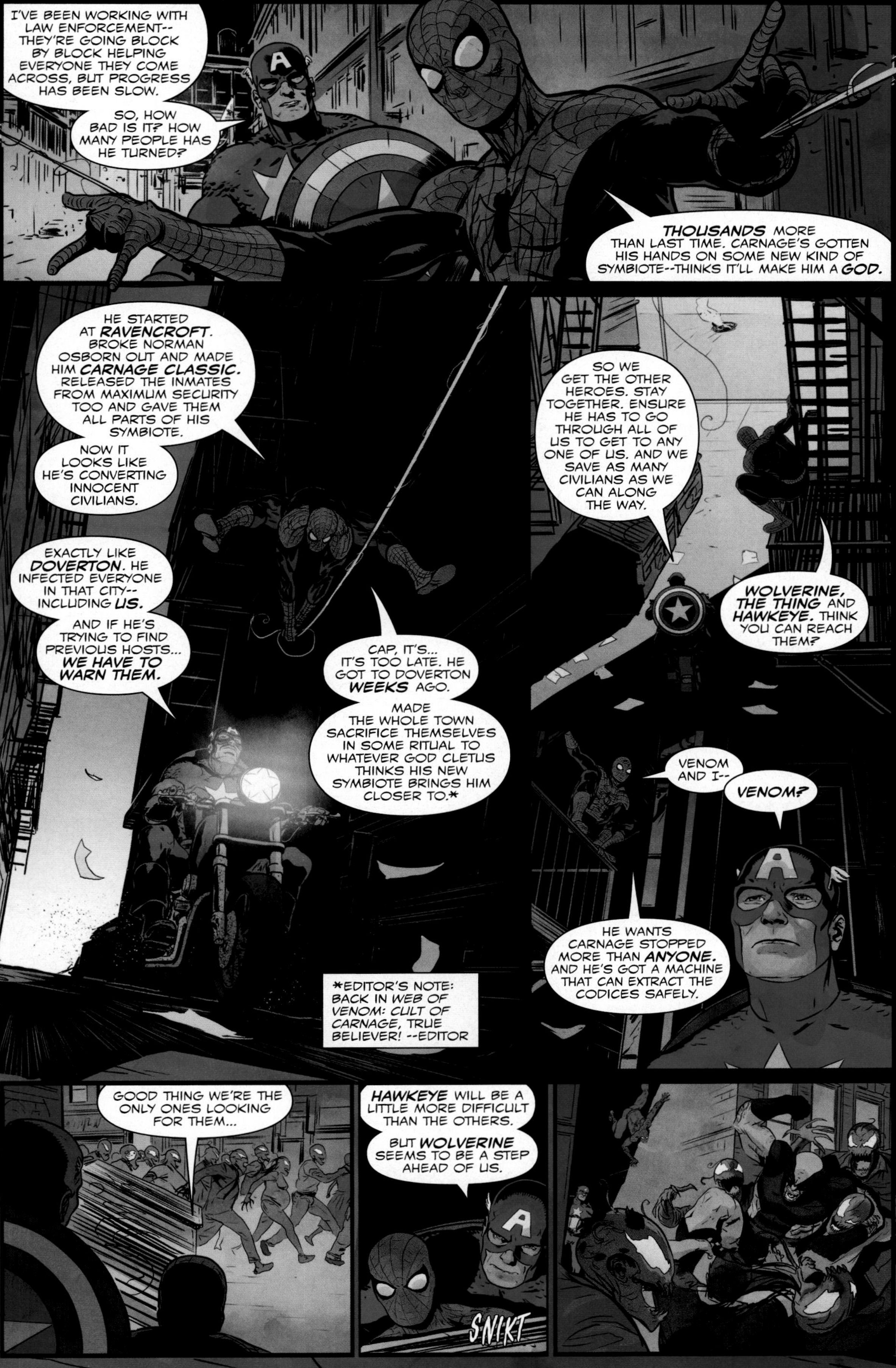
I'VE BEEN WORKING WITH LAW ENFORCEMENT-- THEY'RE GOING BLOCK BY BLOCK HELPING EVERYONE THEY COME ACROSS, BUT PROGRESS HAS BEEN SLOW.
SO, HOW BAD IS IT? HOW MANY PEOPLE HAS HE TURNED?
THOUSANDS MORE THAN LAST TIME. CARNAGE'S GOTTEN HIS HANDS ON SOME NEW KIND OF SYMBIOTE--THINKS IT'LL MAKE HIM A GOD.
HE STARTED AT RAVENCROFT. BROKE NORMAN OSBORN OUT AND MADE HIM CARNAGE CLASSIC. RELEASED THE INMATES FROM MAXIMUM SECURITY TOO AND GAVE THEM ALL PARTS OF HIS SYMBIOTE.
NOW IT LOOKS LIKE HE'S CONVERTING INNOCENT CIVILIANS.
EXACTLY LIKE DOVERTON. HE INFECTED EVERYONE IN THAT CITY-- INCLUDING US.
AND IF HE'S TRYING TO FIND PREVIOUS HOSTS... WE HAVE TO WARN THEM.
CAP, IT'S... IT'S TOO LATE. HE GOT TO DOVERTON WEEKS AGO.
MADE THE WHOLE TOWN SACRIFICE THEMSELVES IN SOME RITUAL TO WHATEVER GOD CLETUS THINKS HIS NEW SYMBIOTE BRINGS HIM CLOSER TO.*
*EDITOR'S NOTE: BACK IN WEB OF VENOM: CULT OF CARNAGE, TRUE BELIEVER! --EDITOR
SO WE GET THE OTHER HEROES. STAY TOGETHER. ENSURE HE HAS TO GO THROUGH ALL OF US TO GET TO ANY ONE OF US. AND WE SAVE AS MANY CIVILIANS AS WE CAN ALONG THE WAY.
WOLVERINE, THE THING AND HAWKEYE. THINK YOU CAN REACH THEM?
VENOM AND I--
VENOM?
HE WANTS CARNAGE STOPPED MORE THAN ANYONE. AND HE'S GOT A MACHINE THAT CAN EXTRACT THE CODICES SAFELY.
GOOD THING WE'RE THE ONLY ONES LOOKING FOR THEM...
HAWKEYE WILL BE A LITTLE MORE DIFFICULT THAN THE OTHERS.
BUT WOLVERINE SEEMS TO BE A STEP AHEAD OF US.
SNIKT

LOS ANGELES,
CALIFORNIA,

THE SHAPE OF
THE NIGHTMARE
IS A *SPIRAL.*

AND THERE'S
A *VOICE*
WITHIN IT.

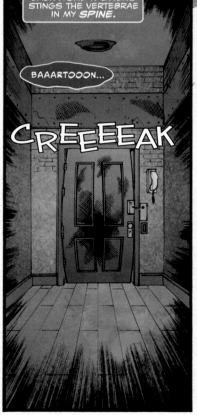

EACH WORD IT UTTERS
STINGS THE VERTEBRAE
IN MY *SPINE.*

BAAARTOOON...

CREEEEAK

BUT I
REFUSE TO
LISTEN.

AND YET
I HEAR IT.

TELLING ME,
"GOD IS COMING,
GOD IS COMING."

BAAARRTON!

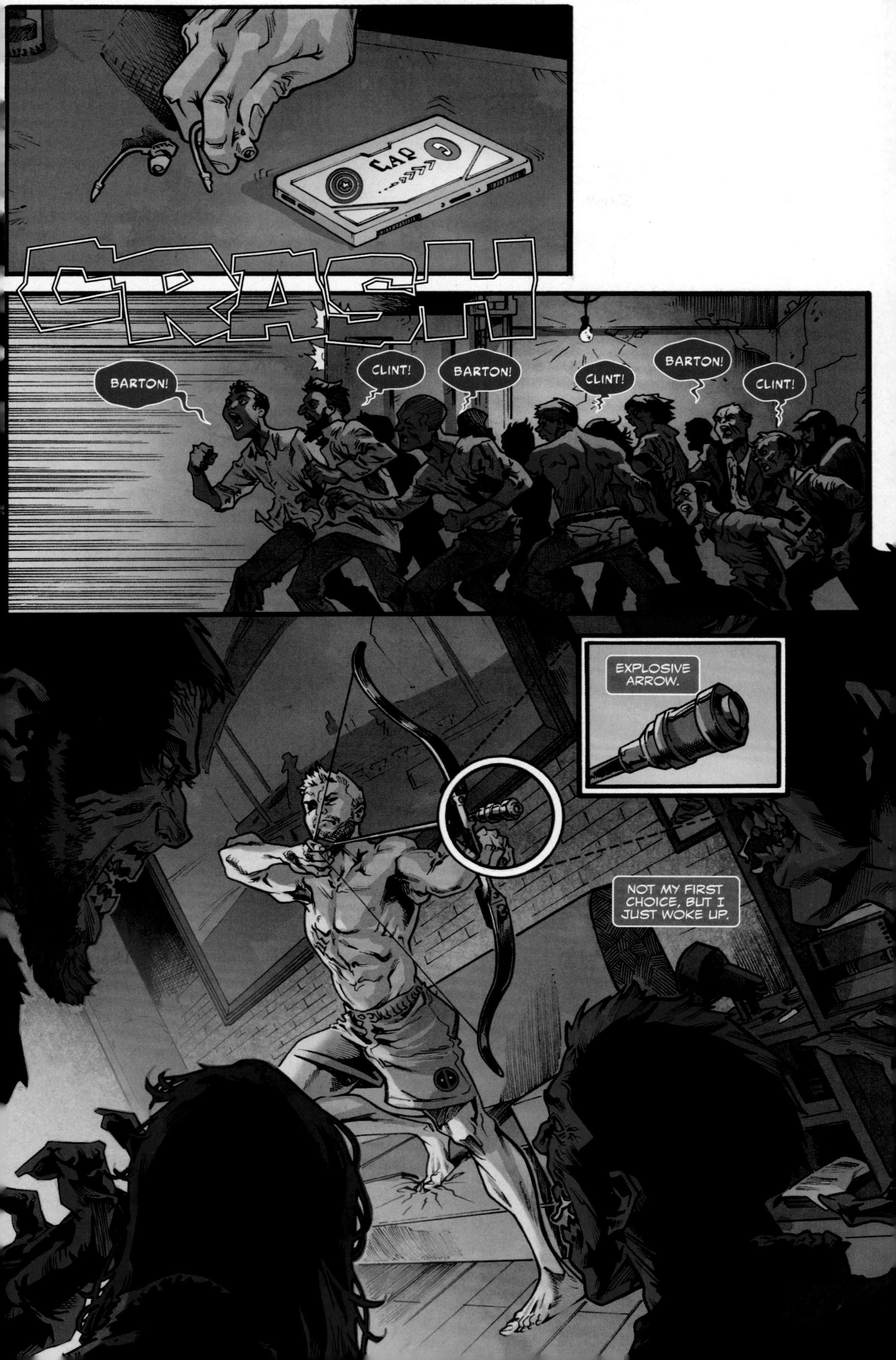
CAP
CRASH
BARTON!
CLINT!
BARTON!
CLINT!
BARTON!
CLINT!
EXPLOSIVE ARROW.
NOT MY FIRST CHOICE, BUT I JUST WOKE UP.

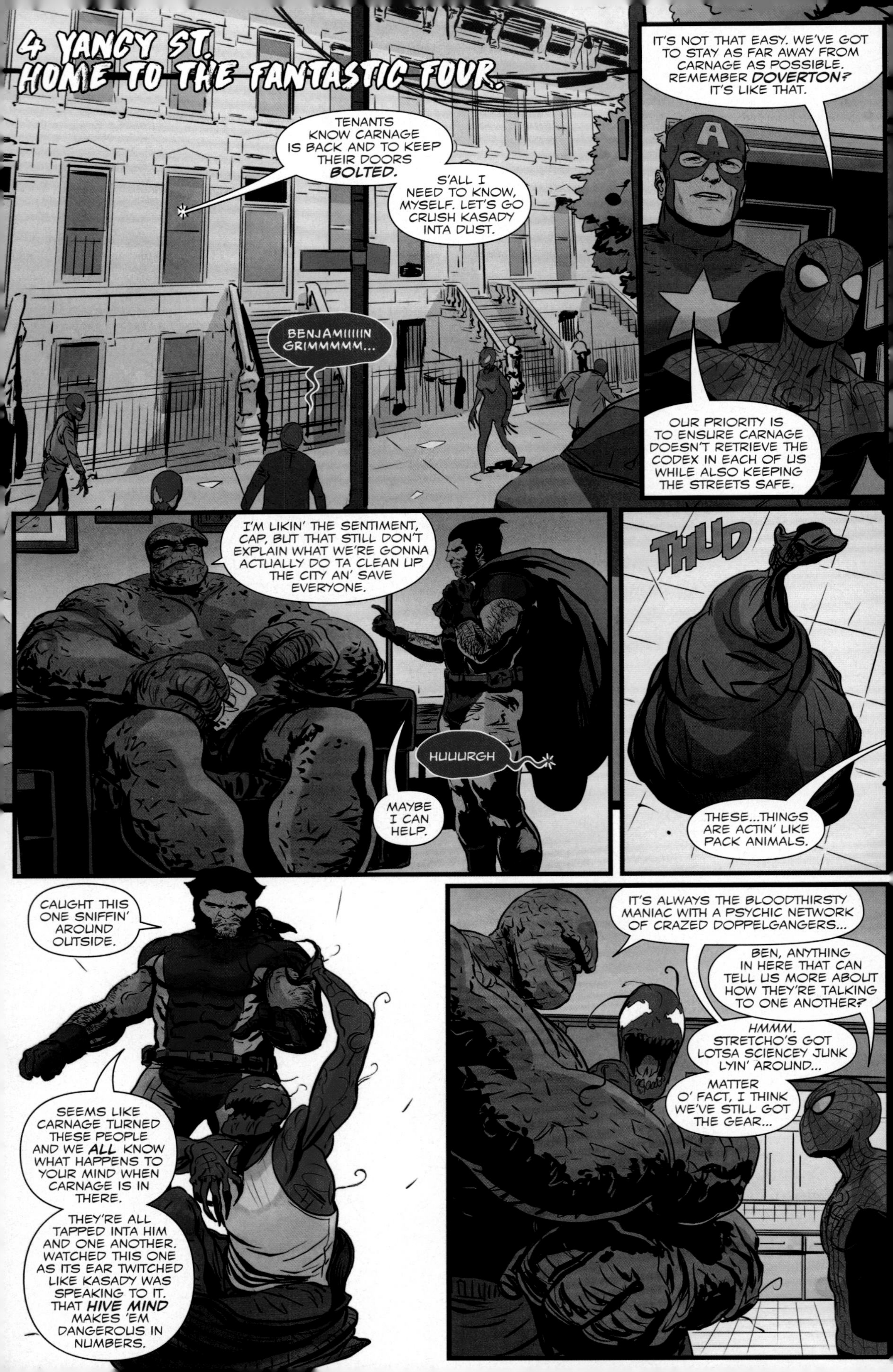
4 YANCY ST. HOME TO THE FANTASTIC FOUR.
TENANTS KNOW CARNAGE IS BACK AND TO KEEP THEIR DOORS BOLTED.
S'ALL I NEED TO KNOW, MYSELF. LET'S GO CRUSH KASADY INTA DUST.
BENJAMIIIIIN GRIMMMMM...
IT'S NOT THAT EASY. WE'VE GOT TO STAY AS FAR AWAY FROM CARNAGE AS POSSIBLE. REMEMBER DOVERTON? IT'S LIKE THAT.
OUR PRIORITY IS TO ENSURE CARNAGE DOESN'T RETRIEVE THE CODEX IN EACH OF US WHILE ALSO KEEPING THE STREETS SAFE.
I'M LIKIN' THE SENTIMENT, CAP, BUT THAT STILL DON'T EXPLAIN WHAT WE'RE GONNA ACTUALLY DO TA CLEAN UP THE CITY AN' SAVE EVERYONE.
HUUURGH
MAYBE I CAN HELP.
THUD
THESE...THINGS ARE ACTIN' LIKE PACK ANIMALS.
CAUGHT THIS ONE SNIFFIN' AROUND OUTSIDE.
SEEMS LIKE CARNAGE TURNED THESE PEOPLE AND WE ALL KNOW WHAT HAPPENS TO YOUR MIND WHEN CARNAGE IS IN THERE.
THEY'RE ALL TAPPED INTA HIM AND ONE ANOTHER. WATCHED THIS ONE AS ITS EAR TWITCHED LIKE KASADY WAS SPEAKING TO IT. THAT HIVE MIND MAKES 'EM DANGEROUS IN NUMBERS.
IT'S ALWAYS THE BLOODTHIRSTY MANIAC WITH A PSYCHIC NETWORK OF CRAZED DOPPELGANGERS...
BEN, ANYTHING IN HERE THAT CAN TELL US MORE ABOUT HOW THEY'RE TALKING TO ONE ANOTHER?
HMMM. STRETCHO'S GOT LOTSA SCIENCEY JUNK LYIN' AROUND...
MATTER O' FACT, I THINK WE'VE STILL GOT THE GEAR...

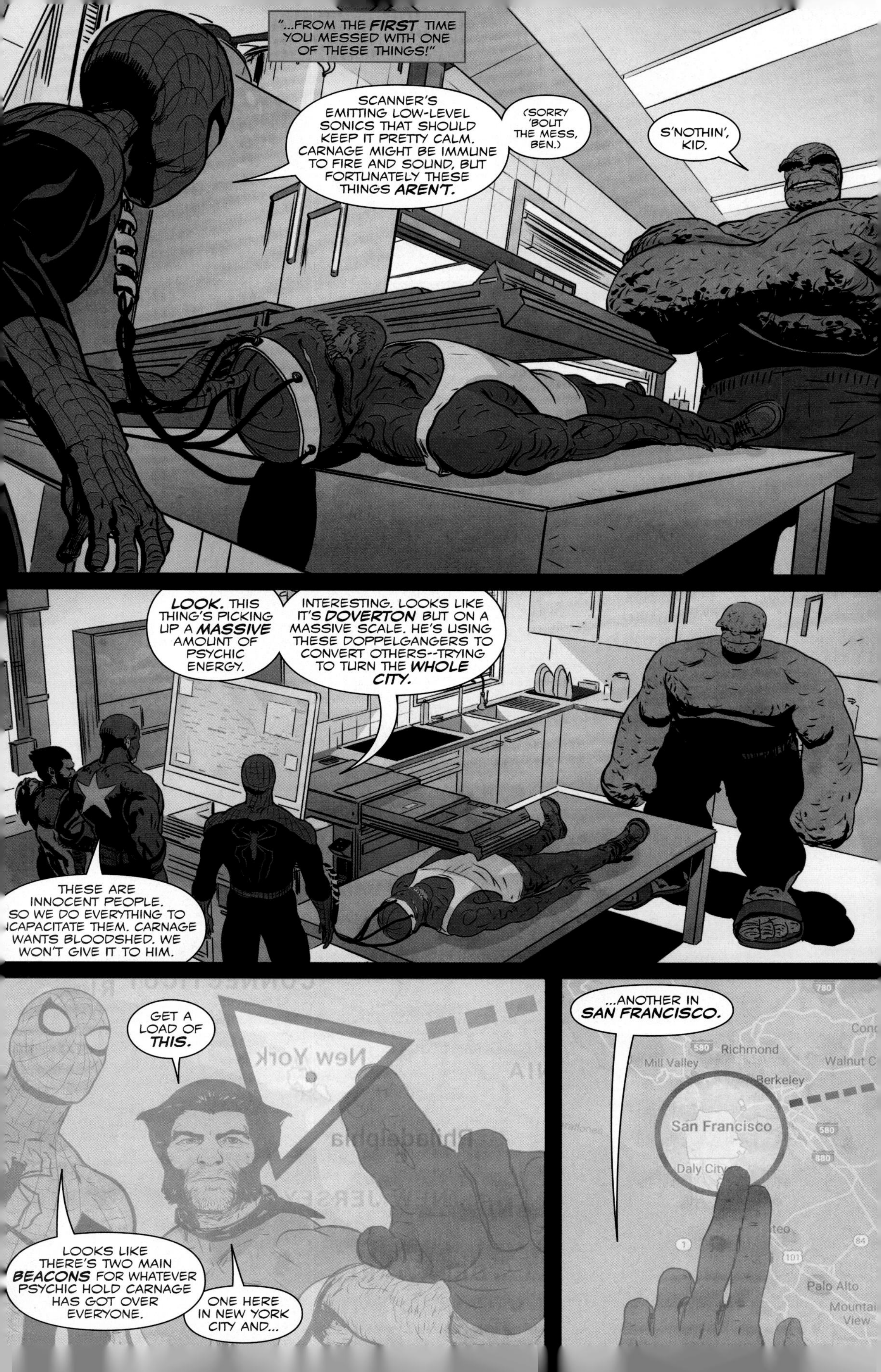
"...FROM THE FIRST TIME YOU MESSED WITH ONE OF THESE THINGS!"
SCANNER'S EMITTING LOW-LEVEL SONICS THAT SHOULD KEEP IT PRETTY CALM. CARNAGE MIGHT BE IMMUNE TO FIRE AND SOUND, BUT FORTUNATELY THESE THINGS AREN'T.
(SORRY 'BOUT THE MESS, BEN.)
S'NOTHIN', KID.
LOOK. THIS THING'S PICKING UP A MASSIVE AMOUNT OF PSYCHIC ENERGY.
INTERESTING. LOOKS LIKE IT'S DOVERTON BUT ON A MASSIVE SCALE. HE'S USING THESE DOPPELGANGERS TO CONVERT OTHERS--TRYING TO TURN THE WHOLE CITY.
THESE ARE INNOCENT PEOPLE. SO WE DO EVERYTHING TO INCAPACITATE THEM. CARNAGE WANTS BLOODSHED. WE WON'T GIVE IT TO HIM.
GET A LOAD OF THIS.
New York
Philadelphia
LOOKS LIKE THERE'S TWO MAIN BEACONS FOR WHATEVER PSYCHIC HOLD CARNAGE HAS GOT OVER EVERYONE.
ONE HERE IN NEW YORK CITY AND...
...ANOTHER IN SAN FRANCISCO.
Richmond
Mill Valley
Walnut C
Berkeley
San Francisco
Daly City
Palo Alto

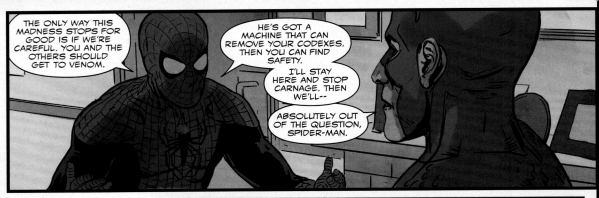

THE ONLY WAY THIS MADNESS STOPS FOR GOOD IS IF WE'RE CAREFUL. YOU AND THE OTHERS SHOULD GET TO VENOM.

HE'S GOT A MACHINE THAT CAN REMOVE YOUR CODEXES. THEN YOU CAN FIND SAFETY.

I'LL STAY HERE AND STOP CARNAGE. THEN WE'LL--

ABSOLUTELY OUT OF THE QUESTION, SPIDER-MAN.

I JUST... DON'T WANT HIM TO HURT ANYONE ELSE. I FEEL TERRIBLE LEAVING HAWKEYE ON HIS OWN...

I DON'T LIKE IT ANY MORE THAN YOU DO. BUT I'M CERTAINLY NOT GOING TO LEAVE YOU OR NEW YORK AT A TIME LIKE THIS.

CAP, THINK ABOUT IT. WE'RE A BIGGER TARGET TOGETHER. *I* CAN MOVE QUICKER THAN *WE CAN.* IN AND OUT.

YOU GUYS CAN GET TO *VENOM.* ONCE YOU'RE FREE AND CLEAR OF THE CODEX--

SPIDER-MAN, WE'RE NOT GOING ANYWHERE. WE'RE IN THIS TOGETHER. END OF STORY.

I JUST *WISH* THIS WASN'T SO MESSY. THAT HE DIDN'T BRING HAWKEYE... EVERYONE INTO THIS...THERE'S ALMOST NINE MILLION PEOPLE IN THIS CITY.

THEN WE'LL HAVE TO MAKE SURE WE DON'T LOSE *A SINGLE ONE* OF THEM

NOT A SINGLE ONE.

THINGS ARE POUNDIN' DOWN THE DOORS OUT HERE! TIME TO GO!

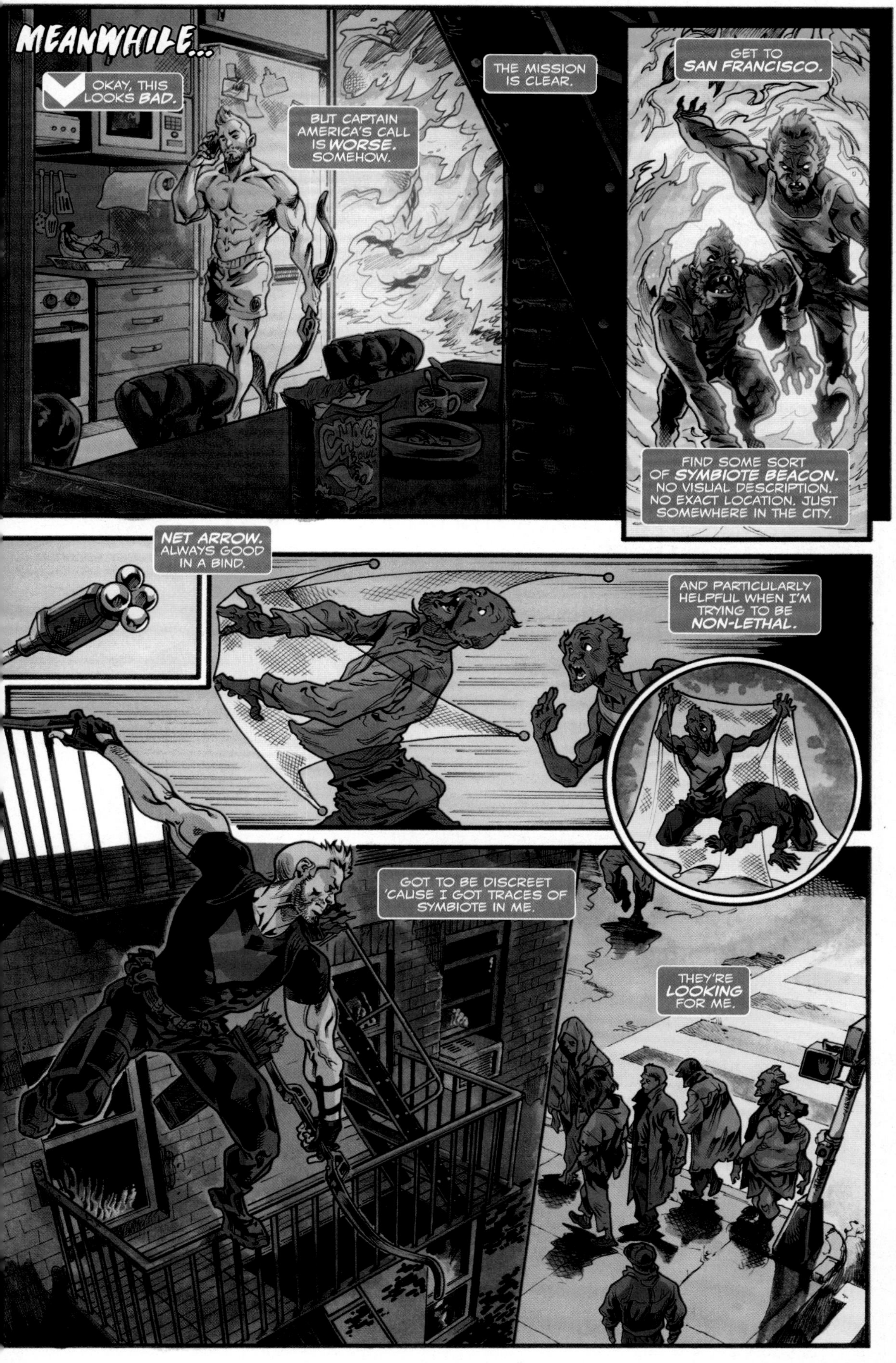

MEANWHILE...
OKAY, THIS LOOKS BAD.
BUT CAPTAIN AMERICA'S CALL IS WORSE. SOMEHOW.
THE MISSION IS CLEAR.
GET TO SAN FRANCISCO.
FIND SOME SORT OF SYMBIOTE BEACON. NO VISUAL DESCRIPTION. NO EXACT LOCATION. JUST SOMEWHERE IN THE CITY.
NET ARROW. ALWAYS GOOD IN A BIND.
AND PARTICULARLY HELPFUL WHEN I'M TRYING TO BE NON-LETHAL.
GOT TO BE DISCREET 'CAUSE I GOT TRACES OF SYMBIOTE IN ME.
THEY'RE LOOKING FOR ME.

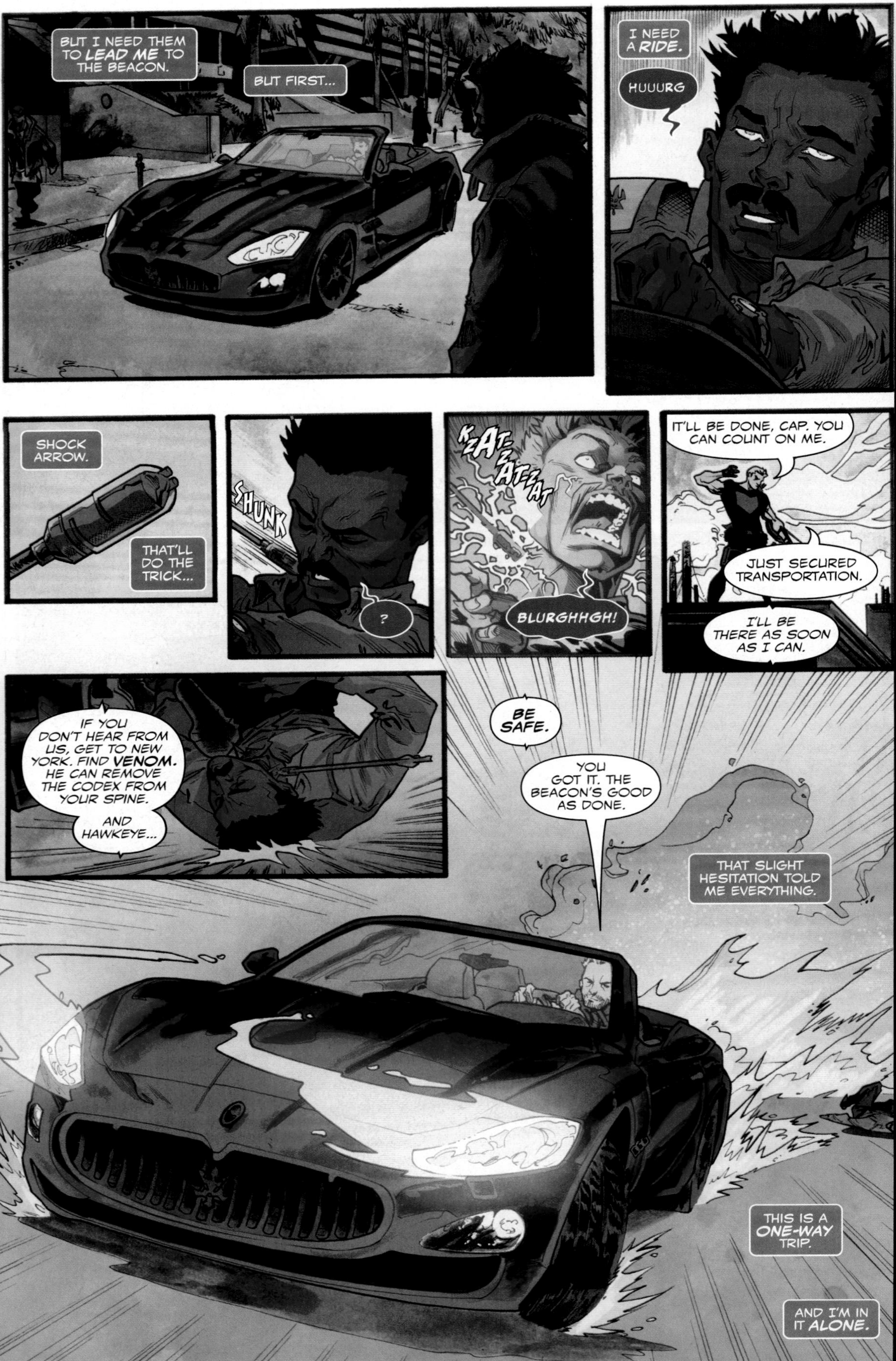
BUT I NEED THEM TO LEAD ME TO THE BEACON.
BUT FIRST...
I NEED A RIDE.
HUUURG
SHOCK ARROW.
THAT'LL DO THE TRICK...
SHUNK
?
KZAT-ZAT-ZAT-ZAT
BLURGHHGH!
IT'LL BE DONE, CAP. YOU CAN COUNT ON ME.
JUST SECURED TRANSPORTATION.
I'LL BE THERE AS SOON AS I CAN.
IF YOU DON'T HEAR FROM US, GET TO NEW YORK. FIND VENOM. HE CAN REMOVE THE CODEX FROM YOUR SPINE.
AND HAWKEYE...
BE SAFE.
YOU GOT IT. THE BEACON'S GOOD AS DONE.
THAT SLIGHT HESITATION TOLD ME EVERYTHING.
THIS IS A ONE-WAY TRIP.
AND I'M IN IT ALONE.

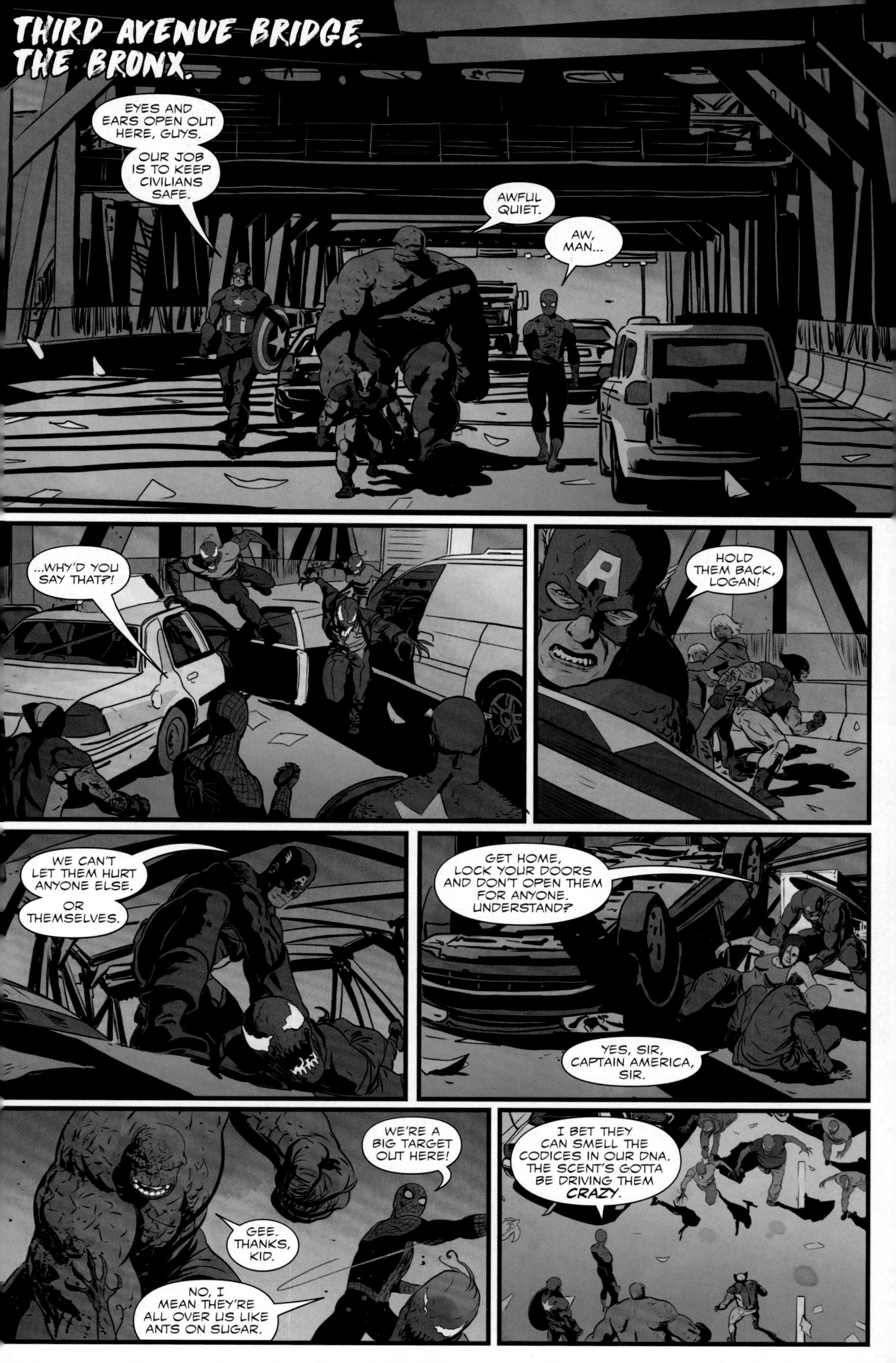
THIRD AVENUE BRIDGE. THE BRONX.
EYES AND EARS OPEN OUT HERE, GUYS.
OUR JOB IS TO KEEP CIVILIANS SAFE.
AWFUL QUIET.
AW, MAN...
...WHY'D YOU SAY THAT?!
HOLD THEM BACK, LOGAN!
WE CAN'T LET THEM HURT ANYONE ELSE.
OR THEMSELVES.
GET HOME, LOCK YOUR DOORS AND DON'T OPEN THEM FOR ANYONE. UNDERSTAND?
YES, SIR, CAPTAIN AMERICA, SIR.
WE'RE A BIG TARGET OUT HERE!
GEE. THANKS, KID.
NO, I MEAN THEY'RE ALL OVER US LIKE ANTS ON SUGAR.
I BET THEY CAN SMELL THE CODICES IN OUR DNA. THE SCENT'S GOTTA BE DRIVING THEM CRAZY.

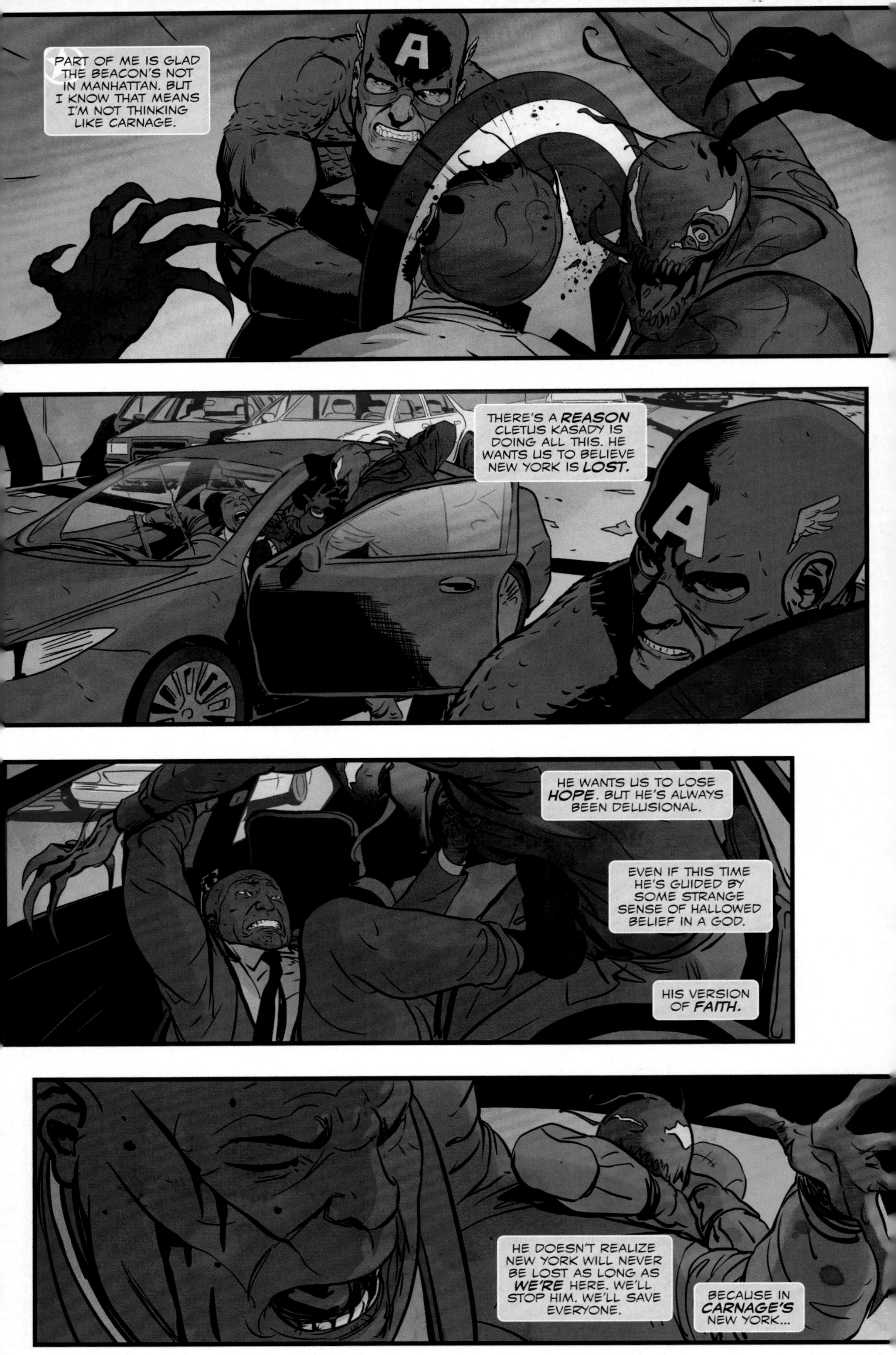

PART OF ME IS GLAD THE BEACON'S NOT IN MANHATTAN. BUT I KNOW THAT MEANS I'M NOT THINKING LIKE CARNAGE.
THERE'S A REASON CLETUS KASADY IS DOING ALL THIS. HE WANTS US TO BELIEVE NEW YORK IS LOST.
HE WANTS US TO LOSE HOPE. BUT HE'S ALWAYS BEEN DELUSIONAL.
EVEN IF THIS TIME HE'S GUIDED BY SOME STRANGE SENSE OF HALLOWED BELIEF IN A GOD.
HIS VERSION OF FAITH.
HE DOESN'T REALIZE NEW YORK WILL NEVER BE LOST AS LONG AS WE'RE HERE. WE'LL STOP HIM. WE'LL SAVE EVERYONE.
BECAUSE IN CARNAGE'S NEW YORK...

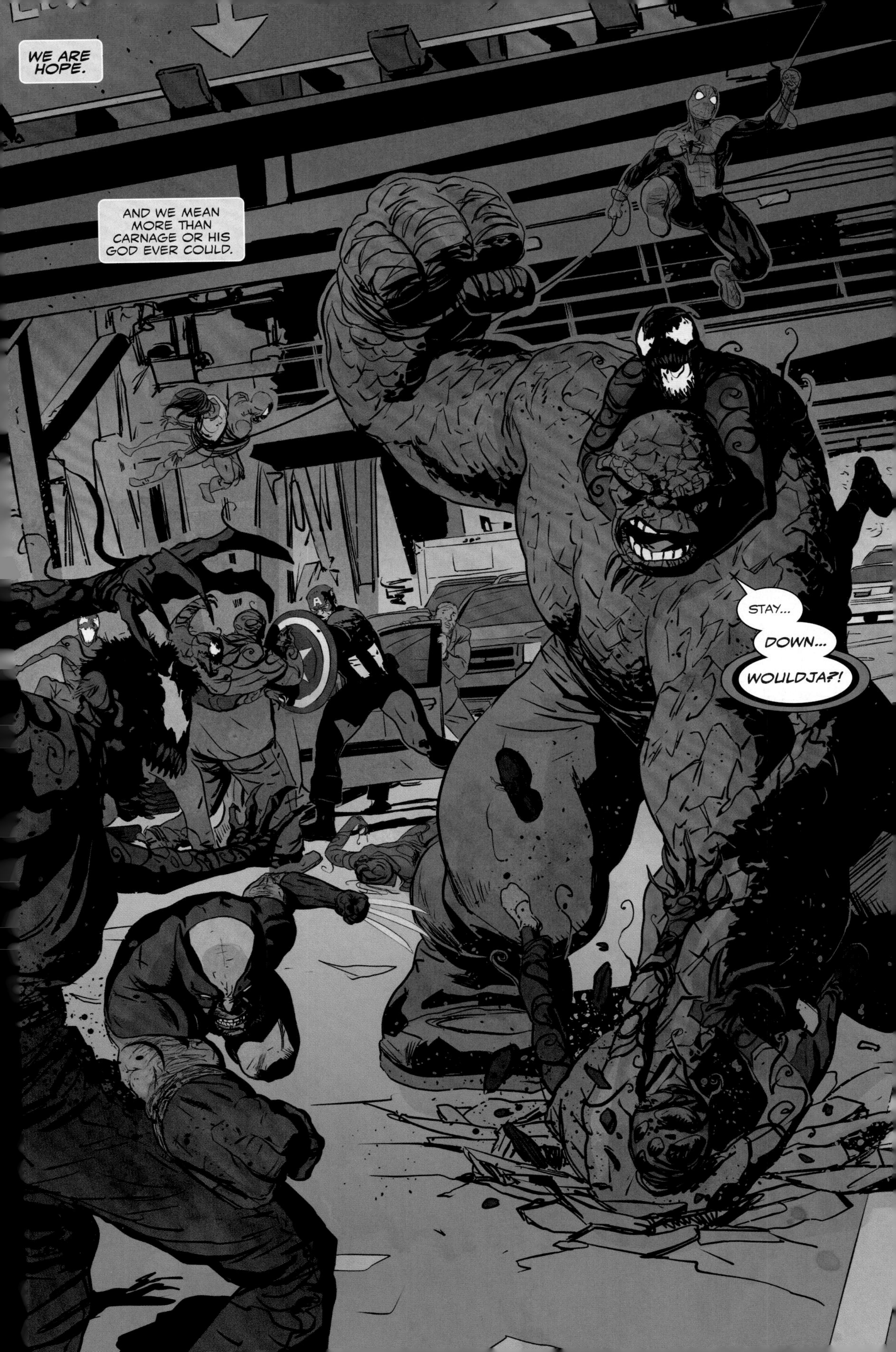

WE ARE HOPE.
AND WE MEAN MORE THAN CARNAGE OR HIS GOD EVER COULD.
STAY...
DOWN...
WOULDJA?!

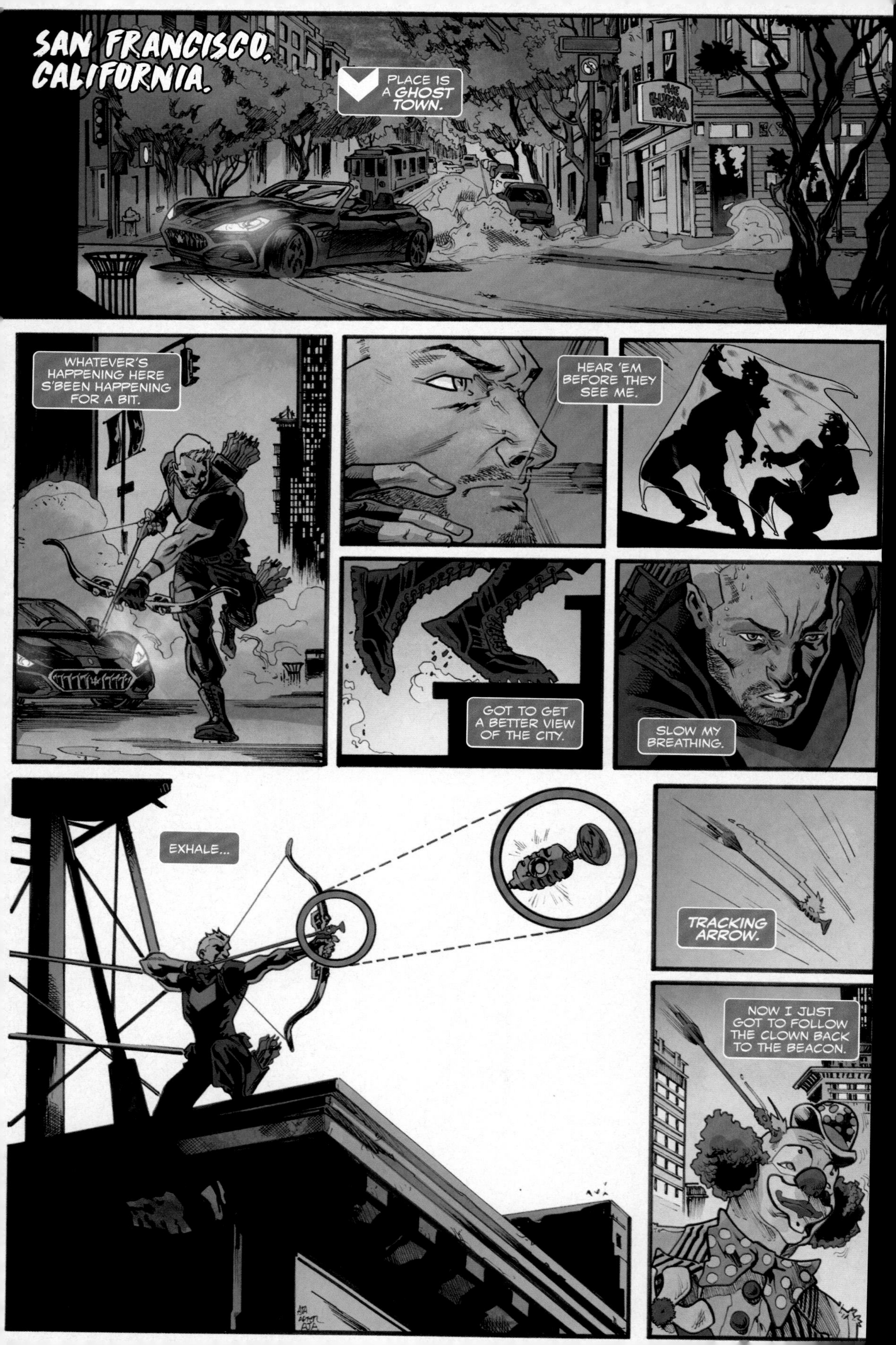
SAN FRANCISCO, CALIFORNIA.
PLACE IS A GHOST TOWN.
THE BUENA MINA
WHATEVER'S HAPPENING HERE S'BEEN HAPPENING FOR A BIT.
HEAR 'EM BEFORE THEY SEE ME.
GOT TO GET A BETTER VIEW OF THE CITY.
SLOW MY BREATHING.
EXHALE...
TRACKING ARROW.
NOW I JUST GOT TO FOLLOW THE CLOWN BACK TO THE BEACON.

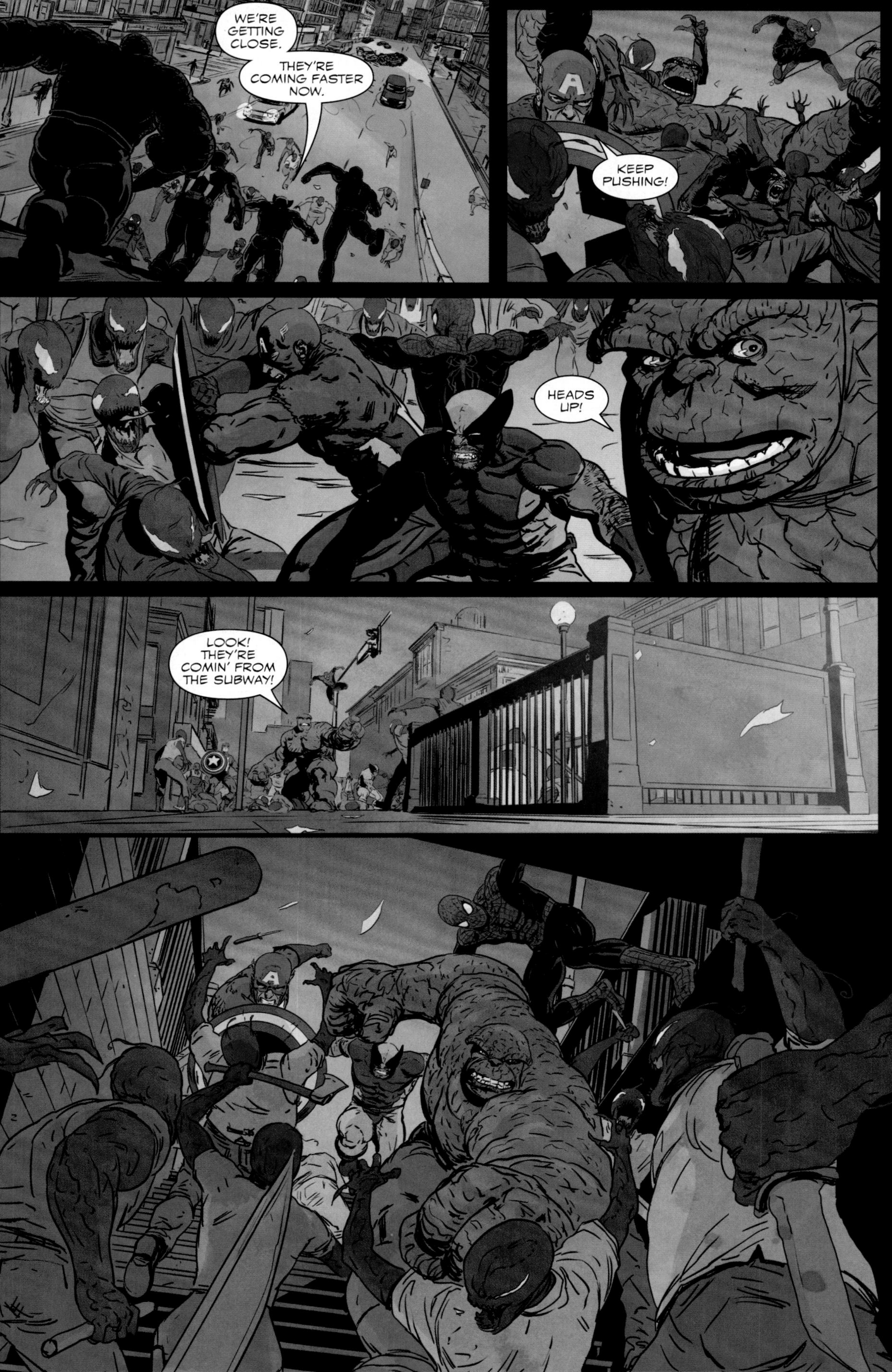
WE'RE GETTING CLOSE.
THEY'RE COMING FASTER NOW.
KEEP PUSHING!
HEADS UP!
LOOK! THEY'RE COMIN' FROM THE SUBWAY!

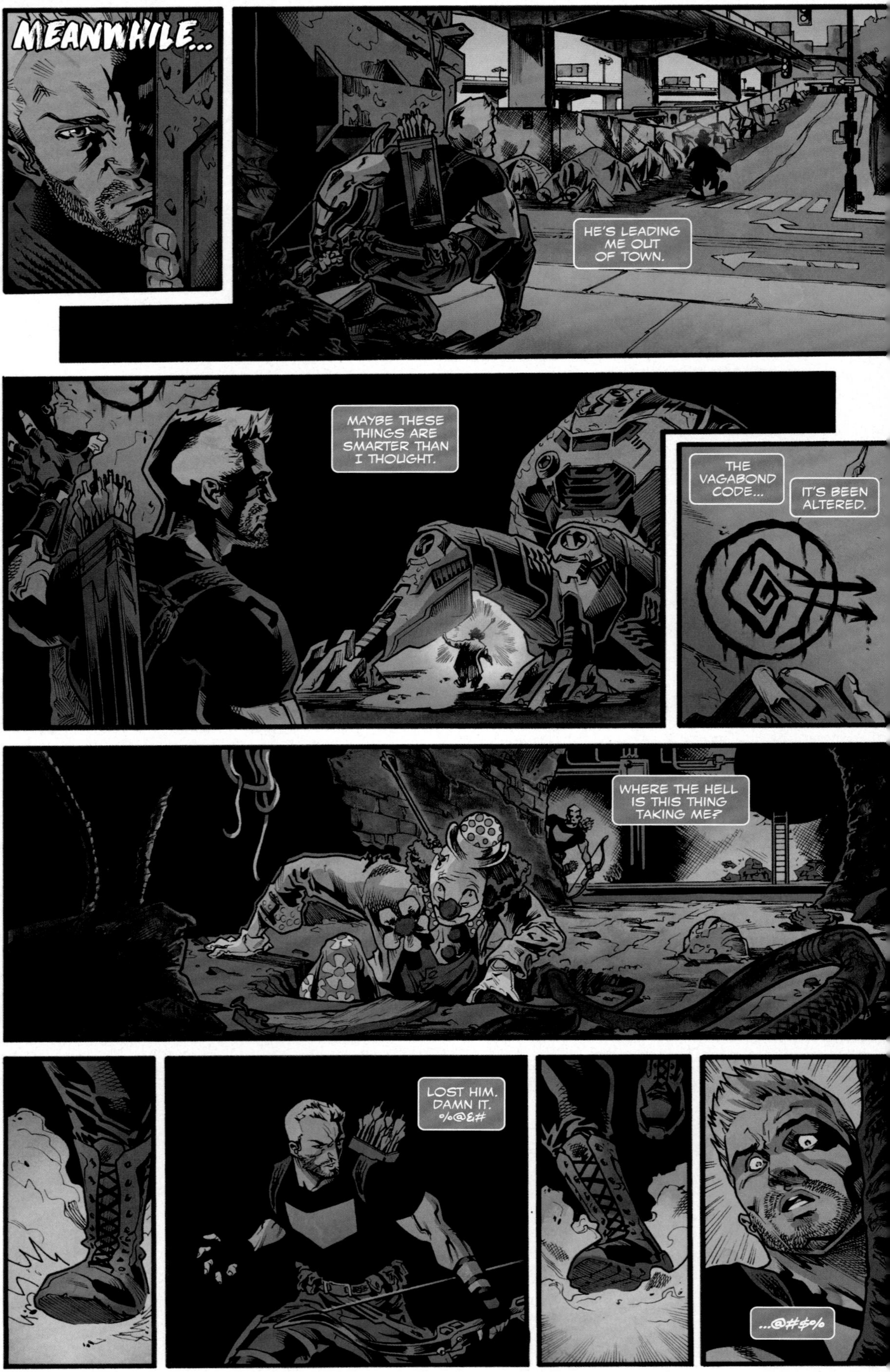
MEANWHILE...
HE'S LEADING ME OUT OF TOWN.
MAYBE THESE THINGS ARE SMARTER THAN I THOUGHT.
THE VAGABOND CODE...
IT'S BEEN ALTERED.
WHERE THE HELL IS THIS THING TAKING ME?
LOST HIM. DAMN IT. %@&#
...@#$%

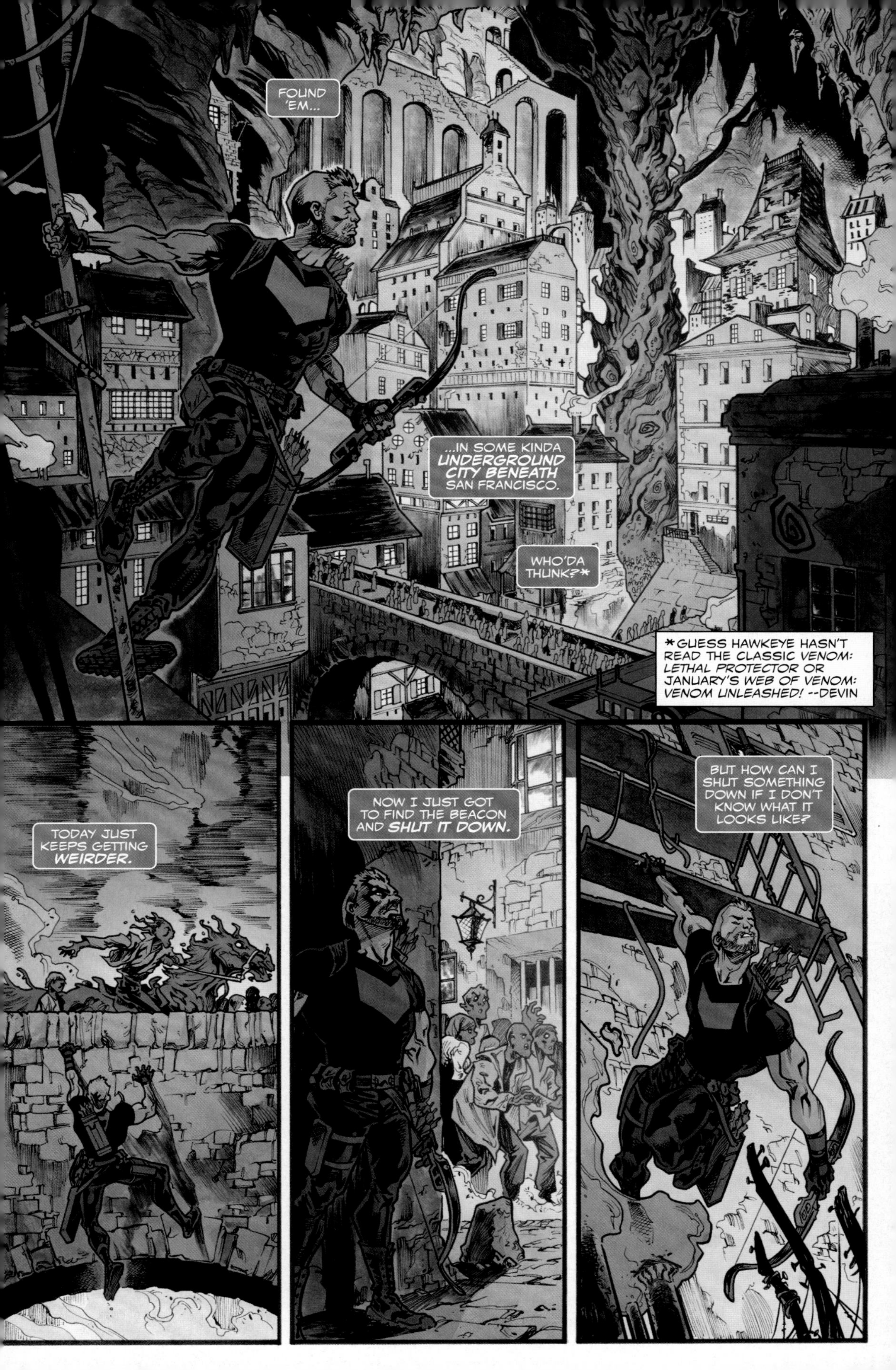
FOUND 'EM...
...IN SOME KINDA UNDERGROUND CITY BENEATH SAN FRANCISCO.
WHO'DA THUNK?*
*GUESS HAWKEYE HASN'T READ THE CLASSIC VENOM: LETHAL PROTECTOR OR JANUARY'S WEB OF VENOM: VENOM UNLEASHED! --DEVIN
TODAY JUST KEEPS GETTING WEIRDER.
NOW I JUST GOT TO FIND THE BEACON AND SHUT IT DOWN.
BUT HOW CAN I SHUT SOMETHING DOWN IF I DON'T KNOW WHAT IT LOOKS LIKE?

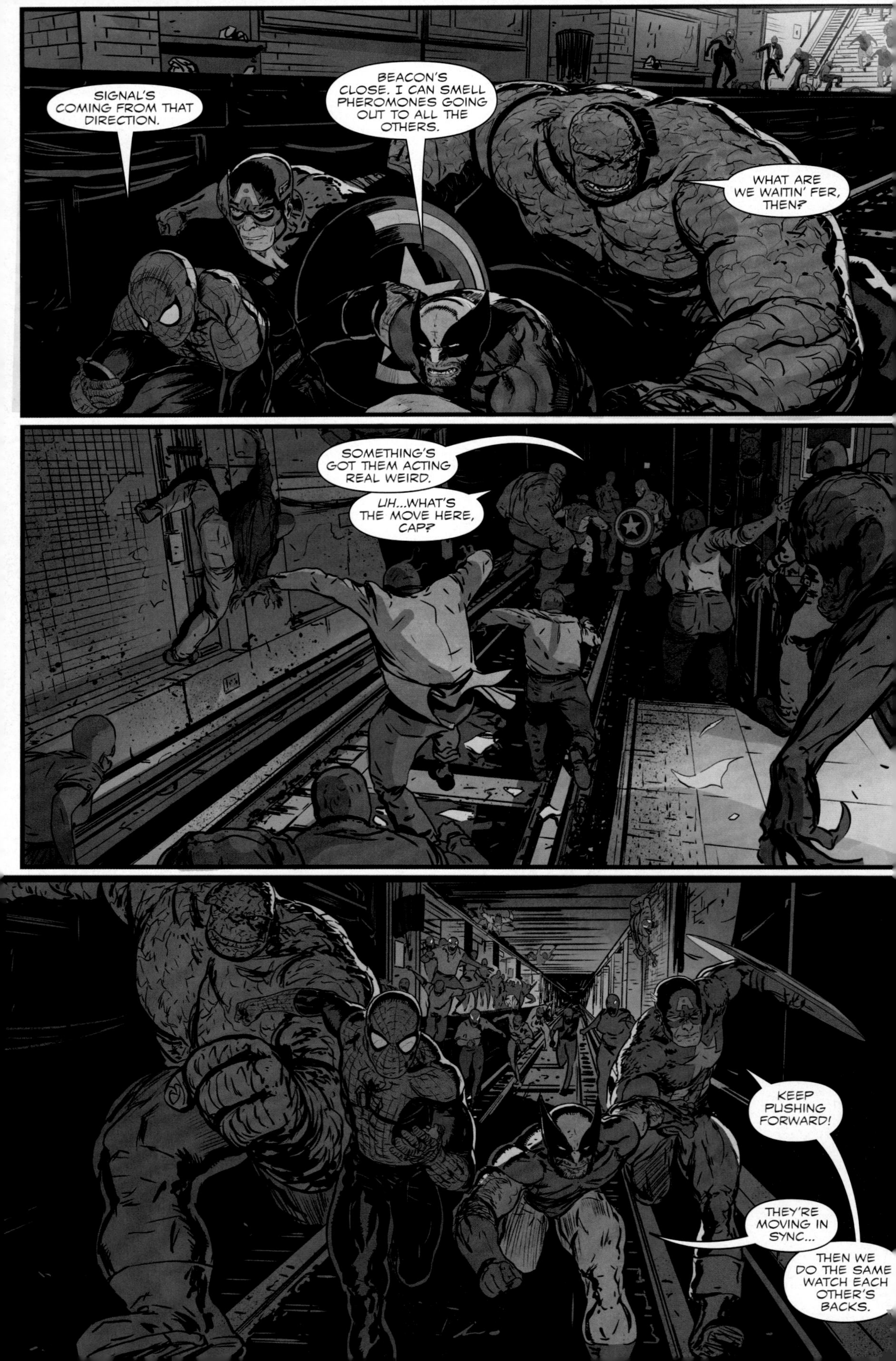

SIGNAL'S COMING FROM THAT DIRECTION.
BEACON'S CLOSE. I CAN SMELL PHEROMONES GOING OUT TO ALL THE OTHERS.
WHAT ARE WE WAITIN' FER, THEN?
SOMETHING'S GOT THEM ACTING REAL WEIRD.
UH...WHAT'S THE MOVE HERE, CAP?
KEEP PUSHING FORWARD!
THEY'RE MOVING IN SYNC...
THEN WE DO THE SAME WATCH EACH OTHER'S BACKS.

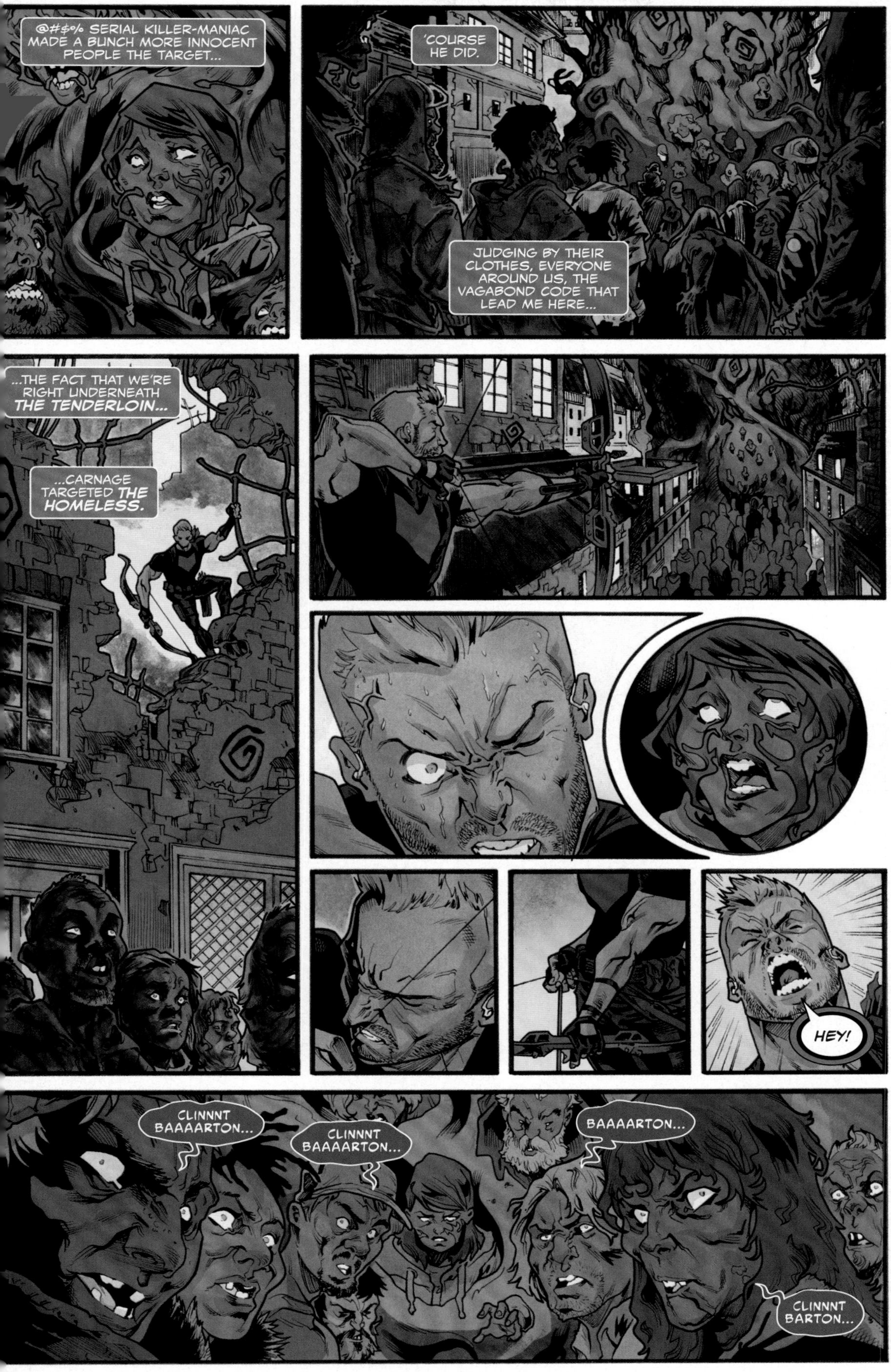
@#$% SERIAL KILLER-MANIAC MADE A BUNCH MORE INNOCENT PEOPLE THE TARGET...
'COURSE HE DID.
JUDGING BY THEIR CLOTHES, EVERYONE AROUND US, THE VAGABOND CODE THAT LEAD ME HERE...
...THE FACT THAT WE'RE RIGHT UNDERNEATH THE TENDERLOIN...
...CARNAGE TARGETED THE HOMELESS.
HEY!
CLINNNT BAAAARTON...
CLINNNT BAAAARTON...
BAAAARTON...
CLINNNT BARTON...

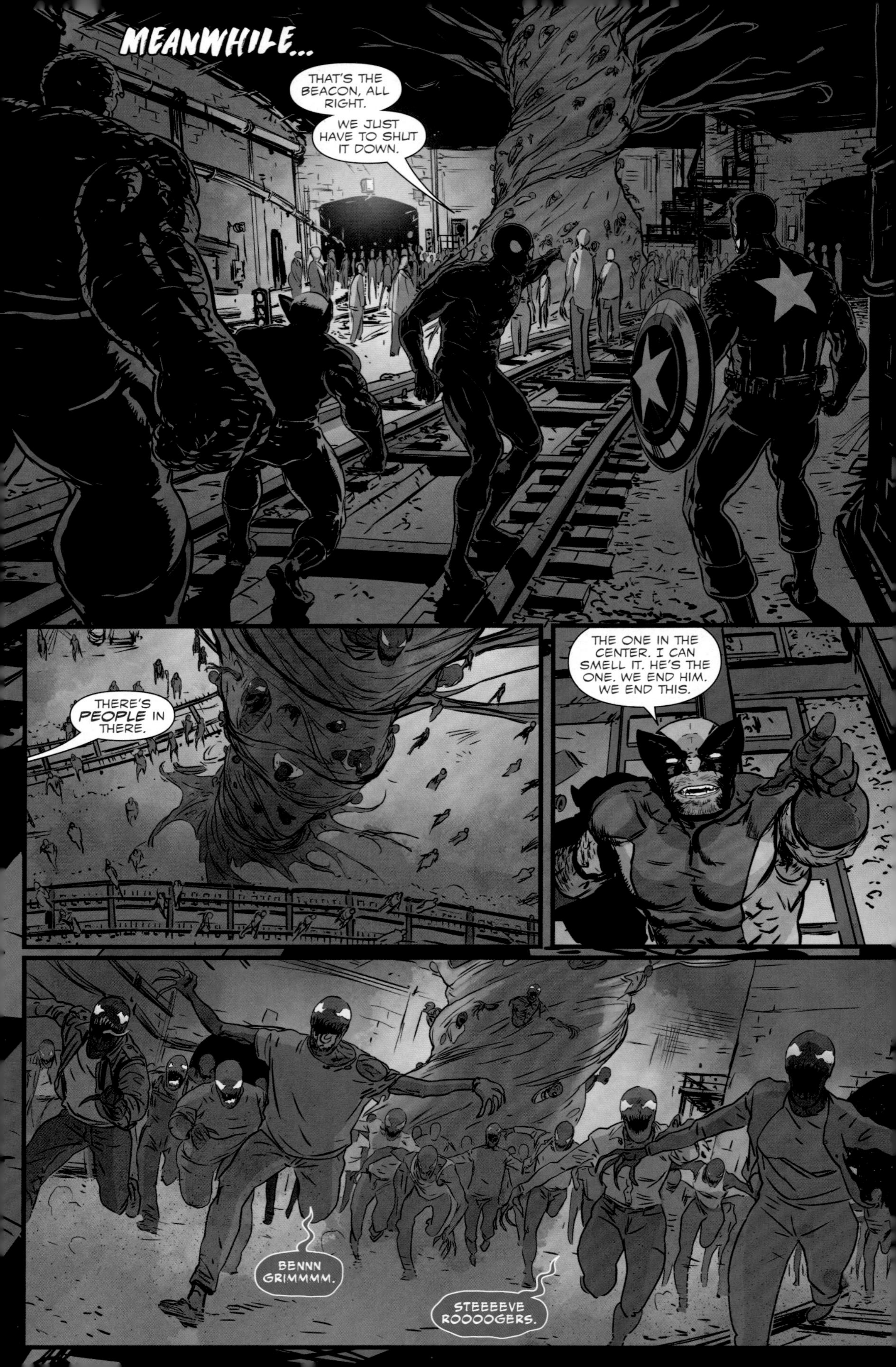
MEANWHILE...
THAT'S THE BEACON, ALL RIGHT.
WE JUST HAVE TO SHUT IT DOWN.
THERE'S *PEOPLE* IN THERE.
THE ONE IN THE CENTER. I CAN SMELL IT. HE'S THE ONE. WE END HIM. WE END THIS.
BENNN GRIMMMM.
STEEEEVE ROOOOGERS.

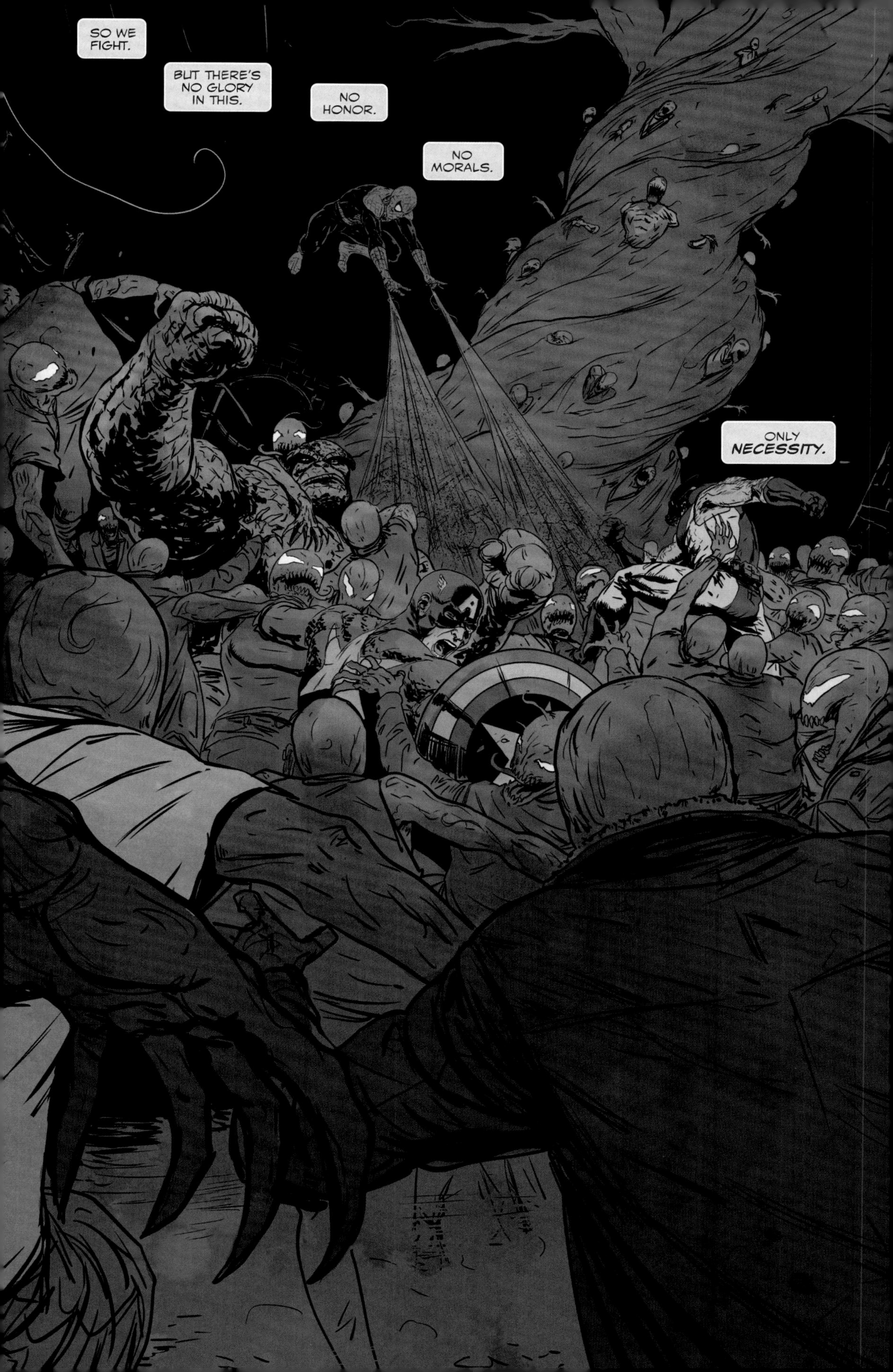

SO WE FIGHT.
BUT THERE'S NO GLORY IN THIS.
NO HONOR.
NO MORALS.
ONLY *NECESSITY.*

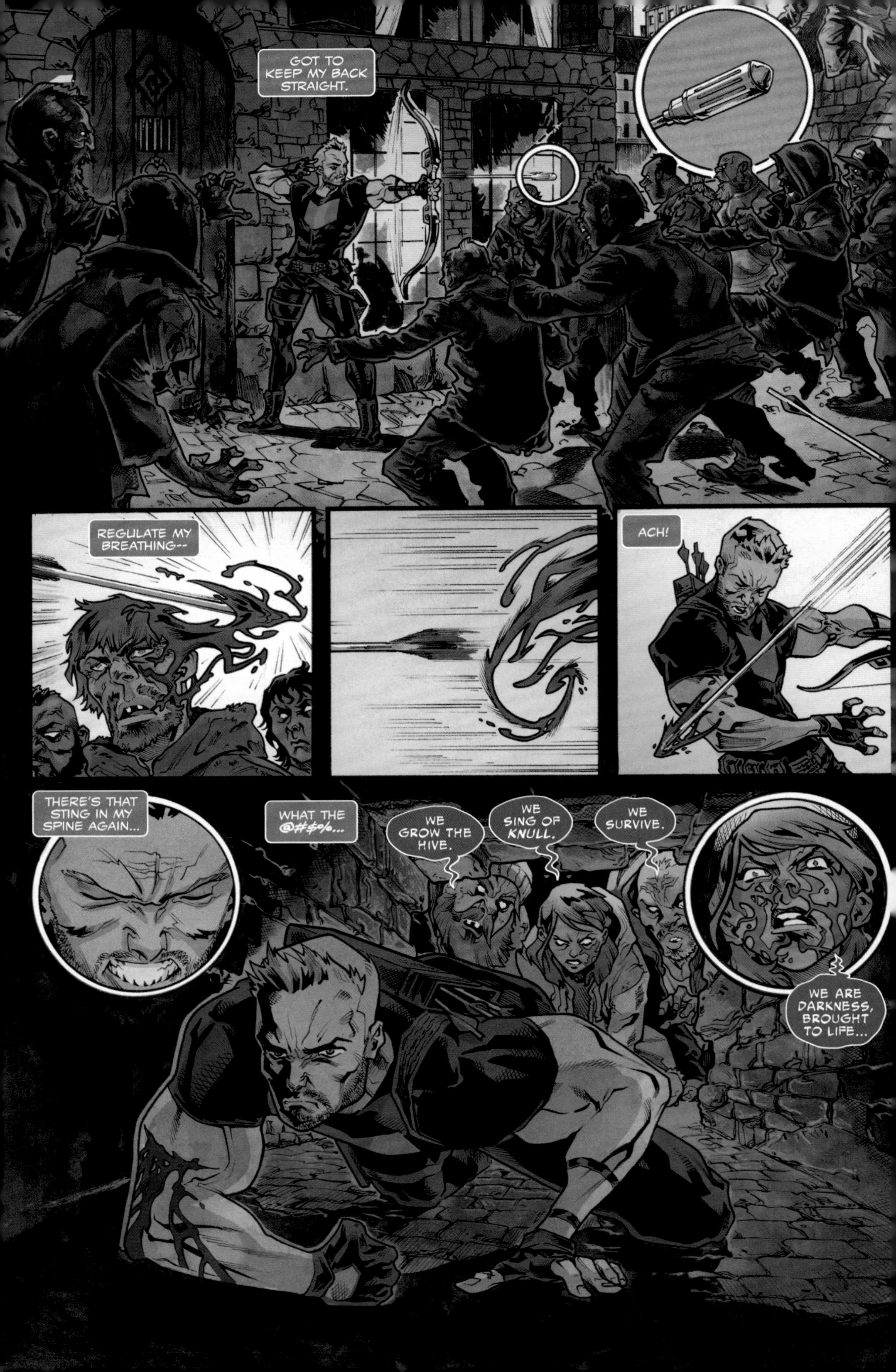

GOT TO KEEP MY BACK STRAIGHT.
REGULATE MY BREATHING--
ACH!
THERE'S THAT STING IN MY SPINE AGAIN...
WHAT THE @#$%...
WE GROW THE HIVE.
WE SING OF KNULL.
WE SURVIVE.
WE ARE DARKNESS, BROUGHT TO LIFE...

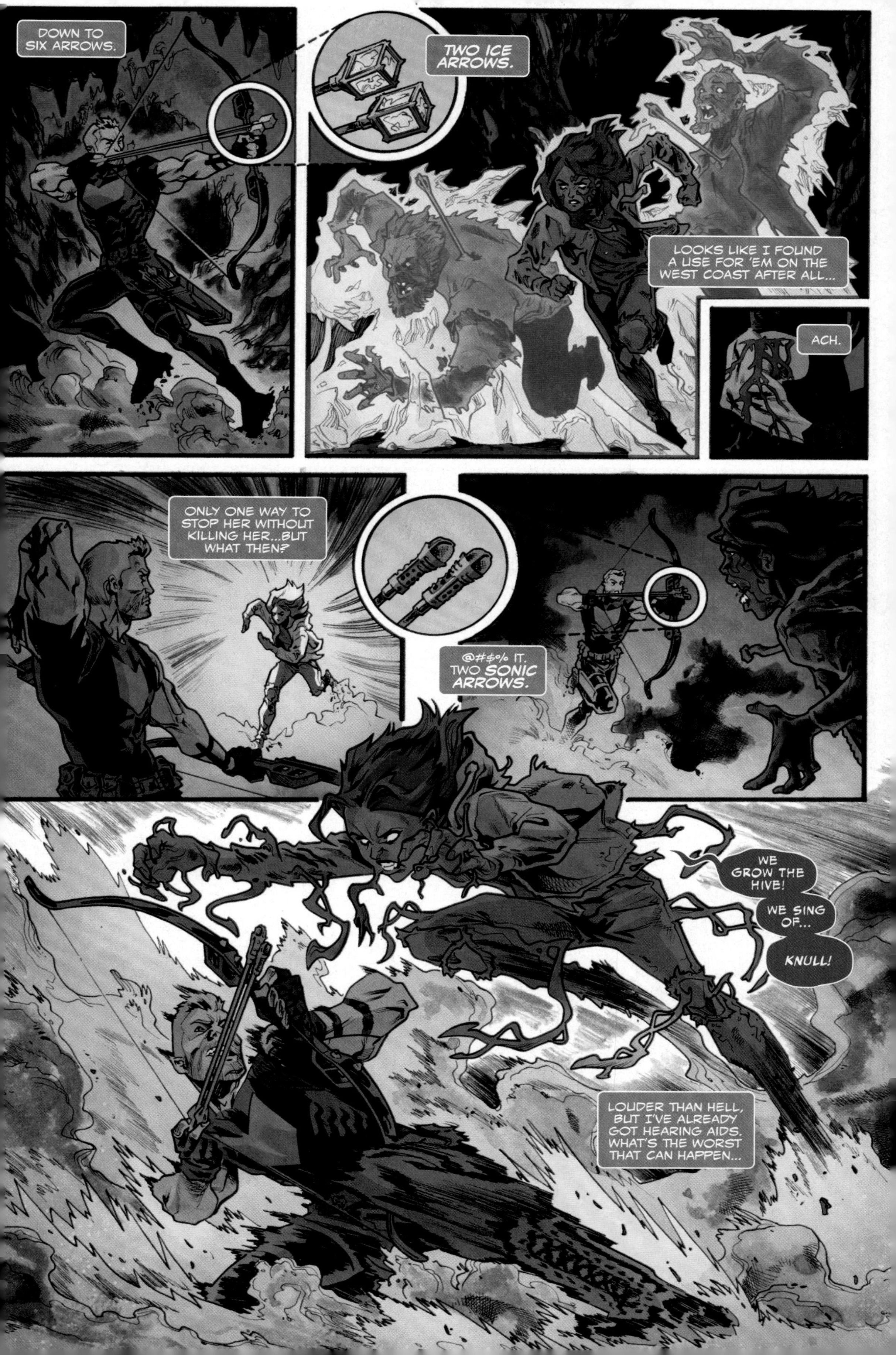
DOWN TO SIX ARROWS.
TWO ICE ARROWS.
LOOKS LIKE I FOUND A USE FOR 'EM ON THE WEST COAST AFTER ALL...
ACH.
ONLY ONE WAY TO STOP HER WITHOUT KILLING HER...BUT WHAT THEN?
@#$% IT. TWO SONIC ARROWS.
WE GROW THE HIVE!
WE SING OF...
KNULL!
LOUDER THAN HELL, BUT I'VE ALREADY GOT HEARING AIDS. WHAT'S THE WORST THAT CAN HAPPEN...

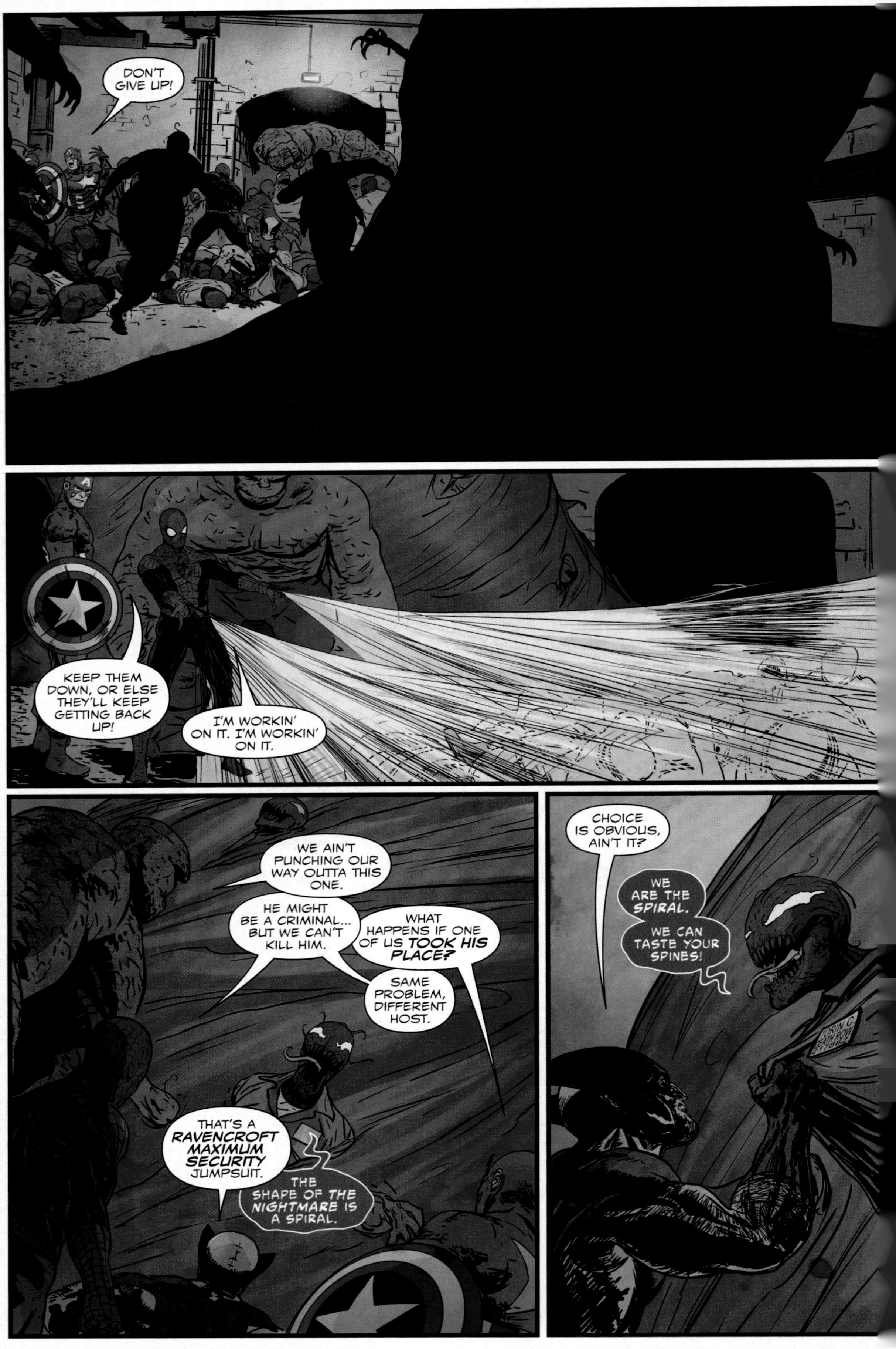
DON'T GIVE UP!
KEEP THEM DOWN, OR ELSE THEY'LL KEEP GETTING BACK UP!
I'M WORKIN' ON IT. I'M WORKIN' ON IT.
WE AIN'T PUNCHING OUR WAY OUTTA THIS ONE.
HE MIGHT BE A CRIMINAL... BUT WE CAN'T KILL HIM.
WHAT HAPPENS IF ONE OF US ***TOOK HIS PLACE?***
SAME PROBLEM, DIFFERENT HOST.
THAT'S A ***RAVENCROFT MAXIMUM SECURITY*** JUMPSUIT.
THE SHAPE OF ***THE NIGHTMARE*** IS A SPIRAL.
CHOICE IS OBVIOUS, AIN'T IT?
WE ARE THE ***SPIRAL.***
WE CAN TASTE YOUR SPINES!

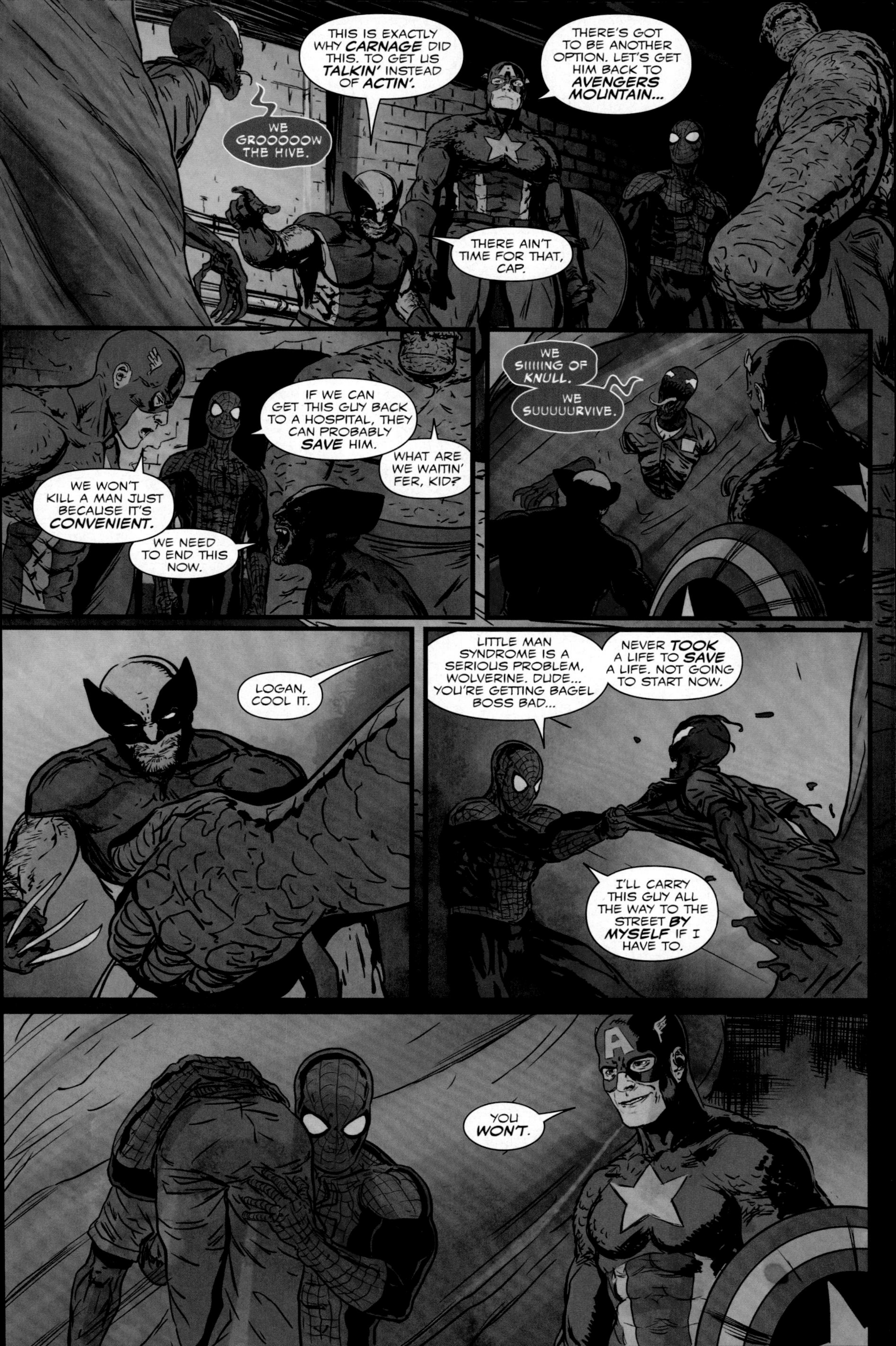
THIS IS EXACTLY WHY CARNAGE DID THIS. TO GET US TALKIN' INSTEAD OF ACTIN'.
WE GROOOOOW THE HIVE.
THERE'S GOT TO BE ANOTHER OPTION. LET'S GET HIM BACK TO AVENGERS MOUNTAIN...
THERE AIN'T TIME FOR THAT, CAP.
IF WE CAN GET THIS GUY BACK TO A HOSPITAL, THEY CAN PROBABLY SAVE HIM.
WHAT ARE WE WAITIN' FER, KID?
WE WON'T KILL A MAN JUST BECAUSE IT'S CONVENIENT.
WE NEED TO END THIS NOW.
WE SIIIING OF KNULL.
WE SUUUUURVIVE.
LOGAN, COOL IT.
LITTLE MAN SYNDROME IS A SERIOUS PROBLEM, WOLVERINE. DUDE... YOU'RE GETTING BAGEL BOSS BAD...
NEVER TOOK A LIFE TO SAVE A LIFE. NOT GOING TO START NOW.
I'LL CARRY THIS GUY ALL THE WAY TO THE STREET BY MYSELF IF I HAVE TO.
YOU WON'T.

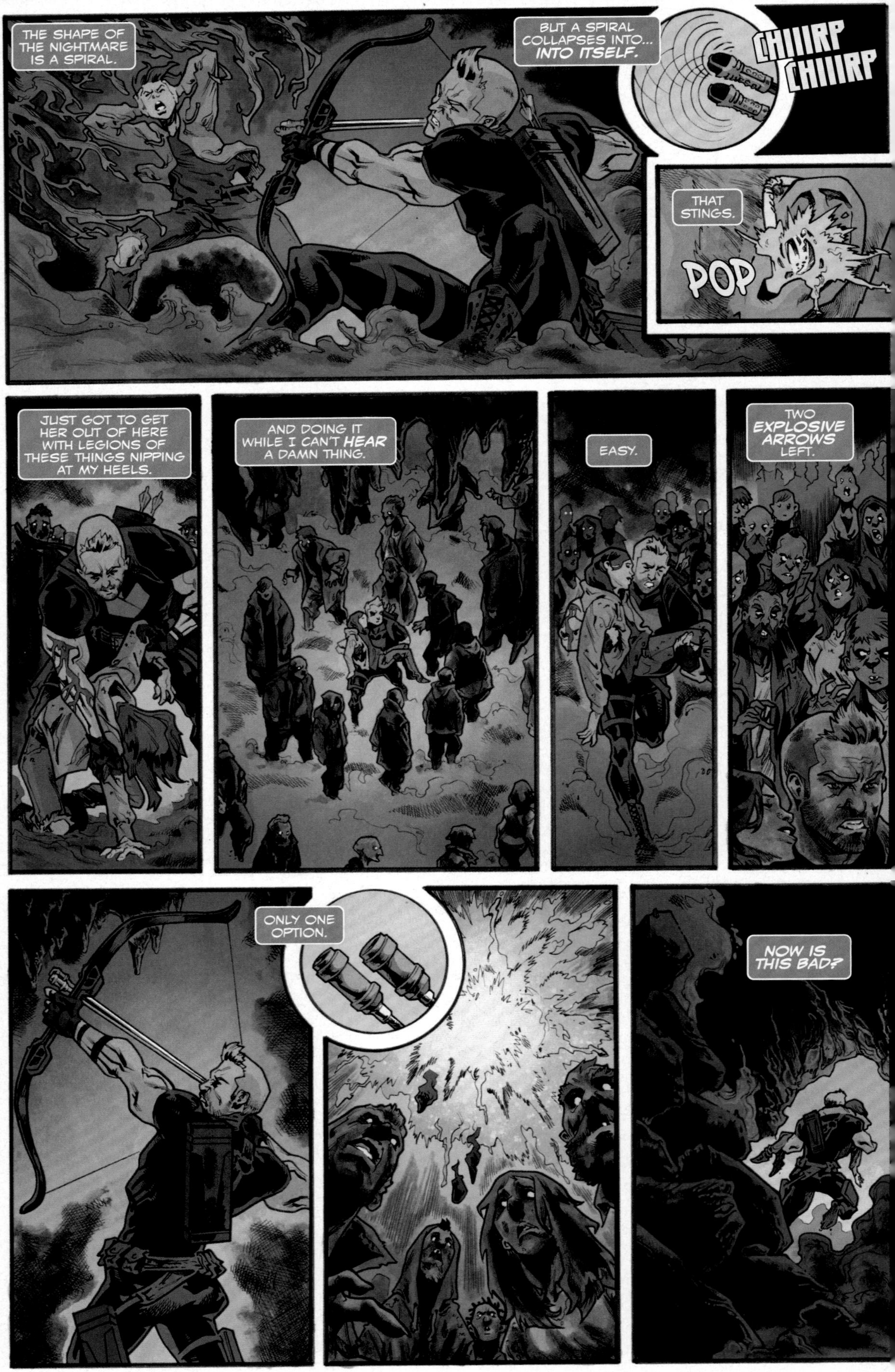
THE SHAPE OF THE NIGHTMARE IS A SPIRAL.
BUT A SPIRAL COLLAPSES INTO... INTO ITSELF.
CHIIIRP CHIIIRP
THAT STINGS.
POP
JUST GOT TO GET HER OUT OF HERE WITH LEGIONS OF THESE THINGS NIPPING AT MY HEELS.
AND DOING IT WHILE I CAN'T HEAR A DAMN THING.
EASY.
TWO EXPLOSIVE ARROWS LEFT.
ONLY ONE OPTION.
NOW IS THIS BAD?

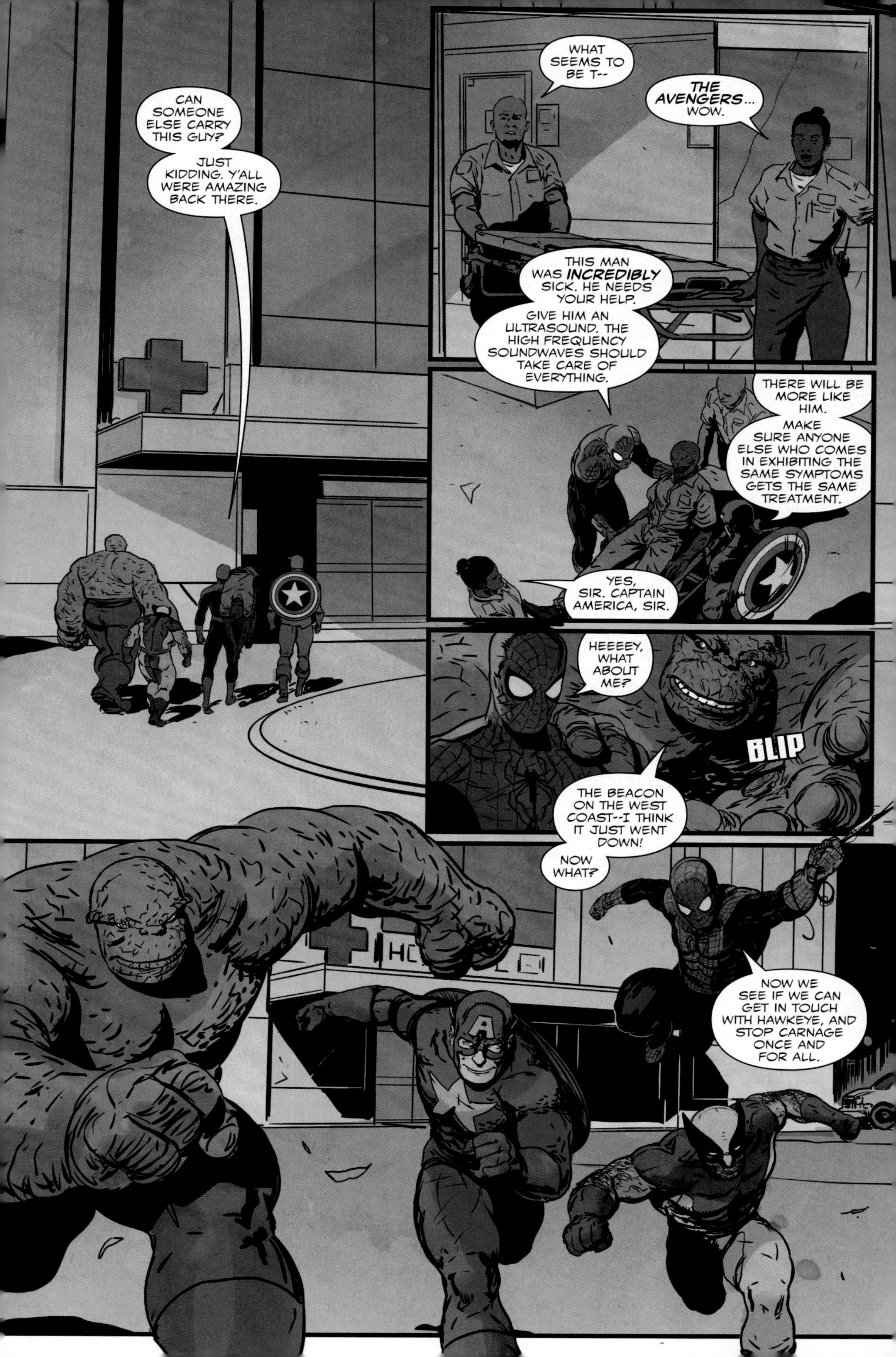
CAN SOMEONE ELSE CARRY THIS GUY?
JUST KIDDING. Y'ALL WERE AMAZING BACK THERE.
WHAT SEEMS TO BE T--
THE AVENGERS... WOW.
THIS MAN WAS INCREDIBLY SICK. HE NEEDS YOUR HELP.
GIVE HIM AN ULTRASOUND. THE HIGH FREQUENCY SOUNDWAVES SHOULD TAKE CARE OF EVERYTHING.
THERE WILL BE MORE LIKE HIM.
MAKE SURE ANYONE ELSE WHO COMES IN EXHIBITING THE SAME SYMPTOMS GETS THE SAME TREATMENT.
YES, SIR. CAPTAIN AMERICA, SIR.
HEEEEY, WHAT ABOUT ME?
BLIP
THE BEACON ON THE WEST COAST--I THINK IT JUST WENT DOWN!
NOW WHAT?
NOW WE SEE IF WE CAN GET IN TOUCH WITH HAWKEYE, AND STOP CARNAGE ONCE AND FOR ALL.

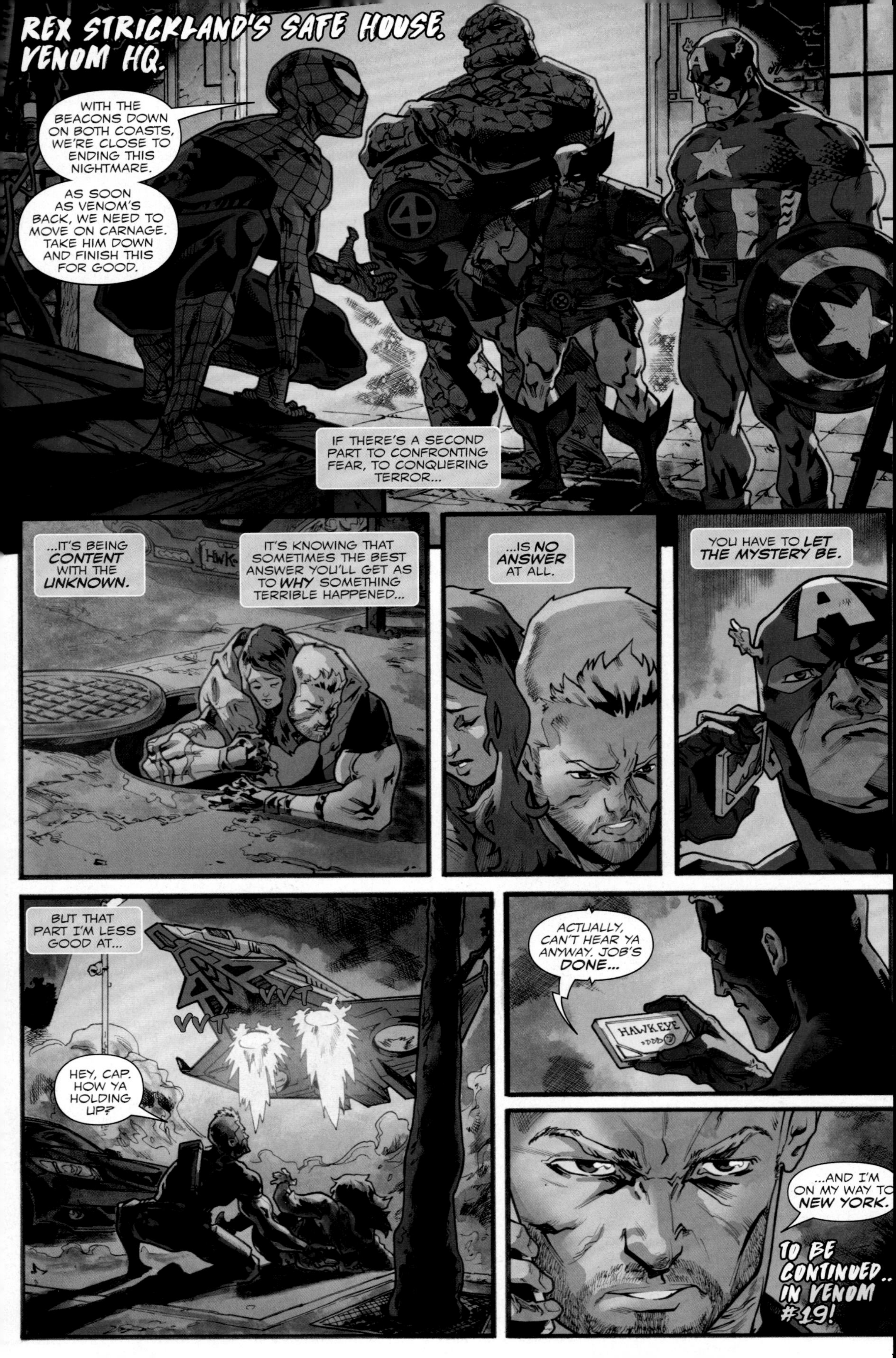
REX STRICKLAND'S SAFE HOUSE. VENOM HQ.
WITH THE BEACONS DOWN ON BOTH COASTS, WE'RE CLOSE TO ENDING THIS NIGHTMARE.
AS SOON AS VENOM'S BACK, WE NEED TO MOVE ON CARNAGE. TAKE HIM DOWN AND FINISH THIS FOR GOOD.
IF THERE'S A SECOND PART TO CONFRONTING FEAR, TO CONQUERING TERROR...
...IT'S BEING CONTENT WITH THE UNKNOWN.
IT'S KNOWING THAT SOMETIMES THE BEST ANSWER YOU'LL GET AS TO WHY SOMETHING TERRIBLE HAPPENED...
...IS NO ANSWER AT ALL.
YOU HAVE TO LET THE MYSTERY BE.
BUT THAT PART I'M LESS GOOD AT...
VVT
VVT
HEY, CAP. HOW YA HOLDING UP?
ACTUALLY, CAN'T HEAR YA ANYWAY. JOB'S DONE...
HAWKEYE
...AND I'M ON MY WAY TO NEW YORK.
TO BE CONTINUED... IN VENOM #19!

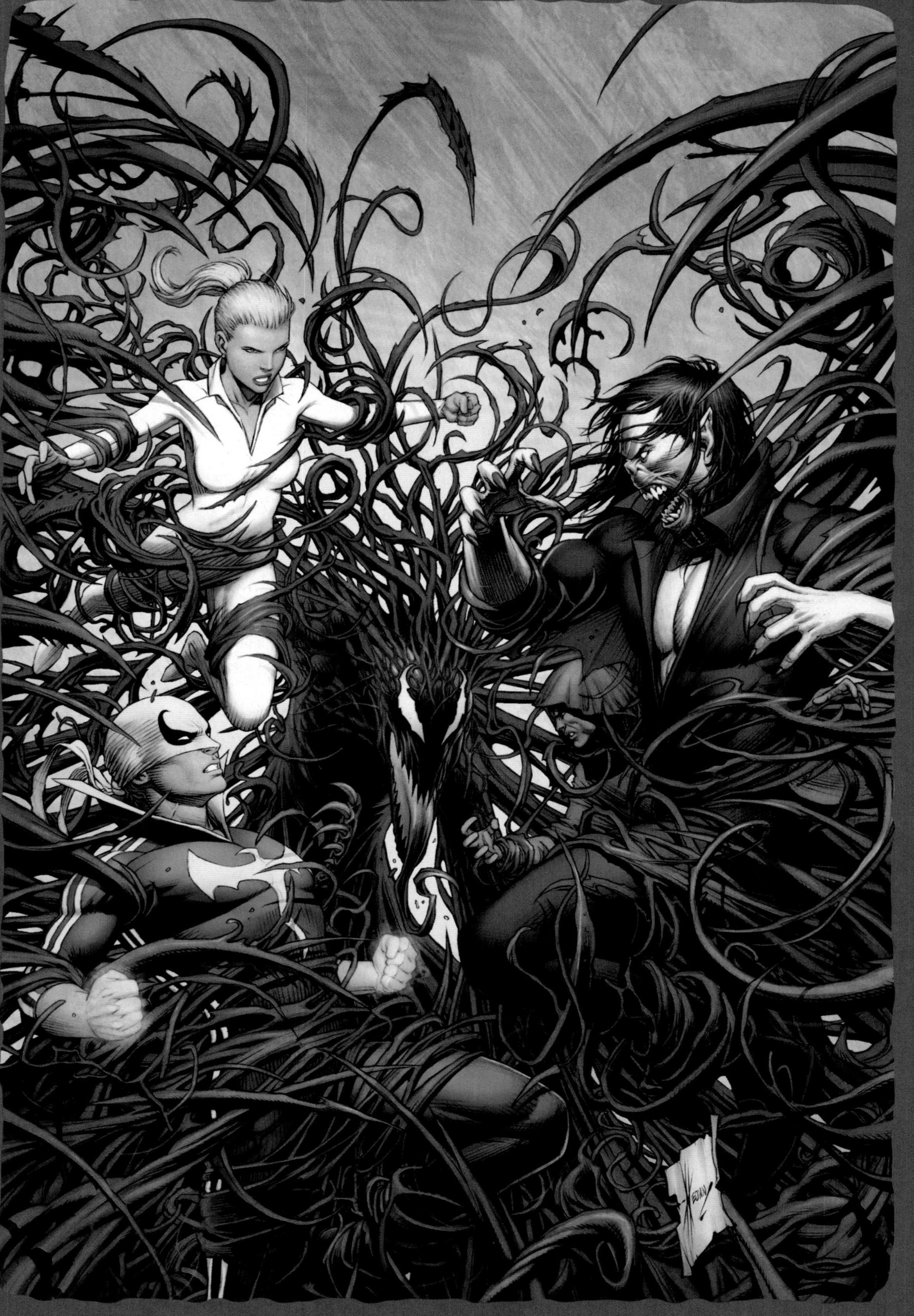

DALE KEOWN & JASON KEITH

LETHAL PROTECTORS #1 Variant

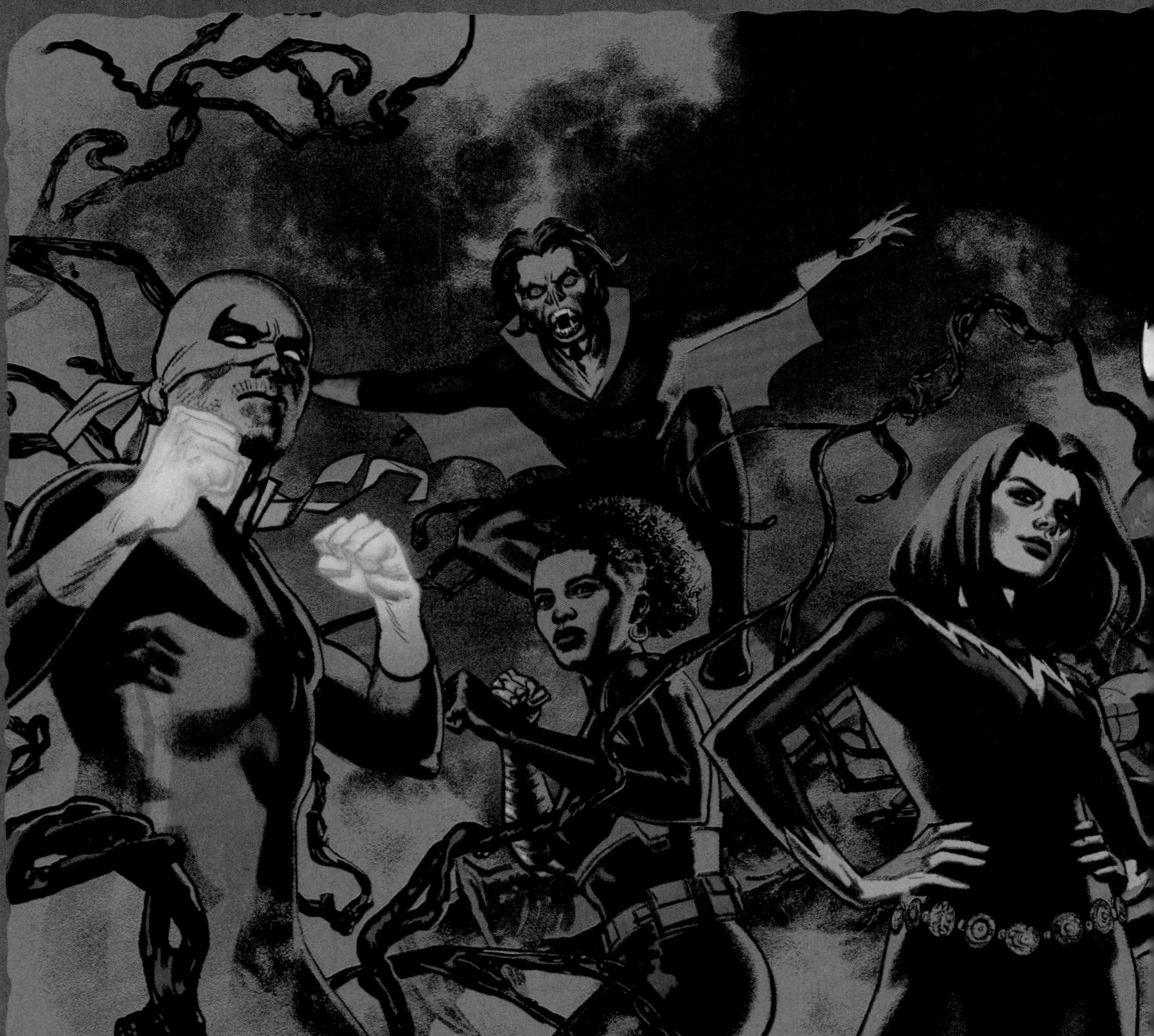

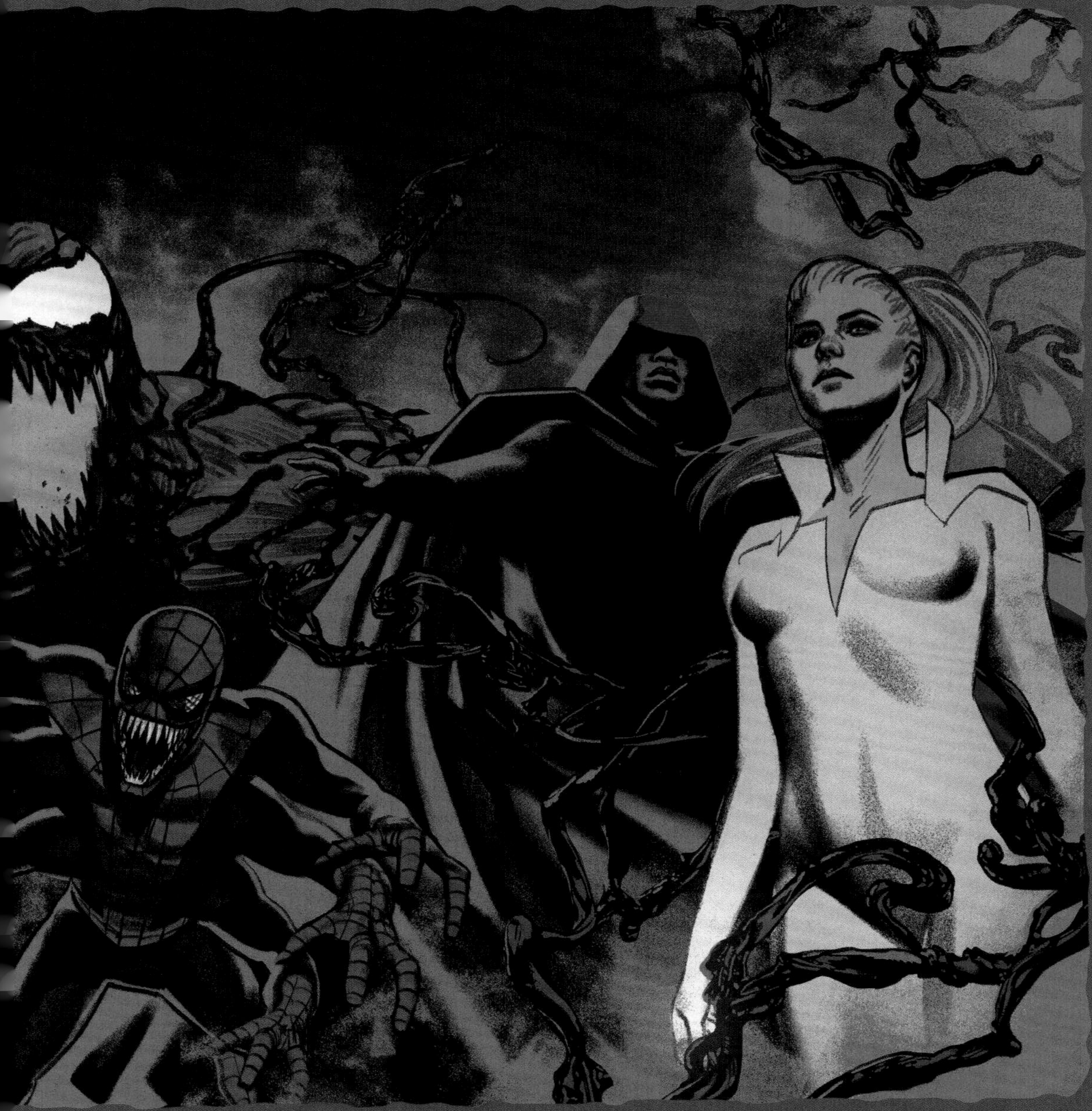

GREG SMALLWOOD

LETHAL PROTECTORS #1-3 Connecting Variants

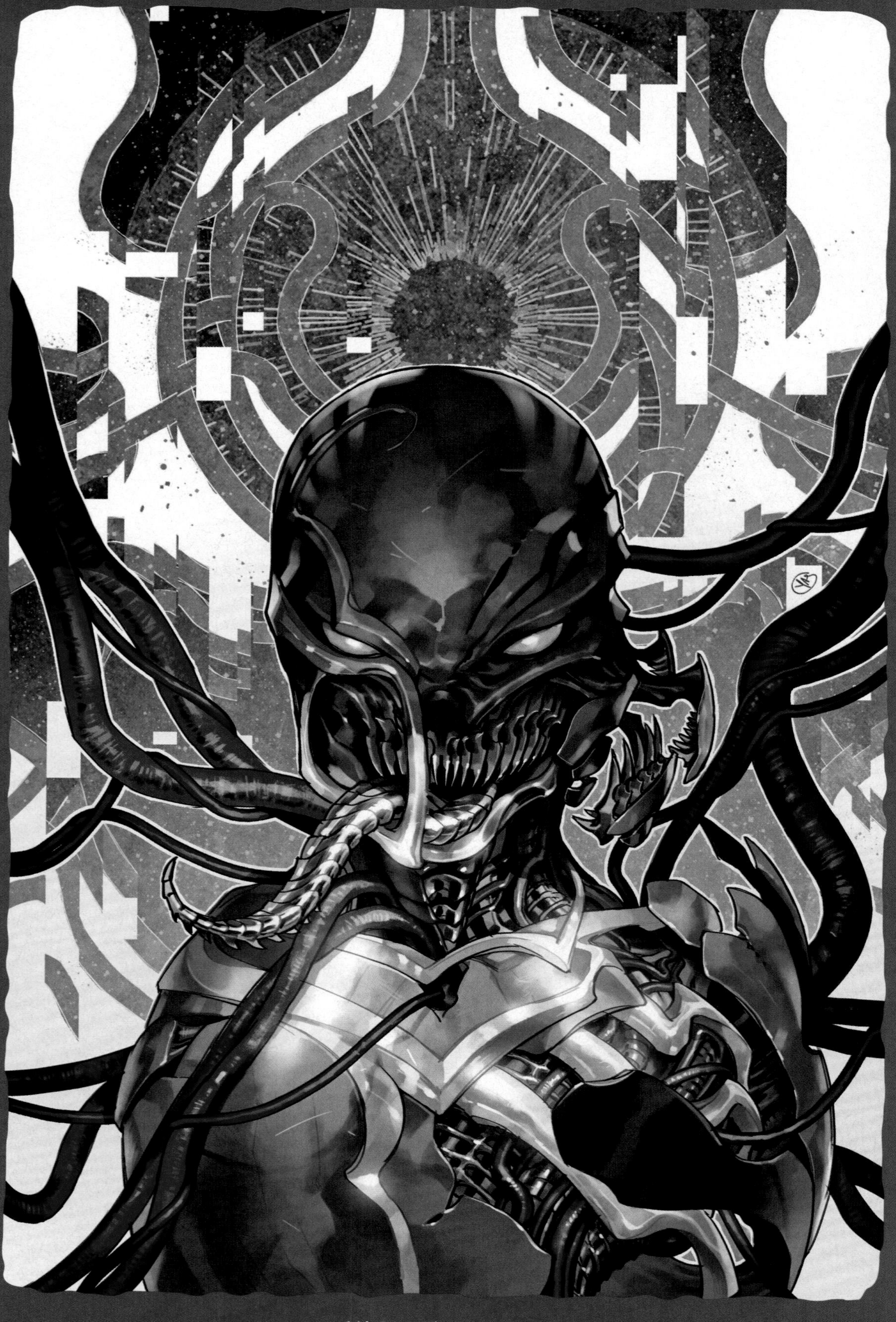

YASMINE PUTRI

LETHAL PROTECTORS #1 Codex Variant

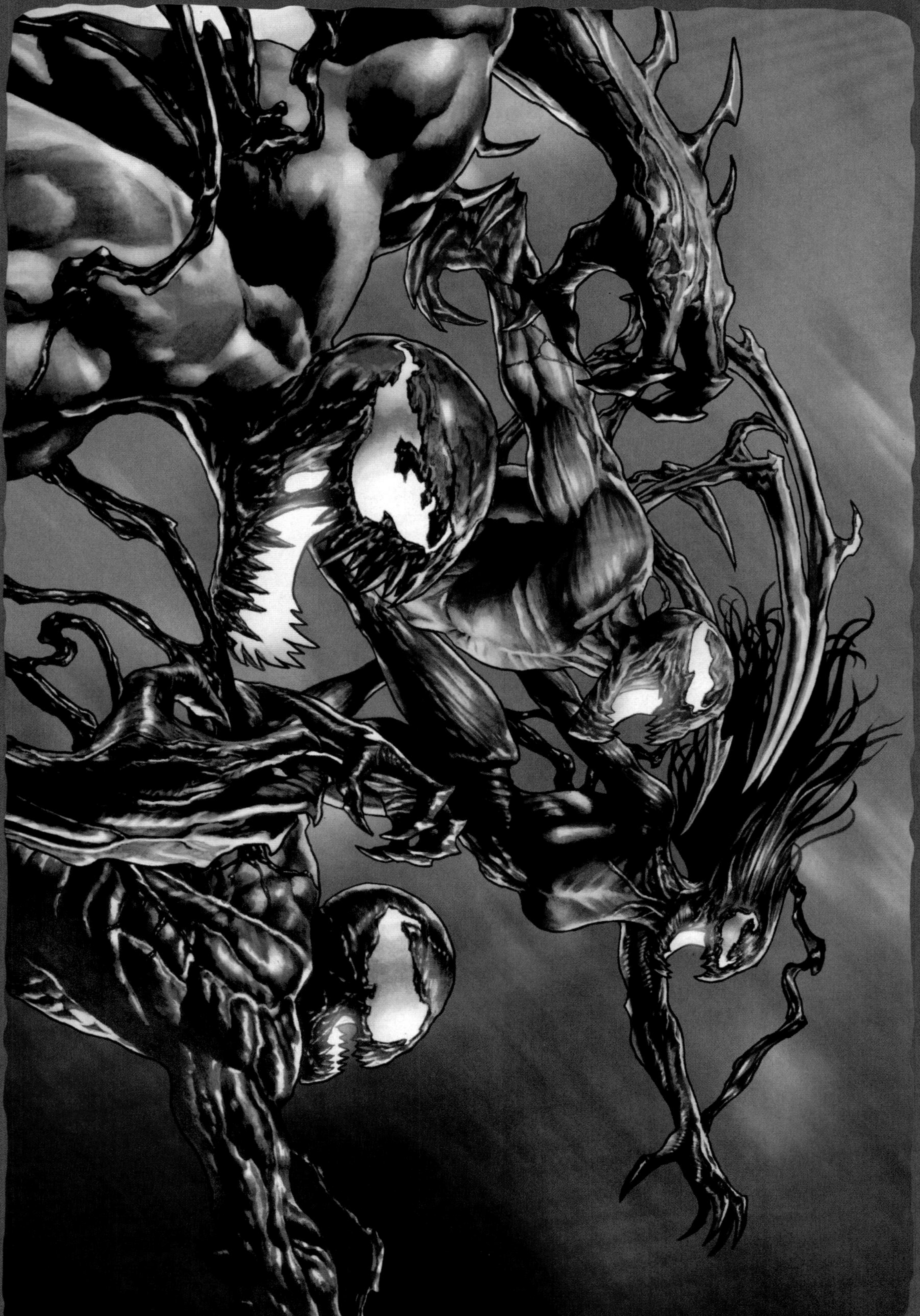

MICO SUAYAN & BRIAN REBER
LETHAL PROTECTORS #2 Codex Variant

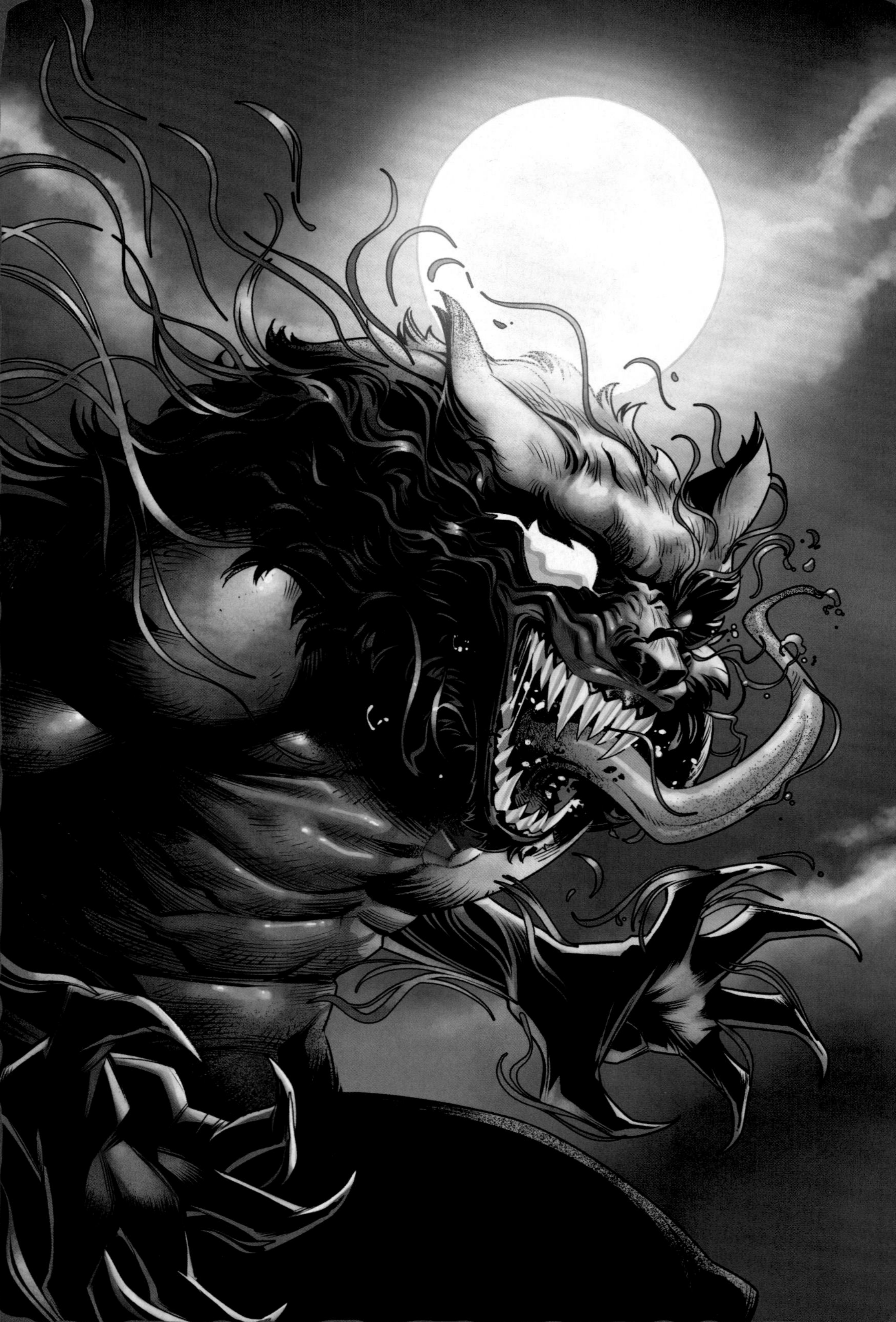

BELÉN ORTEGA & BRIAN REBER

LETHAL PROTECTORS #3 Codex Variant

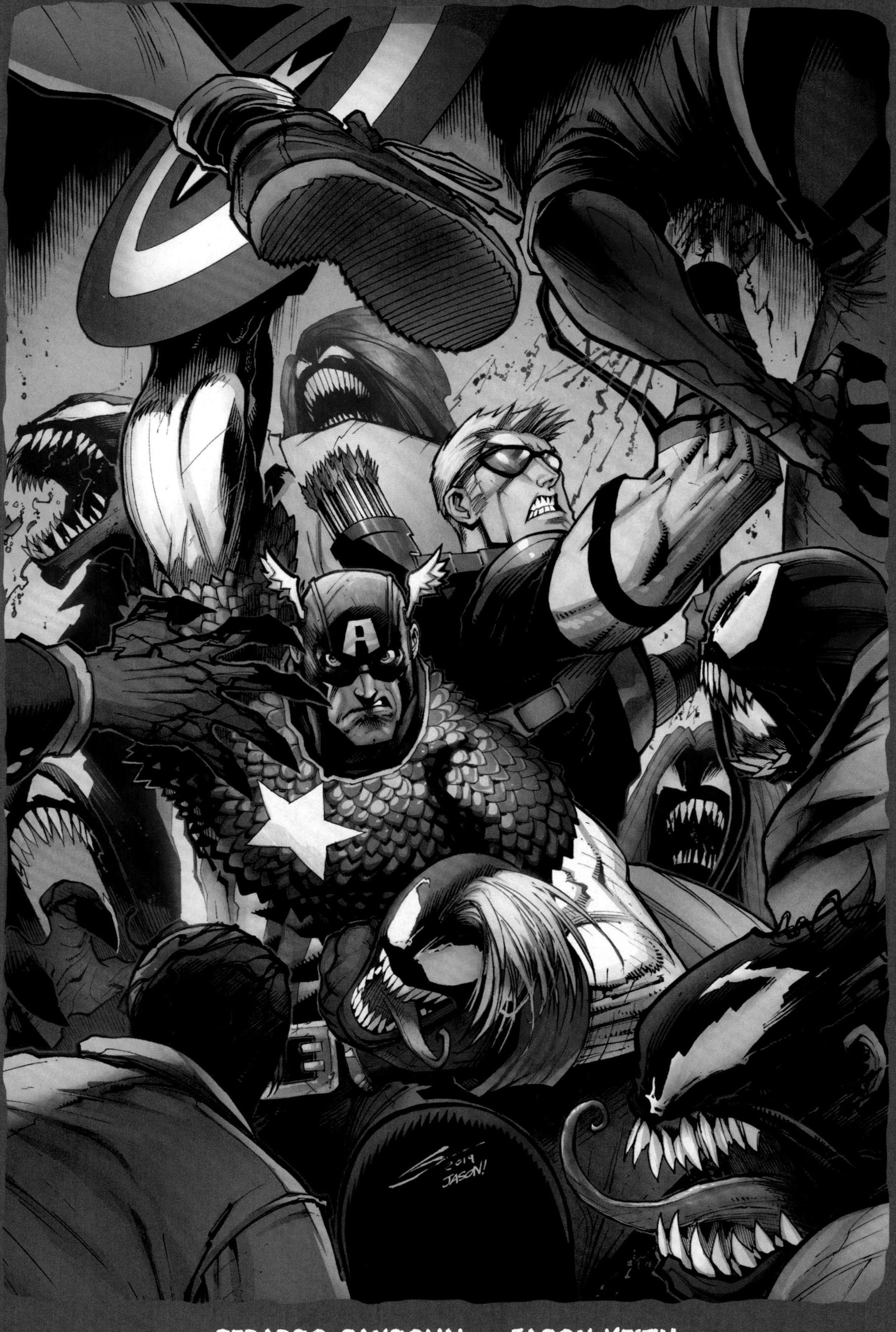

GERARDO SANDOVAL & JASON KEITH

ABSOLUTE CARNAGE: AVENGERS #1 Codex Variant

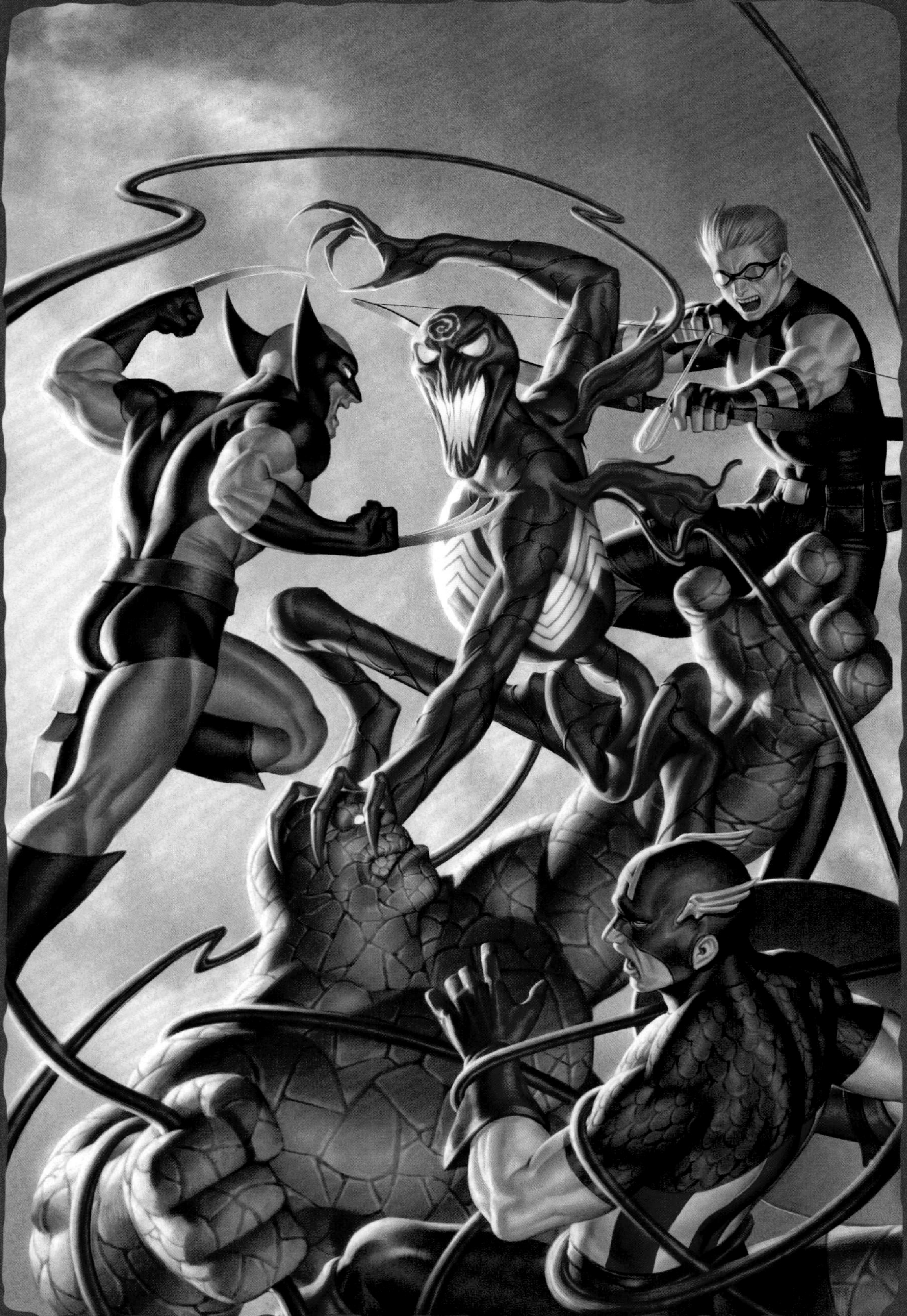

JUNGGEUN YOON
ABSOLUTE CARNAGE: AVENGERS #1 Variant

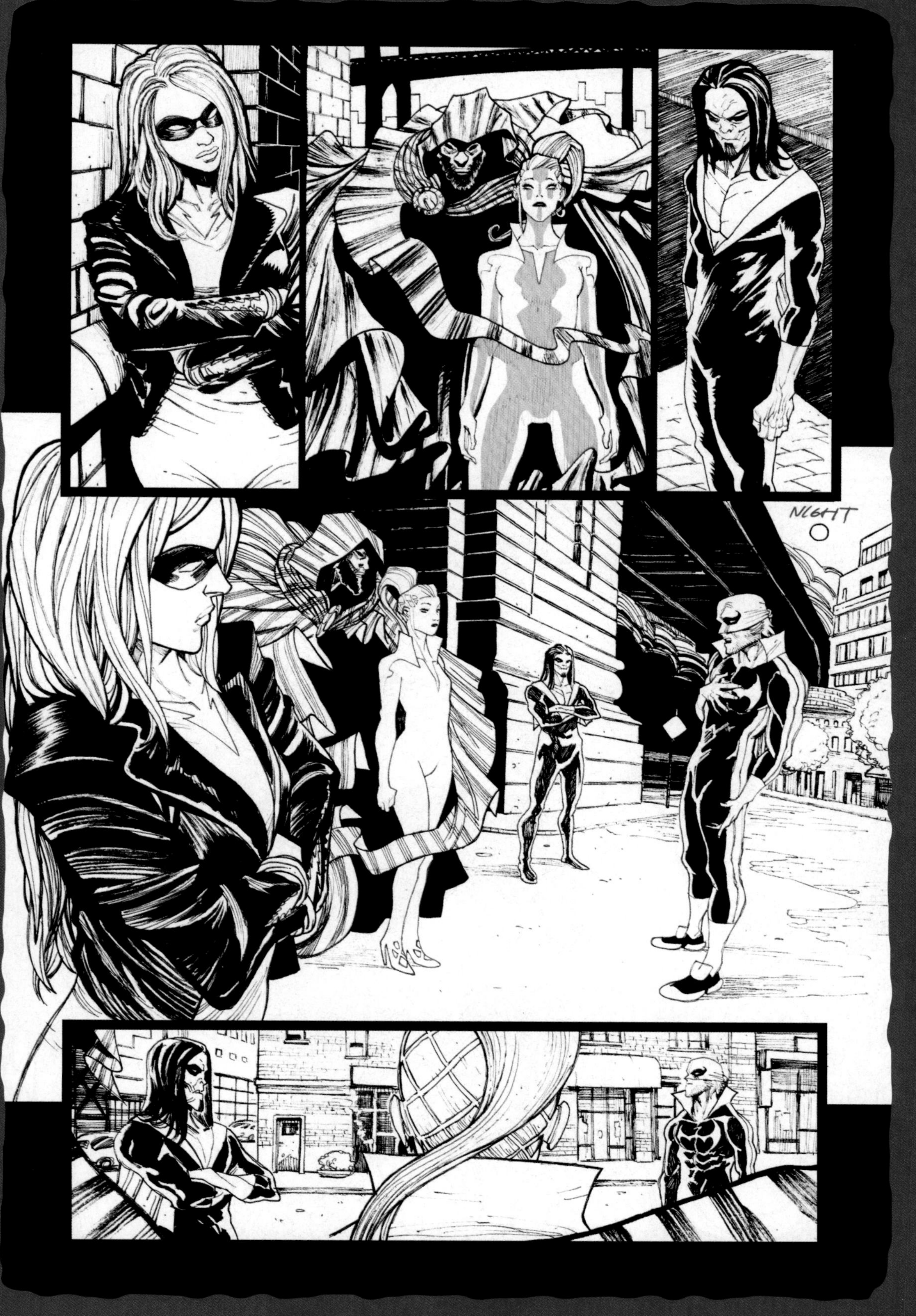
NIGHT

FLAVIANO

ABSOLUTE CARNAGE: LETHAL PROTECTORS #2, page 17 art

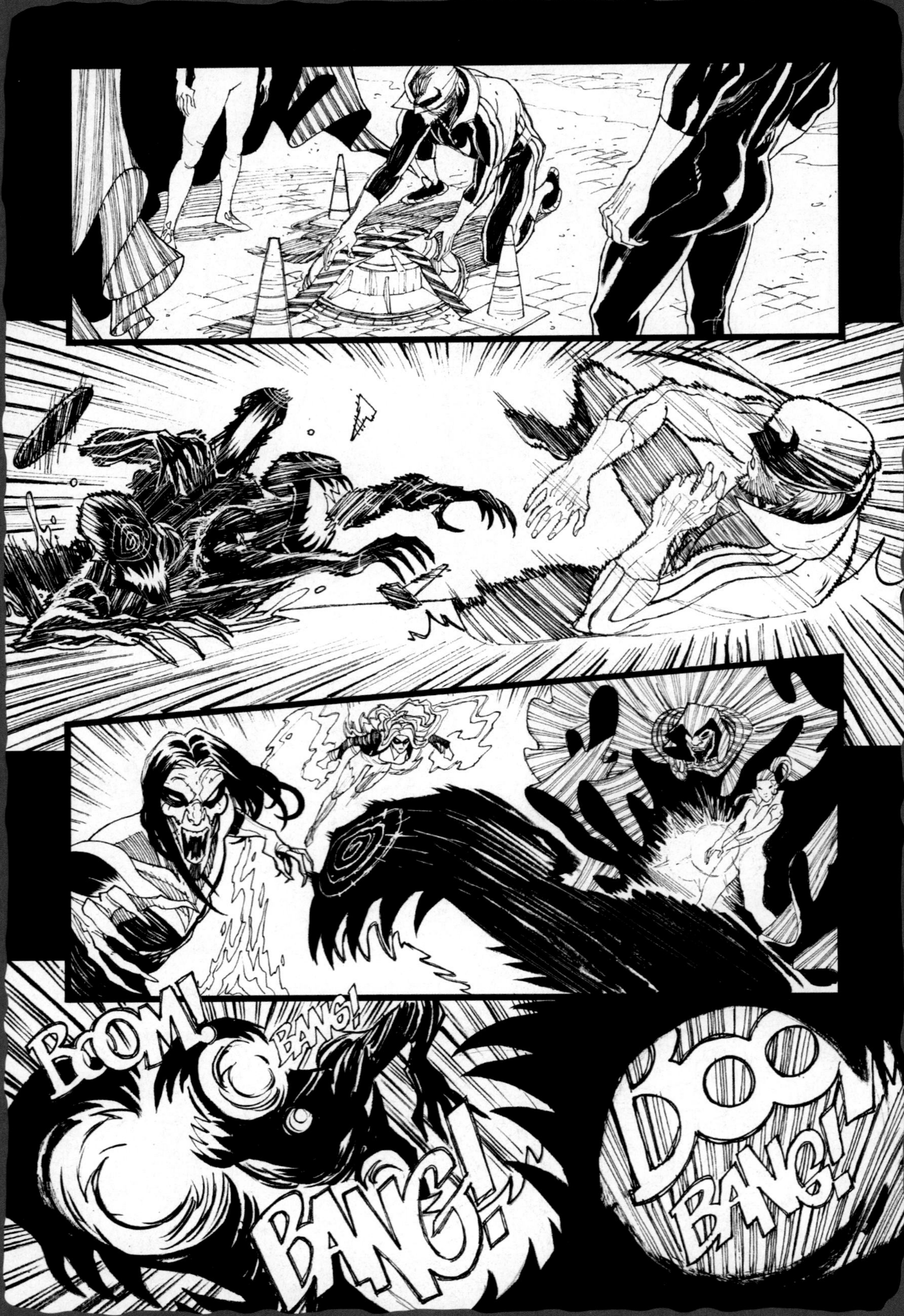
BOOM!
BANG!
BANG!
DOOM
BANG!

FLAVIANO

ABSOLUTE CARNAGE: LETHAL PROTECTORS #2, page 18 art

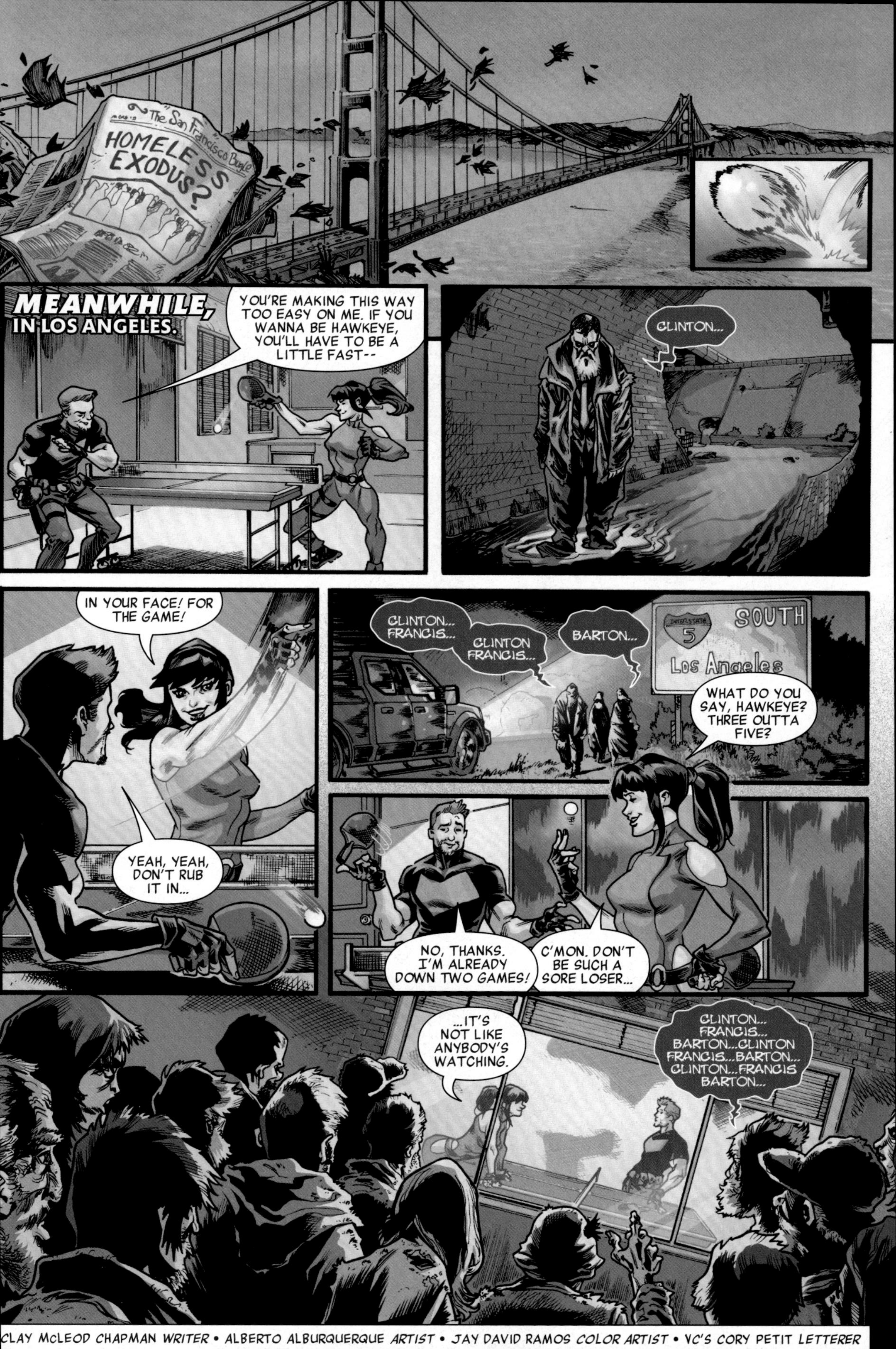
The San Francisco Bugle
HOMELESS EXODUS?
MEANWHILE, IN LOS ANGELES.
YOU'RE MAKING THIS WAY TOO EASY ON ME. IF YOU WANNA BE HAWKEYE, YOU'LL HAVE TO BE A LITTLE FAST--
CLINTON...
IN YOUR FACE! FOR THE GAME!
YEAH, YEAH, DON'T RUB IT IN...
CLINTON... FRANCIS...
CLINTON FRANCIS...
BARTON...
INTERSTATE 5
SOUTH
Los Angeles
WHAT DO YOU SAY, HAWKEYE? THREE OUTTA FIVE?
NO, THANKS. I'M ALREADY DOWN TWO GAMES!
C'MON. DON'T BE SUCH A SORE LOSER...
...IT'S NOT LIKE ANYBODY'S WATCHING.
CLINTON... FRANCIS... BARTON...CLINTON FRANCIS...BARTON... CLINTON...FRANCIS BARTON...

CLAY McLEOD CHAPMAN *WRITER* • ALBERTO ALBURQUERQUE *ARTIST* • JAY DAVID RAMOS *COLOR ARTIST* • VC'S CORY PETIT *LETTERER*

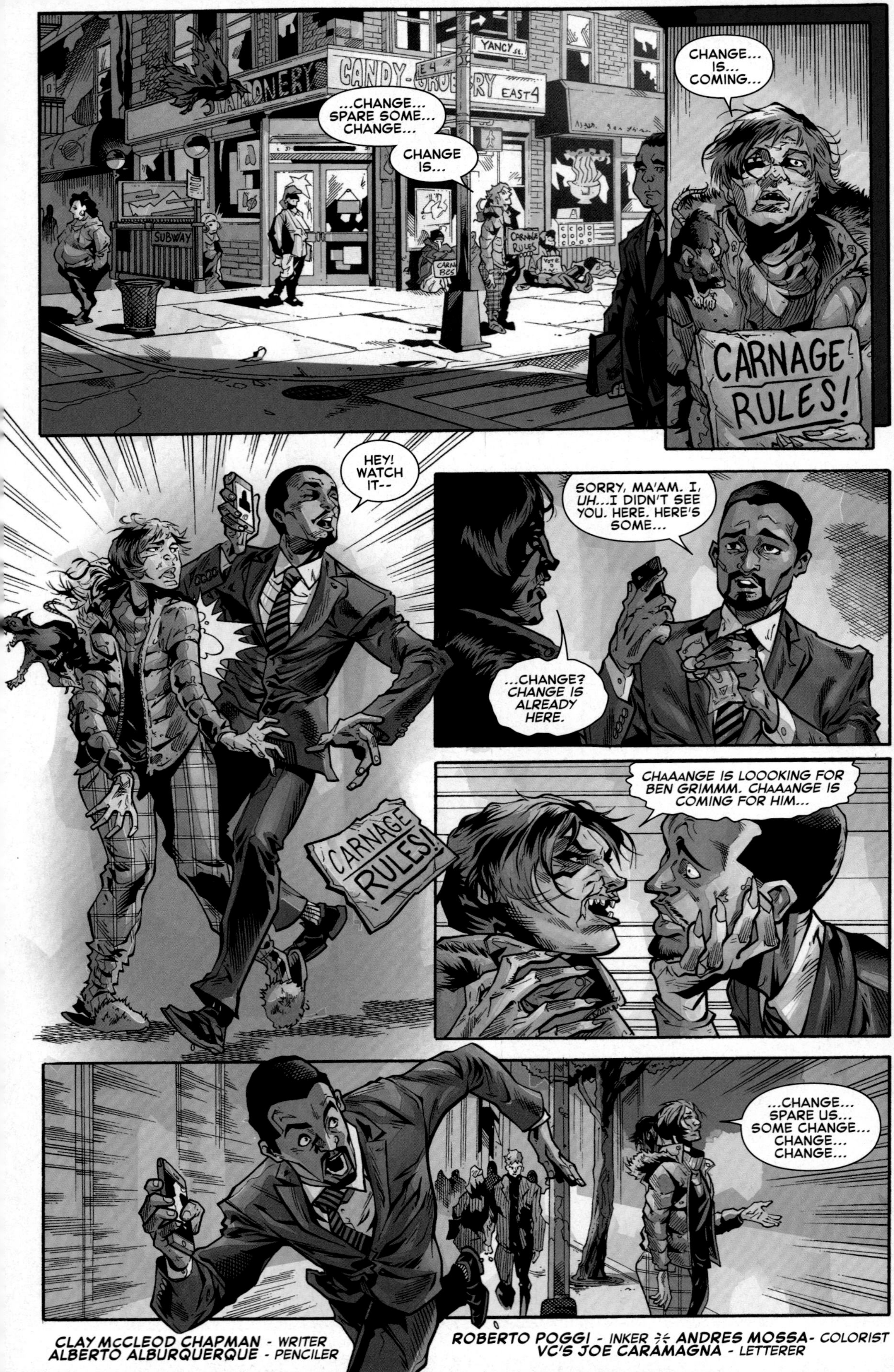
CANDY-GROCERY
EAST 4
YANCY St.
SUBWAY
...CHANGE... SPARE SOME... CHANGE...
CHANGE IS...
CARNAGE RULES
CHANGE... IS... COMING...
CARNAGE RULES!
HEY! WATCH IT--
CARNAGE RULES!
SORRY, MA'AM. I, UH...I DIDN'T SEE YOU. HERE. HERE'S SOME...
...CHANGE? CHANGE IS ALREADY HERE.
CHAAANGE IS LOOOKING FOR BEN GRIMMM. CHAAANGE IS COMING FOR HIM...
...CHANGE... SPARE US... SOME CHANGE... CHANGE... CHANGE...

CLAY McCLEOD CHAPMAN - *WRITER*
ALBERTO ALBURQUERQUE - *PENCILER*
ROBERTO POGGI - *INKER* ***ANDRES MOSSA***- *COLORIST*
VC'S JOE CARAMAGNA - *LETTERER*

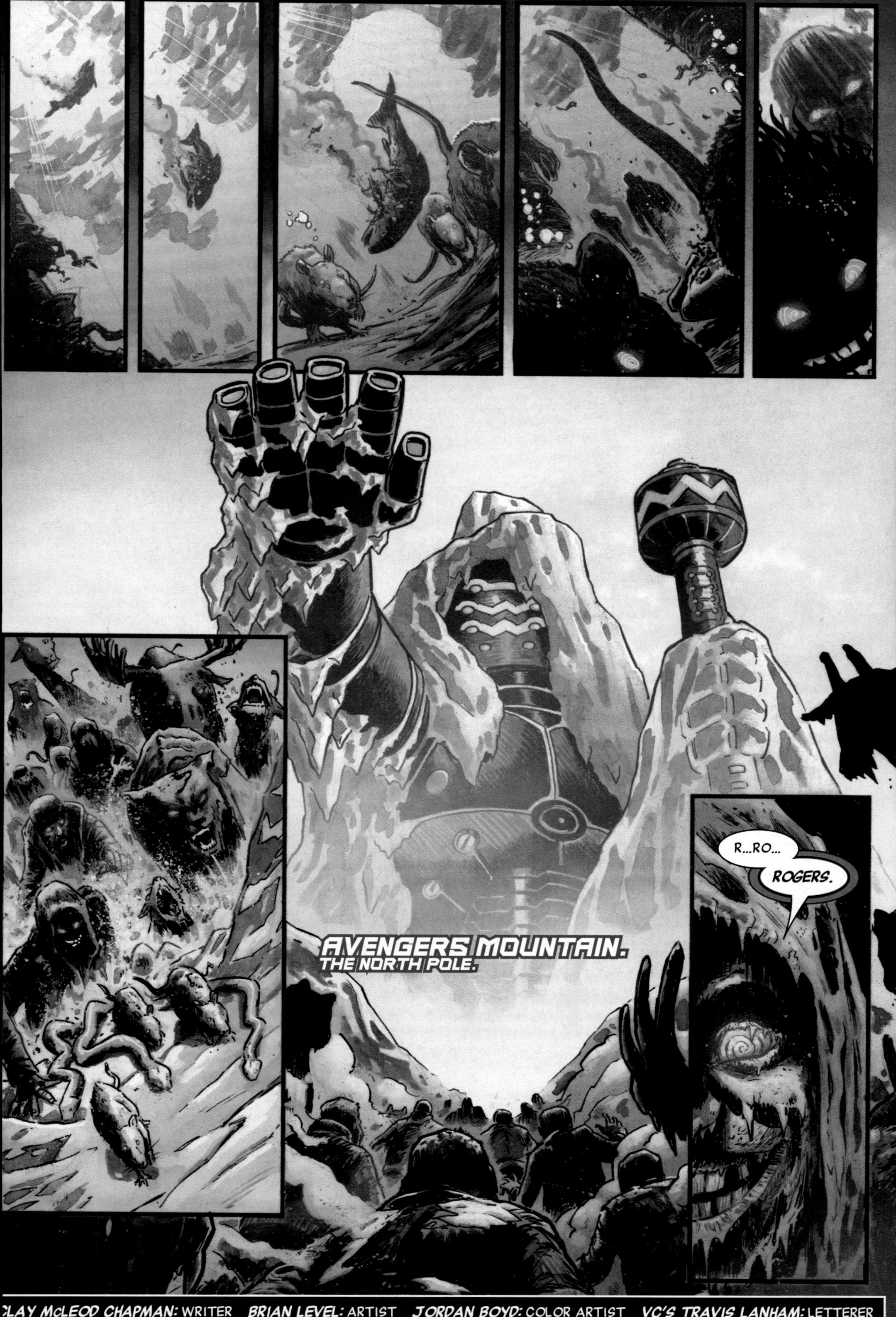
AVENGERS MOUNTAIN.
THE NORTH POLE.
R...RO...
ROGERS.

CLAY McLEOD CHAPMAN: WRITER BRIAN LEVEL: ARTIST JORDAN BOYD: COLOR ARTIST VC'S TRAVIS LANHAM: LETTERER

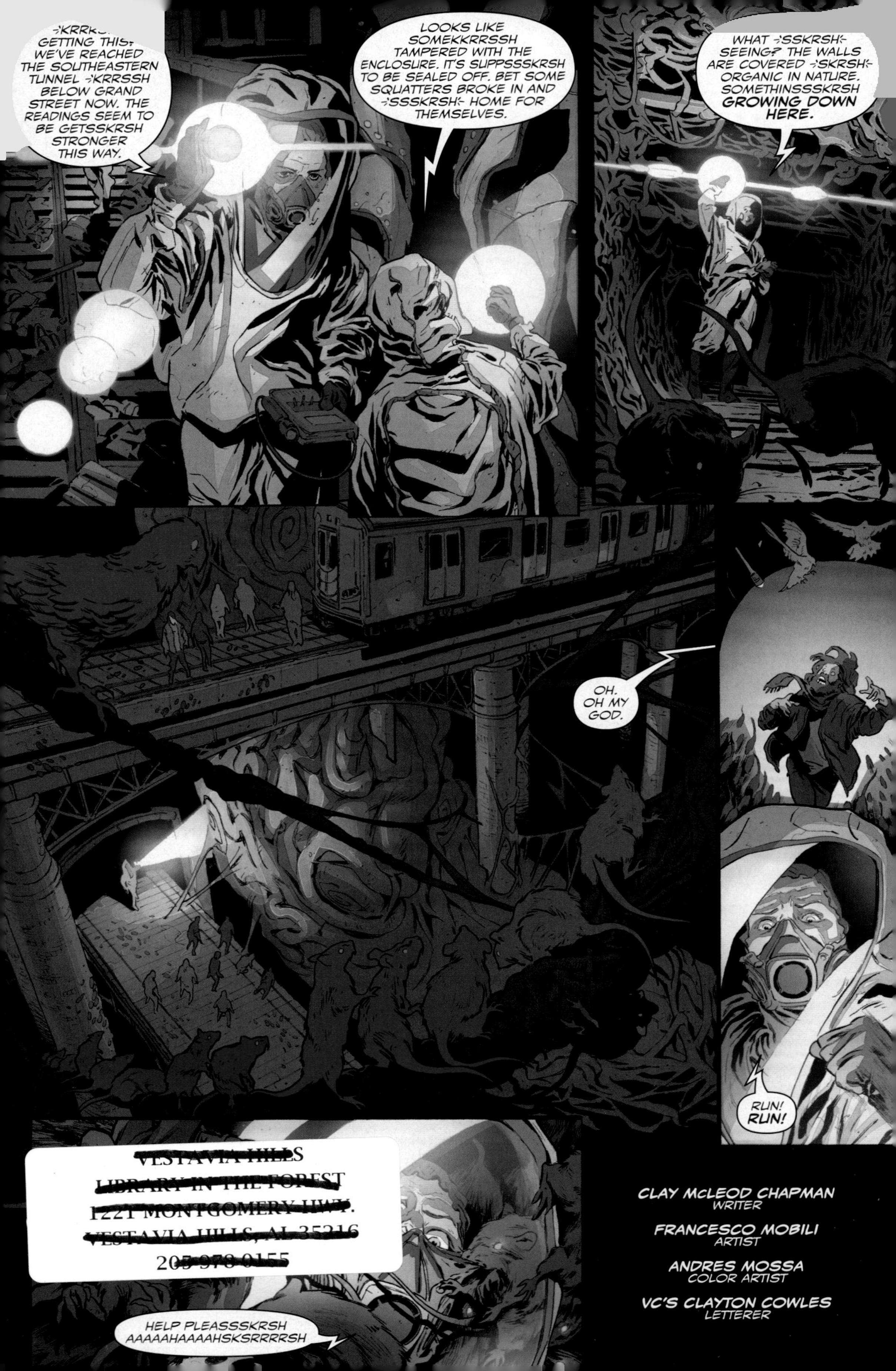

-KRRKS- GETTING THIS? WE'VE REACHED THE SOUTHEASTERN TUNNEL -KRRSSH BELOW GRAND STREET NOW. THE READINGS SEEM TO BE GETSSKRSH STRONGER THIS WAY.
LOOKS LIKE SOMEKKRRSSH TAMPERED WITH THE ENCLOSURE. IT'S SUPPSSSKRSH TO BE SEALED OFF. BET SOME SQUATTERS BROKE IN AND -SSSKRSH- HOME FOR THEMSELVES.
WHAT -SSKRSH- SEEING? THE WALLS ARE COVERED -SKRSH- ORGANIC IN NATURE. SOMETHINSSSKRSH **GROWING DOWN HERE.**
OH. OH MY GOD.
RUN! **RUN!**
HELP PLEASSSKRSH AAAAAHAAAAHSKSRRRRSH
CLAY McLEOD CHAPMAN WRITER
FRANCESCO MOBILI ARTIST
ANDRES MOSSA COLOR ARTIST
VC'S CLAYTON COWLES LETTERER